Hidden N' The Light

William Thompson Jr

Copywrite 2009
by *William Thompson Jr.*
PUBLISHED BY

Write Everlasting Tips,

Publishing company

Unless otherwise indicated, all Scripture quotations are from the King James Version of the Bible.

ISBN-0-9755994-8-8
ISBN-978-0-9755994-8-8

Printed in the United States of America

To contact the author, write
W E T Publishing Co.
7525 Arbor Hill Dr.
Fort Worth, Texas 76120

All rights reserved. Written permission must be secured from the publisher to use or reproduce any part of this book, except for brief quotations embodied in church related publications, critical review or articles.

Contents

Dedication......................IV

Introduction......................V

1. The Light First.....
   pages..21-50

2. His Image.....
   pages 51-84

3. Darkened Perspective......
   pages 85-110

4. Nothing....
   pages 111-138

5. The Breaking of Day.....
   pages 139-170

6. Mystery R' Myth......
   pages 171-212

7. Feet & Paths.....
   pages 213-250

8. Urgency of Emergency....
   pages 251-268

9. Blind Sight........
   pages 269-290

10. But I See Me..........
    pages 299-328

Conclusion
Looking In All
The Wrong Places...
pages 329-346

Dedication

But seek ye first the kingdom of God, and His righteousness; and all these things shall be added unto you. St. Matthew 6:33

To the God of all Glory, The Only Wise God Our Lord and Savior, Soon Coming King; Dominion, and Majesty; Authority and Power; Grace, Love and Peace...........

Kingdom Dwellers and Diligent Seekers...... This work has your interest all over it, written in and throughout the pages in between the lines, that you may be able to atest to the Hidden truths of God that are truly available to all of the Body of Christ....................

Finally: To Mrs. Sharon R. Thompson and again to the Thompson-etts: Antonio, Misty, Aaron, & William III.................

I Love You All,
Much Love

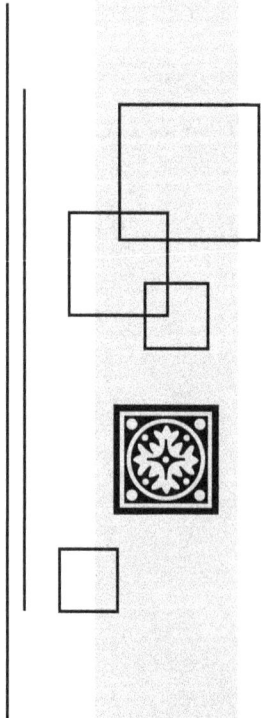

FOREWORD

I count it a privilege to be married to one of the best authors in the world. Bill is an awesome prophet of God. *"Hidden in the Light"* is just one of the many books that he has written and will write. I encourage you to read this book to encounter God in a more excellent way! Once we give our lives to God, sin should no longer rule us and that is the message in *"Hidden in the Light"*, come out of shame and claim salvation, be a part of those Hidden in the Light!

God has ordained him to speak to the masses through revelation and knowledge of God and His power. He really is a man that hates wickedness of all kinds and loves the light (salvation, honesty, righteousness, etc).

He has spent his whole life trying to help the body of Christ come to the Light!

You will not be the same again.

Sharon Thompson

About The Author
William (Bill) Thompson Jr.

Born March 12, 1961 in El'paso, Texas, to the late Rev. William Thompson Sr. & Rev. Daisy Y. Mclawler-Thompson; the family later relocated to Fort Worth, Texas.

He graduated from P. L. Dunbar Sr. High, class of 79' in Fort Worth, Texas. He attended TCJC South Campus, Dallas Theological Seminary, and Vogue Bueaty College.

At 3 years of age he began to express a passion to play the piano and to preach the Gospel; he grew up in the church singing in the choir and learned to study his own bible.

His uncle; the Late Apostle Russell Thompson, laid hands on him at the age of 11, from that point on he knew that there was more for him in the Lord. He moved on to the next level in an effort to gain that which he desired most of the Lord. He is a talented instumentalist, and the Composer of many songs.

Prophet Thompson hails from an extensive linage of dedicated ministers. He's a decendant of the Late; Reverend Vol William McLawler of Louisville, Kentucky; and of the first generation Church of God In Christ. By the grace of God and divine providence, he was realigned with the grass roots of his own spiritual inheritance.

He has been in the church all of his natural life and has the experience of a true churchman that lends the passion for which he ministers the gospel of God. Has been preaching the gospel since Feb. 7,1982, and has been writing and publishing books since October, 1998.

He was ordained an Elder in the COGIC Church since June 1998, He is known and respected as a "True Prophet" of God.

Prophet Thompson has crossed the lines of denominational influences as a friend and brother, enabling him to be identified as a child of God and not Just a Baptist, a Methodist, a Pentecostal, or just another member of the Church Of God In Christ!

He has ministered in music for ministries in the DFW Metro-plex, and OKC, OK. He has traveled with evangelist, and has been the guest musician for many revivals, musicals, weddings, conferences, recordings and etc.

He founded and established the Spoken Word Center, School of Prophetic Excellence 2004.

His endeavor is to serve the people of the Lord everywhere that will receive of the awesome gift of the Holy Ghost to which he has been endowed.

He has been married to Sharon Renee for 25 years and is the father of four children.

Thank You ***

Write Everlasting Tips Publishing Co., & Pastor/Prophet William Thompson Jr. will faithfully continue the Assignment of penning the revealed truths from the Lord, publishing the Excellence of God's Word............

Other Available Topics @ Google, Amazon.com Once Bitten ForEver, Shepherd Wars & Sheep Attacks, Just Let Jesus Do It For You, Word Up, It's Got To Come Out Of Your Mouth........ More to come; and Music By Prophet Bill Thompson

And this is the condemnation, that light is come into the world, and men loved darkness rather than light, because their deeds were evil...   St. John 3:19

Introduction

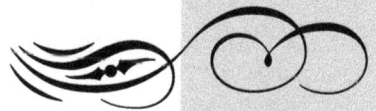

ONE OF THE GREATER BLESSINGS OF OUR LIVES WOULD BE TO DISCOUNT THE MYTH THAT PEOPLE DON'T SEE THE LIGHT OF THE LORD IN OUR LIVES. WHILE JESUS WALKED THE FACE OF THE EARTH, GOD IN THE FLESH; MOST PEOPLE COULD NOT EVEN SEE HIM; THOUGH THEY WERE STARRING HIM RIGHT IN THE FACE.

WE ARE TAUGHT AS CHILDREN TO LOOK INTO THE EYES OF PEOPLE AS THEY TALK TO

Hidden In the Light*

us, and that in doing so we would most likely be able to know when people would be speaking the truth or lying right to our faces. Our teachers were teaching us to be good judges of an individual's character, by looking through the mirrors of the souls of others; right through their eyes!

Even as the people of the geographical surroundings of Jesus' area of residing, who looked into His eyes and listened to the smooth and soothing resinance of His voice, as He told the truth of His own reality; they could neither hear Him, nor could the ever see Him. He was hidden right before their very eyes, in broad daylight!

It is a pitiful thing to be blind and in darkness while having no knowledge of the fact that there is no light in your understanding to brighten your pathway of living at all. What is actually more pitiful is the fact that many people don't feel that there is anything wrong with the fact that they are living in the darkened way of thinking and doing.

As a matter of the fact; people as a whole are no longer ashamed of their wrong doings. The influx of extreme

Hidden In the Light*

WICKED INFLUENCES OVER THE WORLD ENTIRELY HAS COME OUT OF THE CLOSET IN ONE WAY OR ANOTHER. WE WERE TAUGHT EARLY ON IN THE CHURCH THAT MANY THINGS WERE SHAMEFUL AND DISGRACEFUL TO OUR CHARACTER; HOWEVER, MANY PEOPLE APPEAR TO HAVE FALLEN UNDER DARKENED SPELLS FROM SATAN WHEREAS THEY HAVE BEEN ANESTHETIZED TO THE POINT THAT THEY NO LONGER CARE HOW THEY PRESENT THEMSELVES TO OTHER PEOPLE.

MANY PEOPLE HAVE BOUGHT INTO WHAT IS OFTEN REFERRED TO AS "NEW AGE" WAYS OF THINKING AND LIVING. MORE YOUNG PARENTS ARE ALLOWING THEIR CHILDREN TO RAISE THEMSELVES AND TO MAKE THEIR OWN DECISIONS EVEN FROM THE AGE OF 2-4 YEARS. IT IS NO WONDER THAT THE YOUNGER GENERATIONS ARE OUT OF CONTROL AND DISRUPTIVE TO THEIR SURROUNDINGS.

THE TRADITIONAL VALUES OF MORALITY ARE SCORNED AND TOTALLY DESPISED EVEN BY THE PEOPLE OF THE CHURCH WHO PROFESS TO BEING WASHED IN THE BLOOD OF JESUS. SUCH INDIVIDUALS, WHO BELIEVE THAT THEY HAVE BEEN WASHED, SOMEHOW DON'T SEEM TO SHY AWAY FROM THOSE THINGS THAT ARE FORBIDDEN FOR ANYONE WHO CONFESS THE NAME OF JESUS CHRIST AS THEIR SAVIOR AND LORD.

Hidden In the Light*

Use to be that we believed that whenever we sinned that God would get us out of the mess that we had made if we simply ask the Lord to forgive us for doing those sinful deeds. Now many people don't bother to ask the Lord for forgiveness for doing wrong, mainly because wrong has become such a comfortable place of residing among the people of the church now!

> Shame - is the open display of the uncovered embarrassment for doing things that we know are immoral and ungodly. Our conscience convicts us and will not allow us to be at peace within ourselves as a result of guilt.   [William Thompson Jr]

Sin, being so abundant among us in every atmosphere, have caused people to talk themselves out of being ashamed for doing things that are against the word of God. Even people in the church have decided that certain things can't be that bad because they have been told that everybody is doing those things.

Some, foolishly; now even feel that going to hell can't be that bad simply because so many other people are going in that direction. How bad is bad; and how wrong can wrong be since so many people are interested in partaking

Hidden In the Light*

OF IT?

Nowadays certain people will ask you; "Who says that it's wrong to do or to live a particular lifestyle, or to conduct yourself along the lines of what most people would say is disgraceful?"

The desperate lifestyles of the sinfully intrinsic scoffers of our faith in Christ Jesus, are sitting among the pews of the churches more frequently now recruiting the hopeless to follow their ways of living every time that the people of the church failed to reach the same hopeless people.

I don't believe that we as the church are even trying to reach the lost for the cause of Christ as hard as we used to, for the reason of the fact that people who confess to being born of God are put on open display and mocked as a result of their fall. Many people of the church have chosen to give up on the cause of Christ, and have determined that people are not worth their time and effort, since so many people come to the church for attention only while they reject any possibility of a change.

People don't want hope any more, the want help! So they come to the church with sad stories and crocodile tears in effort to move the compassion of the church to help them in many cases to buy crack cocaine, other drugs and alcohol. Whenever they are rejected, they don't hesitate to tell the people of the church that we are all a bunch of hypocrites, and that we are all going to hell for not helping them!

The greater wedge is driven by the people in the congregation who feel that as the church we ought to respond to every need that is presented to the church, especially since they pay tithes and give free will offerings. It doesn't really matter how often you have been responsive to the persons that have come to the church for a hand out, they are mad and angry because you didn't respond every time, no matter what!

Deceived; But Didn't Know It!

We used to have testimony service, which was designed for the people of the church to tell of the goodness of the Lord, and what He had done for them. That particular part of the service would be so hot and powerful that the entire church sometimes

Hidden In the Light*

WOULD BE ELECTRIFIED AND SET ON FIRE. DANCING, LEAPING AND SHOUTING WOULD SEEM TO BREAK OUT ALL OVER THE SANCTUARY. SINNERS WOULD BE CONVICTED, CONVINCED OF THE TRUE POWER OF GOD, AND THEY WOULD EVEN CONFESS CHRIST AS THEIR OWN PERSONAL SAVIOR, WHICH WAS ACTUALLY THE PURPOSE.

THIS WAS ALL FINE AND GOOD FOR THE CHURCH UNTIL CERTAIN INDIVIDUALS WOULD SOON BEGIN TO KNIGHT THEMSELVES AS THE MOST RIGHTEOUS AND SPIRITUALLY EXALTED WITHIN THEMSELVES SO THAT NOT EVEN THE PASTOR HAD INFLUENCE OVER THEM ANYMORE. MANY TESTIMONIES CHANGED FROM TELLING THE GOODNESS OF THE LORD TO GLORIFYING SELF AND PUTTING OTHERS DOWN, WHILE TELLING THE UNKNOWN DETAILS OF OTHER PEOPLE IN THE CONGREGATION THAT WERE DEFINITELY SINFUL.

I BEGIN TO WATCH AS THE PASTORS BEGAN TO CIRCUMVENT THAT PORTION OF THE SERVICES, WHEREAS SOME WHO FELT THAT THEY WERE INDEED ENDOWED WITH THE PURPOSE OF TELLING OTHERS THEIR TESTIMONY, AS THEY WOULD ADAMANTLY RISE TO THEIR FEET TO TELL THEIR TESTIMONY ANYWAY. YOU COULDN'T TELL THEM THAT THEY WERE OUT OR CONTROL IF YOU WANTED TO, EVEN THOUGH THE PASTOR OPENLY rebuked them and asked them to take their seats.

Some would walk the parking lot after the service had ended seeking to convince certain people that had been in attendance of the service that they were mistreated when asked to silence their testimony. They seemed to have convinced themselves that they were indeed exempted from the request of the pastor to omit that portion of the service.

Even though we saw the spirit of the Lord move in the midst of the people during the testimony of those certain people of the church, did not give us the right to launch a campaign against the pastor who is the anointed head of the church. We were led to believe that the pastor had gotten off of the track refusing to allow the spirit of the Lord to have His way in the service.

We were deceived into overlooking the fact that the people had gotten out of control during the worship service whereas God was not even the object of their worship anymore. What used to be a testimony had turned into being just a tale. Many of those persons, who were once thought to be powerful saints of God, had become

Hidden In the Light*

ADVOCATES OF SELF EXALTATION TELLING STORIES AS DRY AS AN EVAPORATED POND. THEY WERE LIKE A CONCRETE SIDEWALK ON A HOT SUMMER DAY; THEY WERE VERY DRY AND CONTINUOUSLY LONG!

So MANY PEOPLE FEEL RIGHT SIMPLY BECAUSE THEY IMPLIMENTED A CERTAIN THING OF THEIR BEHAVIOR EVEN THOUGH IT WAS LATER RECOGNIZED AS WRONG. THEY HAVE BECOME SELF RIGHTEOUS IN THEIR DEMEANOR AND HAVE DEEMED THEMSELVES TO BE QUALIFIED JUDGES OF OTHERS; WHILE OTHER PEOPLE ARE WICKED AND SINFULY INCAPABLE OF EVEN LOOKING ON OTHERS WITH ANY JUDGEMENTAL DISDAIN.

HERE IS WHERE THE DECEPTION COMES IN; MOST PEOPLE OF THE CHURCH ARE TAUGHT THAT JUST AS LONG AS THEY ARE TELLING THEIR STORY TO SOMEBODY, SOMEWHERE; JUST ANYWHERE, THAT THEY ARE BEING THE WITNESS THAT THE LORD IS REFERRING TO IN THE SCRIPTURE. THIS IS ALSO THE REASON THAT SO MANY PEOPLE ARE REFERRING TO THE PEOPLE OF THE CHURCH AS A BUNCH OF HYPOCRITS; THEY SAY ONE THING BUT DO THE TOTAL OPPOSITE.

I BELIEVE THAT WE HAVE TO SPEAK OUT OF OUR MOUTHS. BUT, WE ALSO NEED TO LINE UP WITH OUR SPEECH AND OUR TESTIMONIES SO THERE IS NO CONTRIDICTION AMONG THE PEOPLE WHO hear what we have said to them about Christ.

You should be the first to notice that the anointing of the Spirit of the Lord is not at all flowing as you talk about Him. It is not about what you have to say out of your mouth that makes the difference, it's the anointing of the Lord that makes all of the difference and allows your words to reach all of the way to the inward part of the persons that we are talking to.

Jesus never said that we would talk as witnesses all over the town and the country; rather He said that we would be witnesses unto Him (Acts 1:8). More than anything that we could ever say; it is the lifesyles that we live that is really the witness of Christ living alive in our beings daily among our peers, family and friends, sheding the light on our witness.

People don't usually ask the question; "What is that talking", refering to your mouth; rather we always hear people asking the questions; "Who is that talking!" Many have been deceived into believing that they can do it all without the help of the Lord. Most are only talking because they feel that they are doing the Lord a favor

Hidden In the Light*

of some sort simply by speaking His name.

Often we don't seem to realize that so many others have been robbed of the privaledge to speak the name of the Lord Jesus Christ from birth. They were born into other theocratic idealisms that reject the deity of the name of Jesus Christ.

In these latter generations we are being encouraged and sometimes forced to attempt to find ways to mix with the other religions who openly oppose the name of Jesus Christ. The government is suggesting to us that we need to find ways to get along and to co-exist with non-believers outside of the realms of our true biblical beliefs of the truth and the reality of Jesus.

If it be possible, as much as lieth in you, live peaceably with all men.   *Romans 12: 18*

A very hard truth lies within the fact that we have to be reminded by the secular government to get along with humanity! We don't have to agree with what a person does with their life in order to be kind to them, and just because we have chosen to be kind to people, it doesn't mean that we have to keep close fellowship with them. We must love the people and still hate the

Hidden In the Light*

wrong things that they do. If the scripture hates sin; and it does; then so should you!

We don't have to get it twisted and turned upside down and inside out relative to understanding our place as believers in Christ Jesus; there is to be a noticeable difference between the children of the Lord and the sinners. Eroneous teaching has caused many people of the church to be fearful of showing kindness to the sinners of the world. People fear that they will become sinful and begin to act like the sinners if we show them love.

> *As we have therefore opportunity, let us do good unto all men, especially unto them who are of the household of faith.*   Galatians 6: 10

It's a fact that your company keepers will testify of your true character, because it is not likely that you would be comfortable in the company of others who are totally the opposite of you.

Chapter 1

The Light First*

And God said, let there be light: and there was light. And God saw the light, that it was good: and God divided the light from the darkness.

Genesis 3: 3-4

Hidden In the Light*

*The Light Is!?!?**

Even, as of this late age of existence, we are still attempting to define, and to redefine the true essence of light. Modern Science has also documented the awesome power of light in that it moves at a rate of speed too swift to be documented on speedometers or motion detectors.

Light, itself, is used often to document the rate of speed and the exact motion of most everything tangible that is scientifically tested in the laboratories of our society.

Light cannot be cheated in that never will any object ever pass through light undetected; the illuminated image will cast its shadow on any other lighted surface, exibiting that those objects had just passed through the light.

Light shines from the origin to the destination quicker than our eyesight can behold and see what we are actually focusing our sight upon.

God could have worked from what

The Light First*

WE NOW KNOW OF AS THE DARKNESS, TO STILL CREATE EVERYTHING THAT WAS CREATED, AS EXCELLENT AS IT IS TODAY; BUT, RATHER, He CHOSE TO WORK FROM ONE OF THE GREATER CHARACTERISTICAL ATTRIBUTES OF His OWN BEING; WHICH IS Light!

You have got to know that there is simply nothing to darkened or obscured that could have ever disallowed the handiwork of the Lord, to prevent it from going forth.

Perhaps it would better highlight your own level of intelligence, if you would see the light from God's perspective?

Back in the early 70's, the hippy generation were overwhelmed with what was then referred to as "Black-Light."

Most pot smoking, drug and alcohol abusing individuals referred to the darkened lights as "Trip Lights." Black lights were supposed to enhance the induced altered state brought on by the drug of their choice. They sometimes would hallucinate and see things in the darkened light that would never have been possible to see in the

Hidden In the Light*

whiter, much brighter, light!

The lack-luster illumines of the Black-Light, caused other things to glow, as a result of being painted with what was then referred to as Black-Light paint. Fluorescence paint colors would project the otherwise hidden illumination, under the shower of the Black-Light.

Certain painted images would stand out in highlighted reflection to the strange phenomenon.

It was a bit bewildering to the psychic evaluation, when witnessing the production of highly illuminated images, as result of the much lowered state of light, from what had previously been just another picture on the wall.

Without the Black Light; the pastel colors could be clearly visualized, but, the interestingly exciting and awe striking reflection of the painted images would almost appear to dance forth in the darkness of the room.

God could have worked from this perspective but, He chose not to, and here is the reason why;

The Light First*

God said; "Let there be Light!" and it was so!

Everything about God is Light; this is the reason that the greater things of God are discovered underneath the hidden revelations of the light.

The individuals of which originally orchestrated the Easter Egg Hunt; whereas the eggs are hidden in plain sight; perhaps they might have gotten the revelation of God; in that He is hidden in the Light, out in the open atmosphere for everyone to see Him?

God hides in plain sight; so excellently that only those that diligently seek Him with all of their hearts, can find Him, and only so, because He discloses Himself to those seekers.

It amazes me how that people look all around God and never ever see Him, when in actuality God is everywhere in plain sight; too big to be missed!

If there is any real question as to where God is, relative to the placement of mankind in the earth, the fact that

Hidden In the Light*

God shined the light down on the earth, ought to lend a perspective scope of reasoning for us to take into consideration, that God is indeed shining down on us from Heaven!

God only shined the light where there was clearly no light in the atmosphere to begin with? The bible never give us an indication that God ever had to shine the light up in Heaven, because wherever God is, so is the light!

God never works or performs a miracle in the dark without bringing the light to that darkened place first. The earth was dark and void (formless without shape and splendor), until God commanded the presence of the light in the earth, and began to work.

But, now allow me to reasonably expand upon the understanding of the light of the Lord:......................

The light of the Lord is not to be ascertained as if to be parallel in characteristics to that of the fluorescence in the light-bulbs that we use on a daily basis to illuminate our living spaces, and our work spaces alike.

The Light First*

The light of the Lord is the glory of the Lord! Whatever God does in the earth since from the beginning of time, His glory must always precede His entrance.

Light already existed within the glory of God, therefore God really did not have to create the light, or to even recreate the light, because even as He always is, the light always was and still is to this very day.

While we study God's schedule during the 7 days in which He created the heavens and the earth, we will discover that the glory of the Lord was first over the atmosphere of the earth; even before the greater glory of the sun, and the lesser glory of the moon and the stars.

While God did create a light to light the way for humanity in the earth, He did not totally deplete the darkness that was indeed over the face of the earth, he simply divided the time that the light would be allowed to impact growth stimulation in the earth.

Light is characteristically just like

Hidden In the Light*

God, of which no man can change that fact! The things in the earth grow and progress in the light, the same as we as people grow and spiritually progress in the Lord each moment that we are in the glorious presence of the Lord.

Things rest and pause in the lessened light of the night of what we know of as the darkness. However, in the presence of total darkness, things literally stop and cease progressive stimulation, to the point that they even die and deteriorate as a result of having no light at all!

Things as we know of them today, would grow out of control on the land and even in the sea if all we had was the light! With that being said; let's not get too excited about the darkness, as it is no place to be caught hanging around. We all should desire to walk in the light, as He is in the light also!

> *This then is the message which we have heard of him, and declare unto you, that God is light, and in him is no darkness at all. If we say that we have fellowship with him, and walk in darkness, we lie, and do not the truth: But if we walk in the light, as*

The Light First*

he is in the light, we have fellowship one with another, and the blood of Jesus Christ his son cleanseth us from all sin.   I John 1: 5-7

Just Because We Have It Doesn't Mean That We're Thankful!

All that is hidden in the light would probably be much sooner revealed if we were more determined to reside in the light to discover that those things of the light are in motion with the movement of the light itself!

Therefore, those things of the light would eventually find its way to the presence of any individual that is not only abiding in the light, but also determinately attentive to the light of the Lord.

It has simply become too common for many people who confess Christ, to desire to only temporarily pass through the light, rather than to abide in the light on a daily basis.

Many people will only pass through the light on a Sunday morning during a worship service, only to avoid the light until the very next Sunday for which they will routinely repeat the same behavior of passing through the light.

Hidden In the Light*

It is even of a greater benefit to us if we would allow the light to pass through us while we visit the local worship services on Sunday which would have an even greater lasting affect, motivating us to desire the presence of the properly lighted atmosphere; which is God!

We have developed a very sinister respect, if not only a casual acknowledgement of the light itself, in that we are satisfied with just knowing that the light is still shining, while choosing to do our deeds in the dark or at least only in the shadows of the light.

Most people don't even really pay attention to the light until if the light goes out! Thankfully the Light of the Lord is everlasting and it can never go out!

It has been my observation, that people who don't mind dimly lit atmospheric surroundings in their homes, churches, businesses, or even in their work spaces, that those same people usually do not appear to see the need for placing themselves in the proximity of the glory of the Lord where the light could shine forth through their deeds to illuminate their lives and the lives of

The Light First*

OTHERS.

THEY COULD BETTER FULFILL THEMSELVES WITH AN ENTERTAINING MOVIE RATHER THAN TO BUCKLE THEMSELVES DOWN IN PRAYERFUL DIALOGUE BEFORE THE PRESENCE OF THE LORD. MAYBE YOU DIDN'T KNOW IT, BUT, THERE IS ABSOLUTELY NOTHING DULL ABOUT THE LORD!

I PERSONALLY; CAN'T STAND TO BE IN A ROOM WHERE THE LIGHT IS TOO DIM OR DULL. I HAVE BEEN IN CHURCHES WHERE THE LIGHTING IN THE SANCTUARY IS VERY DULL AND DIM, AS A RESULT, THE SERVICES ARE ALSO VERY DULL AND DIM, AND THE PEOPLE ARE OFTEN LULLED TO SLEEP RIGHT IN THE MIDST OF THE SERVICE, EVEN DURING THE DELIVERY OF THE PREACHED WORD.

I HAVE NOT BEEN ONE TO FREQUENT NIGHTCLUBS AND CAFÉ SURROUNDINGS, WHEREAS THE ATMOSPHERE IS USUALLY DARK OR DIMLY LIT FOR THE PURPOSE OF INTOXICATED EASE OF RELAXATION. PEOPLE GET AWAY TO SUCH PLACES FOR THE PURPOSE OF ESCAPING TO WHAT IS CONSIDERED TO BE THE GOOD TIMES OF DANCING, ALCOHOL CONSUMPTION, AND INTERMINGLING WITH OTHER PEOPLE OF THE SURROUNDING COMMUNITIES THAT MAY BE PARTAKERS OF DRUGS; EITHER AS A USER, OR AS THE PROVIDER.

THE DARKER PLACES OF RECREATION ARE

Hidden In the Light*

SOCIABLY INTOXICATING THEMSELVES, IN THAT PEOPLE HAVE OFTEN FOUND THEMSELVES LONGING TO RETURN TO THE "BAT-CAVE-LIKE" GET AWAY, OUTSIDE OF THE NORMAL EVERYDAY NECESSITIES OF LIVING, AS SOON AS THEY HAVE DEPARTED THOSE DOORS.

And this is the condemnation, that light is come into the world, and men loved darkness rather than light, because their deeds were evil. St. John 3:19

Why?

A LOT OF EXCUSES ARE MADE FOR DOING THE THINGS THAT ARE NOT SUPPOSED TO BE DONE. MOST OF THE REASONS ARE SO LAME; AND INSUFFICIENT TO SUCCESSFULLY SHED LIGHT ON THE PURPOSE AND THE DETERMINATION FOR PRESSING ON FORWARD INTO THE DIRECTIONS OF SIN AND THE UTTERLY SHAMEFUL PRACTICES OF LIVING LOWDOWN IN THE SOCIETAL GUTTERS OF SOCIABLE INTERACTIONS WITH OTHER LOW-LIFE DERELICTS OF THE DARK!

WHATEVER THE REASONS, THE FACT IS THAT THE DEEDS ARE SERIOUSLY EVIL, INTENTIONALLY! AT ONE TIME OR ANOTHER IN EVERY ONE OF OUR LIVES, WE HAVE ALL BEEN; "(QUOTE-UN QUOTE)", A LITTLE BAD!

BUT I'M NOT TALKING ABOUT BEING A LITTLE BAD EVERY NOW AND THEN, I'M

The Light First*

referring to what the scripture has described as the darkened intentional ills of mankind, which makes for an even more dangerous and deadly society, of which the behavioral patterns are described as evil.

Evil people usually flee the presence of any light to avoid the possibilities of exposure and to escape the inevitable rewarding penalty for their actions.

It is amazing to me how that many people will do whatever they feel that they are indeed adult enough to do on a consistent basis, yet their preference is that their actions would remain concealed away from the light of public knowledge.

In this self centered society, many people live outlandishly atrocious relative to the immoral sub-standards of our daily social behavioral structure, who likewise also have no mind to be responsible for their own actions. The same people live hidden under the fog of their own deceptive portrayals of living righteous, though soon exposed for their own evil wrong doings.

Exposure is no accident; nor is it by way of the slight unintentional gesture of an individual's hands mistakenly moved in the wrong direction

Hidden In the Light*

to uncover that which should have been otherwise continually blanketed under the deception of the wicked liar!

No one would ever ask you to expose them for their wrong doings; at least it is certainly not a common practice!

Many people are actually exposed before they ever have the knowledge of the fact of their exposure. Usually someone else who may have gotten wind of the news of the exposure, will contact the exposed person, informing them that the cover had been blown away!

The big stink of being exposed for doing things that shouldn't have been done in the first place, lies within the fact that the culprits are often focused on the wrong things. All they can think of is the fact that; "Everybody Knows!" In such the case scenario as this one, it is rightfully observed that one has lost all reasonable focus on the one who really matters, which is God!

Somehow, we as people have determined that it is ok to deceive mankind and to lie to one another about our situations and our lifestyles. We can often fool people for a while anyway; but, God already knows the truth about us in totality.

People don't even seem to care that

The Light First*

God sees all and that He's everywhere already, therefore alleviating any true hiding places for us to do our evil deeds. My friend if there were hiding places where we as people could hide from the presence of God, He wouldn't tell us!

God will never be held accountable for telling us the wrong thing! He knows everything there is to know about every individual on the entire face of the universe; therefore He would never tell you how you could get away with sin, knowing that the wages of sin is death! [Romans 6:23]

When you determine to do the sin, simultaneously, you bind yourself to the price of the penalty as well!

This smart generation of people, of which we are living among today, have determined the necessity to rule out any and most all of the absolutes of existence, between the realities of both man and God. People have sadistically mixed and meshed the idea of mankind and the creator of mankind all into one massive container of existence. Here is what I mean!

First of all; men started this madness with the idea of ruling out the bible as the word of God, or at least if it is the word of God, then it must have

Hidden In the Light*

been for the usage of the people in latter times?

Disregarding the word of God; as an established mandate for living, sets the stage for the development of the ideas that God no longer regards the sin that we commit on a daily basis as an evil and ungodly thing of displeasure to the righteousness of God. Somehow they have become comfortable with viewing the light of the Lord, as if it were gray instead of bright white.

Such idealisms as this, produces determinate sinners, sooner beginning at the very early stages of youthful adolescence, both hindering and binding the possibilities of developing the necessary convictions in their hearts that would allow them to reverence God in the light of being an Holy God who requires us to also be holy, as He is holy.

The younger people of these present generations have attempted at the insidious conjugation of the behavior of man and the ability to force the hand of God to be available to them at all times, no matter what.

People now believe that even as God is omnipresent anyway, that because He is wherever they are going to be, they

The Light First*

should be ok doing whatever they choose to do because God knew that they were coming and what they were going to do whenever they got there?

What the younger people don't see, is the fact that they have lost the fear of God, in that they think that they can now tell God what to do or what to accept of their behavior, because, after all they're only human! People have unintelligently resolved with saying for decades now, that if God did not intend for them to behave a certain way, then why did He put all of these things in the earth at our disposal?

The bible tells us what to do with all that God has indeed placed at our disposal. It tells us who, where, when and it even tells us how things are to be done. This is the very reason that God never worked from the darkness;

Light yields the instructional plain for us to gleam the proper know how to perform that which is available to us as inhabitants of the earth. Surely most people were taught the same as I was, that if you don't know for sure then you should ask someone who knows.

Since we are talking bible here, you ought to find some one that is not only literarily astute in the written word of

Hidden In the Light*

God, but someone that has also been filled with the Holy Ghost, to help you to understand the word of God.

Only knowledgeable, non-spiritual people; live dangerously close to the edge of life, however not necessarily knowing just how close they are to falling off the edge of the cliffs into the abyss of sinful destruction.

Sort of to the likes of going into the ocean from the beach, and beginning to swim on the top surface of the water, venturing out further and further not knowing the extreme depths of the ocean floor beneath.

On the one hand an individual might actually be stroking as a swimmer, but at the same time without even realizing, they are also being carried out to the depths by the current of the waves on the ocean moving them out over the ocean much further than they ever intended to venture?

Without the light to guide us, it is possible to end up in places of which we never intended to be in life.

Don't you think for one moment that everyone in the penitentiary started out with the purpose in mind to end up there! Like everyone else there behind prison bars, they all thought that they

The Light First*

would be able to get away with the wrong that they had committed.

Perhaps you have discovered that all people sin and do things that they shouldn't do, that shouldn't encourage you to believe that God doesn't care about what you do, and neither should you determine that you are going on forward as a sinner to live life to the fullest as Hell bound as possible.

You may be one of those intelligent thinkers that have rationalized within your own head that because the people who attend the church regularly, that because they still sin wickedly, many of them anyway, that it doesn't make any sense for you to stop sinning and to turn your life over to the Lord?

Don't ever forget the fact that blind people who cannot even see the light, are in the light every single day of their lives! Just because people attend the church does not constitute that they see the light!

You need to focus on the fact that you see the light and do something about it! Some of the other people that you despise who are at the church but still living in darkness, will possibly be led to the light when you come into the light yourself!

Hidden In the Light*

As sinful as you may be right now in your present state, God is allowing you to see that there are those persons that have not sold-out to Him, that are standing in your way and in the way of other people like yourself, that would come to the Lord if they would be who they are supposed to be.

Nevertheless; seeing them as a hypocrite does not prevent them from the ability to change. They are much more subject to see the light in a lighted atmosphere, than you, straying away from the light. The light of the Lord is as much for them that need to come to the light, even as it is for them that are already in the light.

Peeping-Toms, like to stand out in dark hiding places concealed from visibility to look through the window of a lighted building to monitor the activity of the person/persons in the light.

People of the dark can always either tell the people of the light one of three things, the can tell the people of the light what they have done, what they are doing, or what they ought to be doing. But, they have no desire to be doing those same things themselves!

The Light First*

For we hear that there are some which walk among you disorderly, working not at all, but are busybodies.

II Thessalonians 3:11

And withal they learn to be idle, wandering about from house to house; and not only idle, but tattlers also and busy bodies, speaking things which they ought not.

I Timothy 5:13

Don't Get Caught Peeping***

And when they shall say unto you, seek unto them that have familiar spirits, and unto wizards that peep, and that mutter: should not a people seek unto their God? For the living to the dead? To the law and to the testimony: if they speak not according to this word, it is because there is no light in them.

Isaiah 8:19-20

"Peeping-Toms", look into the windows of another individual's vantage position, to monitor that other person's behavior or activities. But, an even more sinister evil stage of peeping, are the realities of those who have the audacity to seek the authority of satanic spirits to enable themselves to peep into the spirit realm, for the purpose of getting

Hidden In the Light*

heads-up into the past, present and future happenstances in the lives of other people.

I can remember a popular advertisement often played during commercial breaks back in the days of early television advertisement for an Optical clinic; the ad stated:

"Jeepers, Creepers, where'd you get those Peepers;
Jeepers, Creepers, where'd you get those Eyes?"

God would rather that you'd prefer to walk in the light, instead of secluding yourself in a far away place in darkness, choosing materials and apparatuses to enable you to only peep into the light to see what's going on over in the light of the Lord!

The eye's of which an individual might have developed over a period of time that enabled them to look in the dark from a darkened perspective, while searching for the types of things that are only done in the dark, had not been given by God as an asset for the body of Christ; though some being foolishly deceived, have come to believe such lies as being the truth.

You need to know, whom' ever you

The Light First*

may be; that the light is definitely for you! It's your God given benefit as a believer in Christ Jesus.

It is my own personal belief; that people who take the time to peep into the light from their own point of interest; that their ultimate desire is to be a partaker of the things that are happening in the light of the Lord!

I encourage you to take a closer look into the reasons that you are so preoccupied with the activities of the lighted atmospheres of God, though you choose to hide away in the dark, obscure from all visibility.

For centuries now, and even for a couple of millenniums; we have heard of witches who sat at a table behind a dark curtain in a back room peeping into a Crystal Ball; or turning Tarot cards to predict the futures of others, and to even breathe out curses.

There have also been reports of darkened individuals who have resided in outdoor caves, stirring in big black seething pots called caldrons; which would involve some hideously gruesome ingredients for the purpose of insuring the spiritual defeat over the persons of which they were targeting.

King Saul of the "Israelites", passed

Hidden In the Light*

A decree that warranted death for all of those who were found with a familiar spirit, because they were known to peep into Crystal balls, cast spells, curses, vexes and hexes to send out spirits of frustration to hinder the work of God, and more.

Many of them were mastery at calling up the dead to communicate with their spirit, and every other evil work possible for them that relied on the spirit of Satan to empower the working order of their trade.

It is not good to only pass through the light, with no intentions of allowing the light to pass through you! Saul passed through the light with his own agenda in mind to carry out his own wishes when the Lord required him to go and attack the "Amelekites."

God's instructions to Saul were to kill every living creature with the edge of the sword, from the oldest to the youngest, even baby infants. He also told Saul not to bring back any of the spoils from the camp of the "Amelekites." However, Saul had his own agenda; in that he brought back King Agag, and the finer things of the spoils, including sheep and cattle of which they found in the camp.

The Light First*

God's anger was kindled against the King at his outright refusal to obey, as a result, He rejected Saul from being king of Israel, and the kingdom was rent from him. Saul lost fellowship with God, whereas, Saul could no longer hear from God whenever he prayed, he had no way of knowing what God's next move would be; he was totally excluded from all business matters pertaining to God and the people of Israel and Judah.

Saul would eventually get word that the Philistines would be coming to attack Israel and Judah in battle, and as was customary during those times, the King would get word of approval from the Prophet of God, instructing them whether or not to go forth into battle.

Saul could get no word; the Prophet Samuel had died, and God himself had already rejected him, being that he had already proven that he would not follow God's instructions! But Saul being very self aggrandizing decided within himself, that if God didn't want to tell him what he needed to know about going into battle against the Philistines, he would just have to find out on his own.

Saul thought that he would just

Hidden In the Light*

go underground and peep into the next agenda of God by way of the witch of En'dor.

Peeping has a set of penalties and circumstances attached to it that you don't even want to experience firsthand.

In order for Saul to go where he needed to go; exiting the light, he had to camouflage himself to keep from being recognized for who he was as he went away from his own surroundings, and upon his approach to the witch's house. Remember that I told you, that you have to hide if you decide; to peep!

Now would be a good time in your life to make up in your own mind to stay away from the darker places of living as if darkness poses a blanket of obscurity hindering the Lord from being able to see us. God moved darkness for us, not for himself!

God, thought of us, as mankind, too precious and too privileged to be left in the dark. So God, in His infinite wisdom, He spreaded the blanket of His own glory for humanity to see and to witness the splendor of His own awesome handiwork when He spoke forth the light.

Upon Saul reaching his own darkened destination, having traveled

The Light First*

through the night to encounter the forbidden counsel of the ungodly, he begins to converse with the woman of familiar spirit, though yet disguised and undercover.

The woman said to Saul; "you know what Saul has done, how that he has cut off them of the familiar spirit, and wizards out of the land; why are you trying to get me killed? (Paraphrasing)

Saul's way of assuring the woman that her life would not be taken as a result of her devilish craft, he said to her; "As the Lord liveth, there shall no punishment happen to thee for this thing. I Samuel 28:10. As she yields the readiness of her craft to him, she asked him; "whom shall I bring up for thee?"

I'm sure that Saul is thinking and feeling by this time; I've got her going in the dark now! What would take place next would definitely be mind blowing for the both of them. Saul told her to call up Samuel; to their surprise, the encounter was not sensually evil as they might have ascertained; it was godly!

The woman screamed for her dear life, while a sense of fear came over Saul. Something about this encounter shined the light on the true identity of Saul, and the woman recognized him.

47

Hidden In the Light*

The woman said to Saul; I saw gods coming up out of the earth. Saul asked the woman; what form was he of? The woman said to Saul; he was an old man covered with a mantle!

Even a backslider, have the power to turn on the light, but often times without them even knowing that they yet have the power to connect. But don't rejoice just yet, now that you have been informed of the fact that those who have left the fold can still connect with the spirit of the Lord, thou it may often be accidental and unintended.

When God is silent, it is better if you determine to wait until He decides to speak to you. Saul thought that he would force God to speak to him; but he would not have been ready in a thousand years, for what Samuel would tell him.

Samuel said to Saul; God is going to deliver Israel into the hands of the Philistines; tomorrow you and your sons will be with me! Though Saul flipped the light switch from the dark, he was not ready for what would be revealed in the light.

Saul had done in darkness through disobedience, what he had not been willing to do in the light to the will

The Light First*

of the Lord. Saul had been fasting all day long, after hearing the words of Samuel, he lay prostrate on the ground, the same way as we who are saved and sanctified will do before the Lord, as we worship Him.

Saul, in my own opinion, waited rather late to humble himself, because the presence of the Lord had been departed from Saul.

It didn't matter to God that Saul had now decided to surrender to the will of the Lord because his time had run out for him to be everything that the Lord had ordained for him to be.

Saul himself was indeed exposed for doing what he had indeed despised, which was peeping by way of familiar spirit. His consequences were indeed deadly and severe, not only for himself; but also the penalty of death had been pronounced over his sons!

Your disobedience will always effect more than just yourself. The far reaching effect of playing in the dark as a leader, who had been called to walk in the light, will unintentionally touch many of your loved ones that you never expected to suffer as a result of your disobedience.

The price of peeping is often so

Hidden In the Light*

CONCEALED AWAY FROM THE GENERAL POPULOUS, SO MUCH THAT MOST PEOPLE DON'T EVEN HAVE AN IDEA OF THE PRICE THAT IS ACTUALLY BEING PAID NOR THE REASONS FOR BEING PENALIZED.

LOOK INTO THE WORD OF GOD AND YOU WILL FIND THAT THE PRICE FOR PEEPING IS TOO SEVERE TO TAKE A CHANCE ON TRYING TO GET AWAY WITH IT. STEP INTO THE BENEFIT OF THE LIGHT AND YOU WILL SEE THAT EVERYTHING THAT YOU REALLY NEED TO KNOW HAS ALREADY BEEN PROVIDED, AND THE ANSWERS WILL MANIFEST TO YOU IN DUE TIME, IF YOU JUST KEEP THE FAITH AND DON'T LOSE HOPE.

AS THE LIGHT CAME FIRST, SO DID EVERY OTHER THING THAT THE LIGHT WOULD PRODUCE FOR US; IT CAME ALSO. FIRST THE LIGHT, THEN THE REVELATION; FIRST THE LIGHT, THEN THE PATHWAY TO WALK IN; FIRST THE LIGHT, THEN THE ATMOSPHERE TO EXIST IN; FIRST THE LIGHT, THEN THE FIELD TO GROW IN; FIRST THE LIGHT, THEN THE MOVE OF GOD!

Chapter 2

His Image *

And God said, Let us make man in our image, after our likeness: and let them have dominion over the fish of the sea, and over the fowl of the air, and over the cattle, and over all the earth, and over every creeping thing that creepeth upon the earth. So God created man in his own image, in the image of God created he him; male and female created he them.

Genesis 1:26-27

I am the Lord thy God which brought thee out of the land of Egypt, out of the house of bondage. Thou shalt have no other gods before me. Exodus 20: 2-3

Who being the brightness of his glory, and the express image of his person, and upholding all things by the word of his power, when he had by himself purged our sins, sat down on the right hand of his Majesty on high; Being made so much better than the angels, as he hath by inheritance obtained a more excellent name than they. Then said I, Lo, I come (in the volume of the book it is written of me,) to do thy will, O God.   Hebrews 1:3-4, 10:7

Tell Me; Have You Seen Him?

As I pose this question to the body of Christ, let it be known that I have done so with much caution, as if to have already approached a red light at an awaiting intersection telling me to come to a complete stop! Judging the experiences that I've had in and throughout the body of Christ, as well as, with the vast volume of non-believers; I could answer for many and never be ashamed.

Unless I take the time to tell you what it is actually, that I am not making a reference to, you might begin to suspect that I am making a reference to some type of a visual citing, or an epiphany, or even some form of a vision in a dream or during a near death experience? I do believe that these types of occurrences are real and even true; I embrace the authenticity of these experiences having been levied upon the

His Image*

individuals, seemingly as having been God sent, allowing such favorable snapshots into the spirit realm.

But, I think it's very necessary not to waist time standing in the questionable dense fog of those situational occurrences, relative to the many diverse individuals that had those experiences. Don't think me to be insensitive to those personal accounts of reported incidents. I believe them!

However! The average individual would definitely have to answer no to the question posed!

To be honest with you, most people are really not even looking to see God, even in the church; they are interested in the people that make up the crowd. People are over indulged in keeping their eyes on one another in and throughout the body of Christ. They will usually latch on to whatever they feel is acceptable to them, be it good or bad! As long as everyone else does a particular thing, most people are going to embrace it as a thing of necessity for being able to exist as a vital member of the church.

It is not really as easy as one might think to enlighten people that they will never be able to clearly discern the spirit of Christ in the church for the fact

Hidden In the Light*

that their own focus has been fixed on another human being. Some, in the body of Christ that are responsible for having another individual to fixate their focus upon them, they really believe that they mean well. They might even say that it was never their intentions to mislead anyone and to cause them to miss out on clearly seeing God truly, for who He is.

Looking at the gospel of St. John, I have discovered that the Jews biggest problem with Jesus was relative to the fact that He said that He had indeed seen the Father; that He was from the Father; and that He and the Father were indeed one!

Certain ones of the Jews, would enquire of the Father, seeking to see Him. They would also ask for Jesus to show them signs of miracles and wonders to prove that He was indeed who He said that He was.

On an occasion in the sixth chapter of St. John, Jesus is talking of haven seen things that occurred before the present generations of any of the people that were standing in the crowd, instantly they were outraged at what they cited as arrogance. They began to enquire among themselves; "isn't this

His Image*

Joseph's boy?'

They even began to enquire of His actual age as a normal young man. They had no inkling of an idea that He was also simultaneously; God eternal. The very image of His flesh; blocked out the image of the "Son of God" that he is, shadowing the presence of their illuminated atmosphere, as result of having Jesus in their presence, thrusting them into the darkness of their understanding.

On the other hand, there are those individual's who could care less, that other people are being mislead as a result of following them. Some people would have you to believe that whenever you look into their eyes, that you are actually looking into the mirror of God's focus staring right back into your own eyes. They have endowed themselves to be the Lord of their own ministries and have taken on a very dangerous God complex.

People are even told to disregard the bible and to listen to the voices of their leader's instruction. Many leaders have successfully convinced a lot of people that they can lead them wherever they need to go, and that they can supply whatever needs they may indeed

Hidden In the Light*

have, because they are the source of the next individual's supply.

You might just be surprised to know that many of these same individuals have been around the church for as many as 30-60 years, being led blindly, in every direction except in the direction of God.

Personally; I think that this is just crazy, at best! If you know for a fact that you have not discerned the true spirit of the Lord Jesus Christ for yourself; read the word of God, and thoroughly search the scriptures in effort to know the characteristics of one who has indeed discerned and have received the spirit of the Lord; when you will have begun to follow the leadership of any ministry.

You have got to know the spirit of prayer and courageously indulge yourself beneath the inquisition of much meaningful prayerful dialogue. Prayer; the word of God; and then praying according to the word of God, while using the word of God to actually formidably engage the prayer dialogue, will imminently direct you to the place of spiritually discerning within yourself, to position you before the presence of His glory, revealing the blessing of His

His Image*

IMAGE.

God Blockers***

Blessed is the man that walketh not in the counsel of the ungodly, nor standeth in the way of sinners, nor sitteth in the seat of the scornful,   Psalms 1:1
But they also have erred through wine, and through strong drink are out of the way; the priest and the prophet have erred through strong drink, they are swallowed up of wine, they are out of the way through strong drink; they err in vision, they stumble in judgment. For all tables are full of vomit and filthiness, so that there is no place clean. Whom shall he teach knowledge? And whom shall he make to understand doctrine? Them that are weaned from the milk, and drawn from the breast. For precept must be upon precept, precept upon precept; line upon line, line upon line; here a little, and there a little: For with stammering lips and another tongue will he speak to his people. To whom he said, this is the rest wherewith ye may cause the weary to rest; and this is the refreshing: yet they would not hear. But the word of the Lord was upon them precept upon precept, precept upon precept; line upon line, line upon line; here a little, and there a little; that they might go, and fall backward, and be broken, and snared, and taken.   Isaiah 28:7-13

THERE IS SIMPLY NOT ENOUGH OF THE WORD OF THE LORD IN MANY OF THE LEADERS TO SHOW FORTH TO THE PEOPLE OF THE CHURCH, THE VERY IMAGE OF GOD. THEY themselves have missed the big picture! The leaders are full of wine and strong drink?

Sometimes this statement is to be taken literally; as there are many leaders who feel that it is ok to consume alcoholic beverages on a consistent basis, even to the point of alcoholism! At other occasions, the symbolisms of the wine and the strong drink are written and spoken to the intent that both the hearers and the readers of the word of God would both seek out and find the definitive comprehensiveness to these symbols.

The wine; would be symbolic to the very aged and long standing maturation; of religious practices relative to any denominational doctrine, or practical repetitive religious behavior based upon any geographical region.

These practices; perhaps might have been a part of a particular family's religious structure for several generations. Sometimes of course, the practices are the learned behavior as soon as an individual has been placed at the helm of the leadership role of the ministry. The leading persons are often required to observe certain rituals and

His Image*

DENOMINATIONAL RITES, FOR WHICH THEY WOULD NEVER BRING THEMSELVES TO EVER STRAY AWAY FROM SUCH CUSTOMS.

THE LEADERS THEMSELVES BECOME VERY PROUD OF THEMSELVES FOR HAVING BEEN SUCCESSFUL AT AFFIXING THEMSELVES INTO A CUSTOMARY ROLE AS A LEADER, RESPECTIVE TO THE EXPECTED BEHAVIOR OF THEIR OWN DENOMINATIONAL UMBRELLA.

SEE; AS LONG AS THEY KNOW THAT THEY ARE DOING THINGS RIGHT ACCORDING TO THE DENOMINATIONAL STRUCTURE, ANY SEGMENT OF THE WRITTEN WORD OF GOD THAT DOESN'T COMPLY WITH THE TAUGHT BEHAVIORAL STRUCTURE OF THEIR OWN RELIGIOUS AFFILIATED MANDATES FOR BEING A PERSPECTIVE LEADER, IS OVERLOOKED AND TOTALLY DISREGARDED.

STRONG DRINK; WOULD BE SYMBOLIC TO THE AGGRESSIVE NEWLY FOUND IDEAS OF SELF AND THE SOCIETY THAT ONE MAY HAVE SURROUNDING THEMSELVES, WHEREAS THEY HAVE INGESTED THE IDEAS OF THEMSELVES TO MEASURES EVEN GREATER, AND OVER AND ABOVE THAT OF ANY BIBLICAL KNOWLEDGE THEY MIGHT HAVE HAD PREVIOUSLY, OR MIGHT EVEN BE IN NEED OF AT THE PRESENCE.

FAR TOO MANY OF THE LEADERS ARE ONLY RELIGIOUS; THEY ARE NOT AT ALL EVEN SPIRITUAL IN THEIR LEADERSHIP ROLES. A FEW OF THE VERY DISTINCT DIFFERENCES BETWEEN

Hidden In the Light*

THOSE LEADERS THAT ARE ONLY RELIGIOUS AND THOSE THAT ARE INDEED TRULY SPIRITUAL LEADERS, IS MORE CLEARLY PERCEIVED IF YOU SEE IT LIKE SO;

1. The RELIGIOUS leader says: "Look at me; I'm the one; just keep your eyes on me and you can never go wrong?" They are consistently reminding others to applaud them for their accomplishments as the leader. Usually they don't mind citing the fact that they do the job better than anyone else.
SELF-INTOXICATION*
2. The SPIRITUAL leader says: "It's still me Oh Lord; standing in the need of your grace to help me to lead your people every step of the way. They are consistently instructing the people of their congregations; "Follow me as I follow Christ." "Of mine own self I can do nothing."
SPIRIT-FILLED*

THE BOTTOM LINE IS THAT, IN EITHER CASE SCENARIO RELATIVE TO THE WINE AND THE STRONG DRINK, THE LEADERS, MANY OF THEM ANYWAY, ARE DRUNK ON THEMSELVES! THIS, MY FRIEND IS THE REASON THAT SO MANY LEADERS ARE COMFORTABLE WITH ANY BEHAVIOR THAT IS TOTALLY TO THE LEFT AGAINST THE MANDATED LIFESTYLES GIVEN FOR US IN THE WORD OF GOD.

His Image*

Whether it is the manner of behavior in which they carry themselves, or the outright ungodly living of the parishioners that attend their churches, they're just not bothered either way.

It is no wonder that they are out of balance; drunken people can't stand up straight! They are always falling down on the ground, and doing things that otherwise, supposedly they would not do. They like to fight, and they get real loud and extremely talkative, saying things that have no real meaning at all it seems.

Other times they become very disruptive and destructive in their behavior. Does this at all in any way sound like the picture of your leader; either realistically speaking, or figuratively speaking?

If so, you are following the wrong leader; they can't help you, and they certainly can't show you Christ!

You Think That You Discern Satan?

Rather you knew it or not, it is extremely important that we as people of the body of Christ be accurate when identifying the entrance of Satan into our affairs, our worship services, and

Just to put it all in a nut shell, whenever that wrong spirit has infiltrated our atmosphere.

While we have gained the ability to read and to comprehend what we have read most of the time anyway; without even knowing it many times, we have also lost the spiritual sensitivity that would guide us in knowing exactly what might have been underneath what we had just read.

The spirit uncovers the subliminal messages which had been purposely hidden between the lines, and underneath the pictures. The enemy knows that only the diligent would ever be able to clearly discern his hidden messages and the mess that it would cause when left undetected!

We have been lulled to sleep in these perilous times of which we are now living, as a result, we have also put away the power of diligence; as it may often seem that no one is actually taking us serious anyway.

The deceptive lullaby; of the song "Nobody Cares"; has been sung in our spirits all along by Satan. When we are not sure to discern the spirit of Satan, we are left to believe that we are living in the reality of people not really

His Image*

desiring to have us present with them on this earth. Satan is cunning and crafty in knowing just how to cause us to put down the weapons of our warfare.

As believers, many things will take place in our lives that we may not be able to comprehensively explain to others. Other people are not able to understand what we are disturbed about, and they are incapable of responding to our point of need as a result of being indigent relative to what we were trying to convey to them.

At such a point as this, we are more easily pushed to the point of embracing the dreaded reality, though a false reality; that we are left alone to deal with our troubles.

Be mindful of the fact that everything that God's wants to press out of you is not at all bad! That which indeed has come to the point of maturity in the word of God, that is going to work for the good of the body of Christ on the inside of you, must be brought forth out of you in due time.

There must be a birthing process which should take place in all of our lives in the spirit realm, less the babe of excellence would die in our womb! God loves us too much to allow such a

Hidden In the Light*

TRAGEDY TO TAKE PLACE IN OUR SPIRITS.

We are born again into the kingdom of God's dear son, Jesus Christ. While we are born into the kingdom, the kingdom is in-turn birthed into our spirits on the inside of us. As a result, the "King" in us must come out of us; so that the Kingdom of God in the earth might be increased and further established for the purpose of fulfilling the plan of God in the earth.

First of all; when you can't clearly discern the spirit of the Lord; there is no way on earth possible for you to be able to properly discern the spirit of Satan, either!

You have got to be able to know what is; which is God; before you will be able to know what is not! Satan is not God; and neither is he in control of our lives, unless we give the control to him!

For an instance; some things that happen to us in our lives as we go through the run of our days, that may not be pleasant to us necessarily, we may have a tendency to plaster the name of Satan all over it, when in actuality, it was God all of the time!

Sometimes we are just in the right time line of our spiritual growth and

His Image*

THE RIGHT SEASON OF OUR TIME, WHILE ABIDING ON THE VINE, FOR A FLAVOR-ABLE-CRUSHING FROM THE LORD.

IF THE FRUIT OF OUR FAVORITE DRINK BEVERAGES WERE NEVER CRUSHED, WE WOULD NOT HAVE THOSE JUICES TO PARTAKE OF. ALTHOUGH FRUITS AND VEGETABLES MUST BE CRUSHED FOR THE PLEASURE AND THE NOURISHMENT OF OUR BODIES, THEY MUST BE READY TO BE CRUSHED WHILE ON THE VINE BEFORE THEY ARE EVER PLUCKED FROM THE VINES AND THE TREES.

GRAPES YIELD VERY FLAVORFUL JUICES AND WINES ALIKE; BUT THEY MUST BE READY GRAPES THAT ARE CRUSHED IN AN EFFORT TO PRODUCE THAT WHICH IS BENEFICIAL TO US AND EVEN GOOD TO OUR TASTE BUDS.

THE SAME THINGS OF WHICH WE ARE OFTEN MOANING AND GROANING ABOUT, THOSE ARE THE SAME THINGS THAT GOD IS MOST LIKELY USING TO MAKE US AND TO FINISH US OUT SO THAT THE GLORY OF GOD MIGHT BE IMMINENTLY FLOWING OUT OF OUR LIVES. THE HAND OF GOD NEVER TRANSFORMS INTO BEING THE VERY SAME AS THE ENEMY'S HAND.

THE SAME HAND OF THE LORD WHICH BLESSES US, IT ALSO SHAPES US, EVEN WHENEVER IT MAY MEAN THAT HE WILL HAVE TO BREAK US ALSO. GOD KNOWS JUST HOW TO GO ABOUT GETTING THE GOOD OUT US BECAUSE HE KNOWS THAT IT'S THERE. JUST AS WE KNOW

Hidden In the Light*

EXACTLY WHAT TO EXPECT FROM ANY PARTICULAR FRUIT OR VEGETABLE, JUST FROM LOOKING AT IT BEFORE WE START THE CRUSHING PROCESS OF EXTRACTION.

WE ARE OFTEN READY FOR THE MASTER'S USE BEFORE WE KNOW OF IT; VISE-VERSA; WHEN WE MIGHT FEEL THAT WE ARE ALL OF THAT AND A BAG OF CHIPS, WHENEVER WE WERE SURE WITHIN OUR SELVES THAT WE WERE READY FOR THE LORD TO PICK US OUT OF THE CHRISTIAN LINE-UP, SHOULD WE GET PASSED OVER, WE ARE LEFT STRUGGLING WITH WHY IT IS THAT GOD DID NOT SEE IN US, WHAT WE HAVE SEEN WITHIN OURSELVES?

THE GREATER FRUSTRATIONS BEFORE US LIES WITHIN THE WARS WITHIN OUR SPIRITS; WHERE WE ALLOW THE PROFUSE CONFUSION OF OUR FEELINGS AND EMOTIONS TO FUSE RELIGION AND RELATIONSHIP TOGETHER, WHICH IS A MAJOR DECEPTION!

RELIGION TEACHES US TO REPETITIOUSLY FEEL, AS LONG AS WE FEEL GOOD ABOUT WHAT WE ARE FEELING ON A CONSISTENT BASIS, WHILE WE PRACTICE CHURCH REGIMENS AND CALL IT GOD.

RELATIONSHIP ON THE OTHER HAND, TEACHES US TO KNOW GOD THROUGH HIS WORD, AND THE PERSON OF JESUS CHRIST OUR SAVIOR AND OUR LORD, AND THE AWESOMELY WORKING POWER OF THE HOLY GHOST DWELLING ON THE INSIDE OF US.

His Image*

We must know God by faith; faithfully trusting Him to show us the way of living every moment of our lives. The only way to get to know God is through faith in the precious shed blood of Jesus Christ. God always know us; but without faith in action towards God, we can never know God.

> *Even so faith, if it hath not works, is dead, being alone. Yea a man may say, thou hast faith, and I have works: shew me thy faith without thy works, and I will shew thee my faith by my works. Thou believest that there is one God; thou doest well: the devils also believe and tremble. But wilt thou know, O vain man, that faith without works is dead? Ye see then how that by works a man is justified, and not by faith alone. For as the body without the spirit is dead, so faith without works is dead also.*   James 2:17-20, 24, 26

We are actually a lazy generation of people; we (meaning most people) want somebody else to do things for us. Whatever the Lord has done for us, we sometimes want someone else to place it into our hands without any effort on our part, overlooking the fact that God has designed that we participate in the process of receiving from Him.

The works that must be added to our faith is called; "diligence." In past times I had been taught as many of you

Hidden In the Light*

were that the works of which we needed desperately to add to our faith would only be centered on the act of believing.

Faith; is, believing! But, diligence; is retrieving that which we have believed for, from the Lord. Therefore, faith believes; and diligence retrieves! Without diligence, faith stands alone to believe God relatively for nothing, but, on the other hand, diligence without faith has nothing to retrieve.

Faith in itself, can only deliver what grace has already provided for us, and given to us freely by God in Christ Jesus. Where there is no diligence added to our faith, the things provided for us by the grace of our Lord, will have to remain on the shelves of God's store house of blessings.(II Peter1:6)

The scenario could be similar to a hunter on a hunting trip for Wild Game Birds, who takes his Golden Retriever with him actually to go out and to bring back the prize of the hunt.

Faith is like the hunter who finds, recognizes, points and shoots its prey. Once the object of our faith has been captured in the spirit realm, like as unto capturing a picture in the camera lens before actually snapping the photo; it is necessary for our own spirit of diligence

His Image*

TO STEP UP TO THE FOREFRONT OF THE CHALLENGE TO BRING THE GIVEN DESIRE OF THE OBJECT OF OUR FAITH DIRECTLY TO OUR POSSESSION. I'M A BELIEVER WITH A RETRIEVER!

FAITH AND DILIGENCE ARE TO THE LIKES OF THE WRITTEN LETTER OF THE LAW; AND THE LAW ENFORCEMENT OFFICERS PARTNERING TOGETHER, TO DILIGENTLY PATROL THE STREETS OF OUR CITIES. THE LAW IN EFFECT, WOULD BE POWERLESS ABIDING ALONE WITHOUT THE OFFICERS OF THE LAW TO ENFORCE THE LETTER OF THE LAW.

IN THE PAST DECADES, MANY OF THE MINISTERS TAUGHT US THAT ALL WE NEEDED WAS FAITH TO RECEIVE EVERYTHING THAT THE LORD HAD FOR US. BUT IN SEARCHING THE SCRIPTURES FOR MYSELF, I HAVE DISCOVERED THAT FAITH MUST BE COUPLED WITH DILIGENCE.

> *But without faith it is impossible to please Him: for he that cometh to God must believe that he is, and the he is a rewarder of them that diligently seek him.*
> *Hebrews 11:6*

BACK IN THE 1980's & 1990's; MOST OF THE CHARISMATIC PENTECOSTALS WERE TEACHING US THAT ALL WE WERE TO DO TO RECEIVE THE BLESSINGS OF THE LORD, WAS JUST TO NAME IT AND CLAIM IT!

OF COURSE WE WERE TAUGHT THAT IF WE COULD BELIEVE IT, WE COULD ALSO RECEIVE

Hidden In the Light*

it. But as of recent times, many of the same people who took notes during those teaching sessions and the services and revival crusades, bought tapes on the perspective evangelical Orators, and sowed seeds into those ministries, are still in the line waiting to receive.

They still have not taken hold of their desired possessions as a result of the release of their faith, as were promised to many of them. They're still on the waiting list!

There is nothing at all wrong with their faith; it is what it is; but, there are elements that are perhaps missing that would propel the faithful desires of the believers to the point of manifestation.

An airplane without a propeller or a Jet engine is still an Airplane; but, without the propeller of the Jet engine, the plane would never get up off of the ground to take flight to anywhere. Even if it were already on the runway with its fuel tank full! Many people have faith that has been fully established on the word of God, but, the faith that they have is abiding alone without the works.

Whenever I am taking a trip on an airplane, I check my bags at the airport

His Image*

when I arrive to board my flight. Upon arriving at the intended destination, we are directed to the baggage claim to collect our bags and our property which had been previously checked in before we left from our departure.

Upon approaching the baggage claim, the luggage are released and delivered to us on a conveyer belt. Whenever I recognize my bags, I can rightfully name them and verbally claim them, whether it is silently spoken in my own mind, or spoken to someone there to pick me up from the airport.

However, my luggage will continue to circulate around the conveyer, until I actively retrieve them and physically take hold of them to possess them.

It doesn't really matter that the baggage already belong to me; as is likewise the very realistic truth that are relative to the things that we have asked for in faith believing God to give to us.

I had even placed a claim tag on the bags before being taken to be stored in the lower storage compartment of the plane for travel.

Naming and claiming therefore, should only activate the diligence in me, enabling me to lay hold on my

Hidden In the Light*

POSSESSIONS. WITHOUT PUTTING MY HANDS TO MY BELONGINGS, THE GREATER CHANCE IS THAT ONLY AFTER A SHORT WHILE MY LUGGAGE WILL BE SHIPPED TO THE DEPARTMENT OF THE LOST AND FOUND, OR IT COULD POSSIBLY BE STOLEN BY SOME ONE ELSE.

THIS ALL FITS IN TO WHAT I AM SAYING RELATIVE TO THE FACT THAT YOU HAVE GOT TO GO AFTER GOD TO SEEK HIM DILIGENTLY WITH YOUR WHOLE HEART, AND STAY IN PATIENCE TO BE FOUND OF HIM.

YOU MUST HAVE A RELATIONSHIP WITH GOD, BECAUSE IT IS GOD THAT IS GOING TO SHOW YOU SATAN EVEN WHEN HE, HIMSELF WILL ATTEMPT TO HIDE IN THE SHADOWS OF THE PEOPLE WHO ARE WALKING IN THE LIGHT.

PEOPLE, WHO WILL SAY THAT THEY DON'T BELIEVE IN GOD; MOST OF THEM ARE DEMONICALLY POSSESSED AND OFTEN SADISTICALLY INFLUENCED IN THE SPIRIT OF THEIR MINDS, BUT WITHOUT THE ABILITY TO KNOW HOW TO RECOGNIZE THEIR TRUE SPIRITUAL STATUS. THEY FEEL THAT IT IS JUST THEIR WAY OF LIVING, AND THEIR NORMAL BEHAVIOR AND THEIR OWN DESIRES WHEN THEY CHOOSE TO DO DETESTABLE THINGS AND DENIGRATE THEMSELVES.

EVEN MORE ALARMING ARE THE PEOPLE IN AND AROUND THE LOCAL CHURCHES THAT ARE SO IN THE DARK AS TO THE REALITY OF SATAN.

His Image*

Find His Face

The Lord bless thee, and keep thee: the Lord make his face to shine upon thee, and be gracious unto thee: the Lord lift up his countenance upon thee, and give thee peace.   Numbers 6: 24-26

Canst thou by searching find out God? Canst thou find out the Almighty unto perfection? Wherefore hidest thou thy face, and holdest me for thine enemy?   Job 11:7, 13:24

Hear, O Lord, when I cry with my voice: have mercy also upon me, and answer me. When thou saidest, seek ye my face; my heart said unto thee, thy face, Lord will I seek. Hide not thy face far from me; put not thy servant away in anger: thou hast been my help; leave me not, neither forsake me, O God of my salvation. Wherefore hidest thou thy face, and forgettest our affliction and our oppression? Lord, why castest thou off my soul? Why hidest thou thy face from me?   Psalms 27:7, 44:24, 88:14

Behold, the Lord's hand is not shortened that it can not save; neither his ear heavy that it can not hear: but your iniquities have separated between you and your God, and your sins have hid his face from you, that he will not hear.   Isaiah 59:1-2

Then shall ye call upon me, and ye shall go and pray unto me, and I will hearken unto you. And ye shall seek me, and find me, when ye shall search for me with all your heart.   Jeremiah 29:12-13

W<small>HENEVER WE AS HUMANS HAVE SEARCHED FOR</small> G<small>OD AND OF OUR OWN SELVES</small>

Hidden In the Light*

HAVE NOT BEEN SUCCESSFUL AT FINDING HIM; IT IS OFTEN CUSTOMARY TO INVOKE ANY SUBSTANCE-LESS FINDINGS RELATIVE TO THE ACTUAL EXISTENCE OF GOD.

BUT, OF THE NATURAL INSTINCTS OF MANKIND, AS A RESULT OF A TIMID SEARCH, MOST PEOPLE USUALLY EMERGE FROM THE EXPLORATORY ESCAPADE OF DETERMINATE SELFISHNESS TO FIND GOD OUTSIDE OF THE WRITTEN WORD OF GOD WITH MUCH BRUISED EGOS.

PRIDEFUL, PROUD INDIVIDUALS OF EARTHLY STUDIES, HAVE ALL BUT CONCEDED TO THEIR INADEQUACIES, TOO EMBARRASSED TO ACKNOWLEDGE THAT THEY HAD FAILED TO PRODUCE ANY SUCCESSFUL FINDINGS IN THEIR SEARCH TO NATURALLY PLACE A VISUAL GRASP ON THE IMAGE OF GOD.

EGOTISTICAL DOUBTERS, ARE FOR CERTAIN, OF THE WORST AT SUCCUMBING TO THE WIN OF THE FAITHFUL BELIEVERS, WHO CONFESS TO EXPERIENCING THE BENEFIT OF THEIR SEARCH THROUGH THE SCRIPTURE.

THOSE WHO HAVE INDEED FAILED AT FINDING GOD FROM A VERY HUMANISTIC PERSPECTIVE, FIND IT MUCH EASIER TO ATTEMPT AT DESTROYING THE IMAGE OF GOD IN THE SPIRIT OF THE MINDS OF THE FAITHFUL.

USUALLY ANGERED AT THE FACT THAT IT SEEMS THAT GOD WOULD ACTUALLY HIDE FROM THEM AND NOT ENABLE THEIR VERY

His Image*

SECULAR APPROACH TO KNOWING HIM; THEY BEGIN REACHING FOR THE SLEDGE HAMMERS OF THEIR SCIENTIFIC MINDS, WIELDING THE SKEPTIC VERBAL BLADES OF THEIR TONGUES, ATTEMPTING TO POUND THE TRUTH OUT OF OUR REVELATORY COMPREHENSIVE MANIFESTATIONS OF TRUTH AS IS WRITTEN IN THE BIBLE.

I AM WALKING IN THE STRENGTH AND POWER OF WHAT I HAVE FOUND TO BE THE SOUND FIRM TRUTH OF THE REALITY OF THE IMAGE OF GOD. THE FACT IS THAT NOT ALL THAT ARE LOOKING FOR GOD, IN SEARCH OF SEEING HIM LIKE OTHERS HAVE REPORTED OF SEEING HIM; ARE SEEKING HIS FACE!

MOST CARNAL MINDED PEOPLE SIMPLY WANT TO SEE WHAT GOD LOOKS LIKE, BUT THEY HAVE ABSOLUTELY NO DESIRE TO KNOW WHAT GOD IS REQUIRING OF MANKIND. THE EASIEST WAY TO DISREGARD GOD'S COMMANDMENTS FOR HUMANITY IS TO DENY THE REALITY OF HIS EXISTENCE.

WHY IS IT THAT SOME PEOPLE SEARCH FOR GOD AND FIND HIM, WHILE OTHERS CONTINUE TO SEARCH NEVER COMING TO THE END OF THEIR SEARCH FOR GOD?

TO ME; AND TO THE SPIRITUAL LITERATE; TO THOSE OF US WHO STUDY THE SCRIPTURE FROM OUR HEARTS UPWARDS TOWARDS OUR HEADS, SPIRITUALLY REACHING UP INTO THE ATMOSPHERE OF THE HOLY GHOST; THE

Hidden In the Light*

ANSWERS ARE OBVIOUS AND CLEAR............................

God is neither lost, gone, nor either obsolete in these latter ages of the existence of humanity; but, He is hidden; though in plain view.

The tools and the agenda of our search for God is what will more assuredly determine the outcome of our search. What we use to search is equally as important as what we are indeed looking to find as a result of our search.

The greater problem lies within the fact that many people are searching in the natural realm of humanity for a man-like created being, or for some type of a physical sculptured image of stone, metallic, or any other rare substance; for the purpose of finding God who is both a spirit; and the creator of all created beings in the heavens and the earth.

Even, where we implement the initiation of our search, has to be established as an essential consideration for the benefit of the outcome of the search for God.

These latter generations of people have become too open minded, to the point that they don't mind prolonging their search for God, who is presently

His Image*

everywhere all of the time. They have no sense of an urgency as it relates to finding God, as a matter of the fact they feel that they actually have a life time to complete their search.

People usually feel as though they are better equipped to expunge life's realities should they maintain a much broader scope of reasoning, which allows them to look in places other than, within the written word of God (King James Bible), and within the spiritual atmosphere of the Christian body of baptized believers, for what might otherwise be regarded as the Face of God; or His Image.

People choose consistently to look everywhere else for the purpose of finding God in places of which ultimately He will never be found.

None of us human-beings have the power or the skill to bring God to us from hiding away from our visibility to see Him and to know Him, without Him coming forth in the spirit to show Himself to us.

Let's not overlook the fact that men have found other gods in other places that satisfied the curiosity of their minds, while at the same God in which they found was powerless to save

Hidden In the Light*

them from the power of sin, leaving the longings of their souls still void.

To any people that would prefer a God that they could boss and tell Him what to do concerning them, it might appear a bit puzzling and even down right cruel in that God is here all of the time, even directing the search for Him in the spirits of certain individuals that are indeed sincere in their hearts to connect with God.

Coming up in the church as a young boy, I can remember the saints of old singing a song the said; "God's Got a Way That You Can't get Over; Under; or Around; You Must Come In At The Door!" They use to sing; "God's Way Is the Best Way!"

And of course anyone that has been in a church service would have to say that they have heard the church sing; "All to Jesus I surrender; All to Him I Freely Give!"

While it is your search for God; it is His face that you are seeking, therefore allow me to encourage you to align your search with the word of God, so that success will come your way immediately!

Then said Jesus unto his disciples, If any man will come after me, let him deny himself, and take up his cross,

His Image*

and follow me.   St. Matthew 16:24

"SELF' DENIAL" IN THE VERY BEGINNING OF THIS CHAPTER THE QUESTION WAS POSED; "HAVE YOU SEEN HIM?"

I ALSO KNEW THAT I COULD ANSWER THAT QUESTION FOR MOST PEOPLE SIMPLY BECAUSE, MOST PEOPLE OF TODAY ARE PARTICULARLY SELF CENTERED! SELF STANDS IN THE WAY OF MOST EVERY DECISION MADE.

IT HAS BEEN A PROVEN FACT, THAT PEOPLE DON'T MIND BEING A SERVANT IF THEY ARE THE ONE'S GETTING THE BENEFIT OF BEING A SERVANT. JUST TAKE A LOOK AT OUR SOCIETY, RELATIVE TO OUR CONSUMER AFFAIRS, ALL YOU SEE NOW ARE SELF SERVE GAS STATIONS, RESTAURANTS WITH BUFFET LINES AND STEAM TABLES, AND SALAD BARS, GROCERY STORES, DEPARTMENT STORES, HARDWARE STORES AND MANY OTHERS.

HOW FAMILIAR ARE YOU TO THE "SELF-CHECK-OUT" METHODS OF PURCHASING NOWADAYS?

MANY PEOPLE ARE SATISFIED WITH THIS METHOD OF SHOPPING FOR A NUMBER OF REASONS OF WHICH I DON'T THINK THAT IT WOULD BE NECESSARY TO TRY TO EXAMINE THOSE ISSUES AT THIS TIME. BUT OF COURSE, I WILL SAY THAT THE NUMBER ONE REASON FOR THE VOTE OF ACCEPTANCE WOULD DEFINITELY BE FOR THE REASON OF THE FACT

Hidden In the Light*

that people are more selfish. It is easier to hide our selections at the checkout counter, and the quantity of the purchases, without being scrutinized.

By a very similar self serving principle, many want God in their lives on the Secrete Tip; as long as nobody really knows that they have sought the Lord and have invited Him into their life to be their Lord and savior, some people feel that they will just silently enter into the Kingdom of Heaven with every one else, to receive the same reward.

So many people, are even leaving the local churches, forsaking the teachings of the Bible which mandate holy living and consideration for others, above and beyond any selfish behavior that causes one to care more for themselves than they would for anyone else. The reason they say that they are leaving the church, is because they want to serve the Lord in their own way.

Forget about the established method of worshipping the Lord, some people feel that they have found new ways to do what has been done for centuries, according to the written word of God.

People want to find God who never

His Image*

changes His image or His ways, and they expect one day to see Him face to face; quote-un-quote=to see Him just as He IS! Only, most people would rather change the image of God, by way of altering His requirements and commandments for mankind; but, they still want to see Him, as He IS?!???

God, is who He always was, and He is, whom He will always, forever be! God is an ever unchanging God; He is always the same; therefore we can't go looking for someone that no longer matches the description of the God of the Holy Bible, expecting for them to be one and the same. Changed is what we will become whenever we finally come into contact with the powerful presence of God.

Go ahead and take into consideration the fact that we are who we are whenever we begin to search for God, but, we are the person of interest that needs to recognize who we are not.

The key to successfully seeing God's image is incumbent upon the initial act of denying self. The greater the sacrifice you make in seeking God, the greater the blessing you will receive as a result.

God will never be outdone by

anyone, especially when it comes to giving. Young men and young women alike will give their lives for the security of their own countries, and we as people cite those selfless acts of patriotism as remarkable!

But consider the fact that Jesus gave His life for both friend and enemy, good and bad, rich and poor, smart and illiterate, and finally for all mankind.

My dear friend, God is hidden in plain sight and in open view, for all to see Him everywhere. My family and I use to frequently visit a restaurant here in the Metroplex, called the "Black eyed Pea." They would decorate the table with paper table mats with puzzles on them.

The puzzles consisted of cartoon drawings with several scenes. There were several Black eyed Peas hidden on the page in plain view, and we were required to find all of the Black eyed Peas on the page, which required more than just a momentary glance. Initially we had to search for them which kept us a bit occupied until our meal arrived.

Once we gave a thorough examination to the puzzle, to our amazement, there they were; there were peas all over the page everywhere. They

His Image*

had been drawn into every scene as a part of each article that would make up the complete picture. After we completed the puzzle for the initial test we could almost complete the puzzle blind folded, we not only knew what to look for, but, we also knew exactly where to look on the page to find the peas. It was fun!

The puzzle had a few instructions written just at the top of the page for us to follow in an effort to finish the puzzle. As simple as the instructions were, if we followed the instructions, we would simplify our search and find whatever we were looking for much swifter. We knew what to look for!

In the same manner as this principle of the puzzle, the Bible has refined the search for us to assuredly find God in our search. We must be sure to start at the beginning of the instructional manual and be willing to obey the instructions. To your own amazement, you will find that God is hidden everywhere in plain sight.

You may find yourself asking the question; "why didn't I see Him there a long time ago?"

Back then, before you could see God doesn't really matter, all that matters is right now that you have

Hidden In the Light*

FINALLY COME TO THE POINT OF MATURITY IN YOUR SPIRIT, BECAUSE GOD RESIDES IN THE "RIGHT NOW."

THE ULTIMATE BLESSING IS THAT, ONCE YOU HAVE COMPLETED YOUR SEARCH AND HAVE FOUND THE LORD GOD, WHO WAS NEVER LOST TO BEGIN WITH, YOU WILL SOON DISCOVER THAT YOU WILL ALWAYS KNOW WHERE AND HOW TO FIND GOD!

ONCE YOU PLEASE THE LORD BY FAITH, YOU WILL RECEIVE THE BENEFIT OF KNOWING THAT GOD IS EVER OPENED TO YOU, FOR THE REST OF YOUR BEING, BOTH NATURALLY AND SPIRITUALLY.

GOD CAN BE SEEN IN EVERYTHING THAT HE HAS EVER CREATED, BUT YOU HAVE GOT TO BE WILLING TO SEE GOD AND NOT JUST MAN.

DON'T JUST SEEK THE HAND OF GOD BEGGING FOR HIS BLESSINGS, BUT, SEEK HIS FACE FOR THE PURPOSE OF BEING IN HIS PRESENCE.

GOD'S GOT EVERYTHING THAT YOU NEED EVERY TIME HE MANIFEST HIS PRESENCE IN YOUR OWN ATMOSPHERE.

BY THE WAY; WE ARE MADE IN GOD'S OWN IMAGE; SEE YOURSELF IN THE MIRROR OF THE WORD OF GOD AND YOU WILL SURELY SEE THE IMAGE OF GOD.

THAT THE <u>WORLD MIGHT SEE JESUS</u> IN ME AND IN YOU TOO!

Chapter 3

Darkened Perspective

There is none that understandeth, there is none that seeketh God. They are all gone out of the way, they are together become unprofitable; there is none that doeth good, no, not, one. Their throat is an open sepulchre; with their tongues they have used deceit; the poison of asps is under their lips: whose mouths is full of cursing and bitterness: their feet are swift to shed blood: destruction and misery are in their ways: and the way of peace have they not known: there is no fear of God before their eyes.

Romans 3: 11-18

Righteously Invisible!

I HAVE STATED IN OTHER WRITINGS, THAT PEOPLE REALLY HAVE A DESIRE TO SEE GOD! MOST ARE SO FRUSTRATED THAT THEY CAN'T SEE THE LORD FROM THEIR OWN DARKENED POSITIONS OF INIQUITY, THAT THEY CONTINUE TO PUSH ON FORWARD DETERMINING IN THEIR OWN MINDS TO WITNESS THAT WHICH CAN'T EVEN BE NATURALLY VISUALIZED.

THE FOOLISH HEARTS OF MEN, HAVE DECEIVED THEM INTO TAKING ON A BINOCULAR LIKE FOCUS AT GOD FROM THEIR OWN SEPARATED DISTANCES, NOT BEING ABLE TO APPROACH UNTO THE THRONE OF THE LORD COVERED IN THE SLIME OF SIN AND INIQUITY; TO WHICH THEY HAD NO DESIRE TO BE FREED OR RELEASED, BEING THE ONLY REAL PROBLEM THEY HAVE WITH COMING BEFORE THE LORD.

MANY HAVE DETERMINED THAT THEY WILL STAY AWAY DIRTY, AND SEE HIM AS HE IS IN THEIR OWN SKEWED PERCEPTIONS, BASED ON THEIR SINFUL HUMANISTIC INSIGHT, AND STILL BE LIKEWISE FAVORABLY SEEN AND SMILED UPON; OF HIM!

MANY PEOPLE HAVE COME TO ME SEEKING TO HAVE AN EXPERIENCE WITH GOD, ALTHOUGH THEY NEVER DESIRED TO HAVE A RELATIONSHIP WITH HIM. THEIR UTTER DETERMINATION RELATIVE TO GOD; IS THAT

Darkened Perspectives *

He ought to just show up for them to give them a sign of some sort, proving the reality of His existence.

Many are so heavily affixed into positions of self exoneration from the wrath of God, that they have determined in their hearts not to be moved from their sinfulness. They are gone so far under the weight of sin and shame.

The Jews often confronted Jesus brandishing these same like attitudes, relative to their human-ness. The Jews alike many of the people of today, felt that the teachings of Jesus were unrealistic and a major hinderance to the teachings of the synagog, which were already established.

Although that which they had been following for many years had failed them, they weren't interested in following after a surer and a more perfect way of living to please the Lord.

The Jews could see the rabbi, but they could not see the Messiah, the same way that most people of the churches of today can see their pastors, but they have absolutely no revelation of Jesus!

I have had a lot of people say to me, that living by the bible in these modern times is unrealistic to the very necessary evaluation of modern sivilization. The statement has been made often that; "People don't believe that stuff anymore."

Across all racial barriers, those who preach seem to conduct themselves as if God has stepped aside and allowed them to take over, supposedly as having the new authority on the scripture. They themselves have begun seeking to disprove the biblical accounts of the scripture right in the pulpit, during their own sermonic delivery.

My point, before I get too deeply engrossed in the subject of blinded leadership; is however, that many people are standing in the dark and often in the darkened places of their own understanding trying to gain enlightenment and a clear picture of the Lord.

Often times, it's what we already think that we know that keeps us from receiving the knowledge of what we ought to know, that is most important.

They Can't See You Either!

It is very important to keep ourselves unspotted from the world for the sake of how we are going to be perceived by the people who see us on a

Darkened Perspectives *

DAILY BASIS.

Whom, you've become, is not actually who people are going to recognize whenever they look upon you. They remember whomever they thought they might have seen the last time they saw you!

People's perceptions are easily tainted and slurred! It may not have even been you that tainted their perception of you, never-the-less, they have an idea of who they think that you are, and most are not easily bent on changing their minds.

I have discovered that we who are walking in the glorious light of the Lord, we want the people of these latter generations, who for the fact of being spiritually blinded themselves, they cannot even see God to begin with, we are determined for those same people to see God in us!

Believe me; for a truth, they don't even see God; in God! Most for sure don't even have any respect for God in Christ Jesus!

Their blindness has nothing to do with the fact that God shows up in our lives and shines forth for all men to see Him; God's ability to shine in these latter times has not been hampered

Hidden In the Light*

NEITHER HINDERED! THE HEART AND THE MINDS OF THE PEOPLE HAVE BEEN FOOLISHLY DARKENED FOR REASON OF THE FACT THAT MANY PEOPLE HAVE BEEN TAUGHT TO DISRESPECT THE DEITY OF CHRIST!

LET ME ENCOURAGE YOU NOT TO BE SO CARRIED AWAY WITH YOURSELF, THAT YOU SUPPRESS YOUR TRUE CHARACTER AND PERSONALITY FOR THE FACT OF BELIEVING THAT YOU'RE THE CAUSE THAT PEOPLE DON'T SEE THE PRESENCE OF THE LORD ON YOUR LIFE!

HAVE YOU EVER STOPPED TO THINK ABOUT THE FACT THAT SOME PEOPLE ARE WEARING MENTAL BLINDERS AND THE DARK SHADES OF STINKING THINKING ON A DAILY BASIS; THAT KEEPS THEM FROM SEEING CLEARLY TO DISCERN THE TRUTH ABOUT ANYTHING OR OF ANYBODY?

PEOPLE ARE TAUGHT TO ASSIGN A DIFFERENT FORM AND SPIRITUAL PERSONA TO OUR GOD OTHER THAN WHAT HAS BEEN GIVEN TO US IN THE HOLY BIBLE. SO WHAT YOU AND I KNOW OF, AND RESPECT AS THE TRUTH ABOUT GOD RELATIVE TO THE SCRIPTURES, IS FOREIGN KNOWLEDGE TO THEM THAT ARE WILLFULLY BLINDED.

CERTAIN PEOPLE BELIEVE THAT YOU AND I ARE REDICULOUS HILLS, AND WEAK FOR SELLINBG OUT TO THE REALITY OF GOD, WHO IS INDEED INVISIBLE AND CANNOT BE SEEN WITH THE NAKED EYE.

Darkened Perspectives *

Secular huministically thinking people, feel that we choose Christ for the simple reason of needing something or someone to believe in other than ourselves, as a result of truly being less fortunate than the very rich in finances and having fewer opportunities than the wealthier people of our society.

Somehow they don't see us being sound in our minds and in our choices, as we choose Jesus Christ; as our Lord and our savior.

We are to assume the positions of being reflexive to the light of the Lord whenever we come to be saved. Often times we are doing a good job of reflecting the light and the life of Christ in our lives; but, what we are projecting forth from our lives is not what many people are looking to see from us.

We often make the mistake of believing and trusting in the fact that people are looking through the clean filtered intellects of their own mind, with the ability to actually see us for who we really are!

As we focus our attention of looking from a darkened perspective; or standing in a dark place looking into the light, it is paramount that we

Hidden In the Light*

RECOGNIZE THE TOTAL ABSENCE OF AN ILLUMINATION IN THOSE DARK PLACES.

THE LIGHTS HAVE ALL BEEN TURNED OUT! THE OBJECTS THAT ARE CAPABLE OF DISSPELLING DARKNESS AND LIGHGTING THE PATHWAYS HAVE BEEN ELIMINATED. SOMEONE HAS ALLOWED THE LIGHT TO GO OUT.

Then all those virgins arose, and trimmed their lamps. And the foolish said unto the wise, Give us of your oil; for our lamps are gone out. But the wise answered, saying, not so; lest there be not enough for us and you: but go ye rather to them that sell, and buy for yourselves. Watch therefore, for ye know neither the day nor the hour wherein the son of man cometh.   *St. Matthew 25: 7-9, 13*

Dark- 1. Without light; with very little light:
    4. Hard to understand or explain:
    5. Secret: hidden:
    6. without knowledge or culture; ignorant; unenlightened:
    7. evil; wicked:

Darken –made to become dark or darker; dim:

Blessed is the man that walketh not in the counsel of the ungodly, nor standeth in the way of sinners, nor sitteth in the seat of the scornful,   *Psalms 1:1*
Because that, when they knew God, the glorified him not as God, neither were thankful; but became vain in their imaginations, and their foolish hearts were darkened.   *Romans 1:21*

Darkened Perspectives *

Who Turned Out The Lights?

I have had conversations with certain people discussing the goodness of the Lord and the word of God. The persons of which I had engage to discussion, were so darkened in their understsnding, they could not even begin to fathom the truthful reality of my dialogue.

Though our conversations lasted for hours sometimes, they were never able to be enlightened to perceive the truth about God.

> *The entrance of thy words giveth light; it giveth understanding to the simple.*   *Psalms 119: 130*

Contrary to the teachings of many Christian circles; just because the word of God is spoken and mentioned during a discussion, doesn't mean that the word has actually entered into the heart of the listener. It is one thing to want to hear a particular thing, but, it is altogether a totally different thing to know how to actually receive that to which you may have desired to hear.

To those of us who are very present of reasonable understanding, it is often bewildering to us and baffling as we

Hidden In the Light*

ENCOUNTER THOSE PERSONS WHO ARE ACTUALY VOID INDEED OF UNDERSTANING. AT TIMES IT IS EVEN HEART BREAKING AND TOTALLY UNSETTLING TO REALIZE THAT CERTAIN PEOPLE ARE IN THE SHAPE THAT THEY ARE IN, SIMPLY BECAUSE THEY CANNOT SEE FOR THEMSELVES, THE WAY OUT OF THEIR OWN SITUATIONS, THE SAME WAY THAT ANYONE ELSE SEES THE WAY OUT FOR THEM.

A VERY GRUELING FACT IS THAT THEY WERE ACTUALLY TRICKED AND TRAPPED INTO BELIEVING IN THE DECEPTION WHICH LED THEM TO WALK INTO THE SECRET CLOSET OF THEIR OWN BLINDNESS, AND TO DISBELIEVE IN THE WAY OUT OF THE DECEPTIVE SITUATIONS OF THEIR MINDS, OF WHICH THE ACTUAL WAY OUT OF THEIR BLINDNESS, IS ONLY GOING TO BE FOUND IN THE WORD OF GOD.

OFTEN, AS PEOPLE ARE TAUGHT TO GET UNDER THE BLANKETING FOG OF THE UNTRUTH, THEY ARE LIKEWISE, SIMULTANEOUSLY TAUGHT TO BLOCK OUT THE LIGHT OF THE LORD IN THEIR MINDS, WHICH IS THE VERY POWER TO HOLD THEM UNDER THE SPELL OF DARKNESS.

REMEMBER, THE SCRIPTURE TELLS US THAT THE ENTRANCE OF THE WORD GIVES US LIGHT. WHICH IS TO BE TAKEN IN THE REFFERENCE OF KNOWING THAT THE TOTAL ACCEPTANCE OF THE TRUE UNDERSTANDING OF THE WORD OF GOD, WILL ILLUMINATE OUR

Darkened Perspectives *

MENTAL PERCEPTIONS OF THE TRUTH OF GOD AND OF THE WRITTEN WORD OF GOD, ALLOWING US TO RECEIVE THE TRUTH AS A MANDATE FOR TASTEFUL HEALTHY CLEAN LIVING; TO WALK THEREIN.

> *Teach me, O Lord the ways of thy statutes; and I shall keep it unto the end. Give me understanding, and I shall keep thy law; yea; I shall observe it with my whole heart. Thy word is a lamp unto my feet, and a light unto my path.* Psalms 119:33-34, 105

NOWADAYS, THROUGH VERY WILLFUL ERRONEOUS TEACHINGS IN THE CHURCHES, THE LIGHT FOR MANY PEOPLE HAVE BEEN TURNED OUT! MANY OF THE SUPPOSEDLY WELL TRAINED THEOLOGICALLY ASTUTE MINISTERS WHO PREACH FROM THE PULPITS, USE THEIR OWN DARKENED IMAGINATIONS TO FLIP THE SWITCH ON THE LIGHT OF THE WORD OF GOD, CAUSING THE PEOPLE WHO HAVE COME TO THE CHURCH, TO COME BEFORE THE LORD, TO RETURN TO THE DARKENED CAVES OF SIN IN WHICH THEY HAVE BEEN LIVING, THINKING THAT IT WAS ALL TOTALLY UNNECESSARY TO HAVE THOUGHT OF HAVING TO COME OUT IN THE FIRST PLACE!

PEOPLE ARE OFTEN ENCOURAGED TO BELIEVE THAT THEY ARE ALRIGHT JUST AS THEY ARE. SIN IS OFTEN GLORIFIED FROM THE PULPITS IN MANY OF THE CHURCHES. PEOPLE ARE LED TO BELIEVE THAT THEY ARE COMING

Hidden In the Light*

INTO THE CHURCH TO HELP THE CHURCH AND THE LORD. THEY BELIEVE THAT THEY ARE DOING THE LORD A FAVOR BY COMING INTO THE CHURCH, OUT OF THE WORLD. WE, THE CHURCH; HAVE ALLOWED THE PEOPLE OF THE WORLD TO BELIEVE THAT THE CHURCH IS A BORING INSTITUTE OF CHANGE, FOR WHICH THE JOY OF LIVING WILL BE HINDERED AND TAKEN AWAY.

MANY PEOPLE ARE BEING TAUGHT THAT GOD NEEDS US! PEOPLE ARE NOT ALWAYS BEING TAUGHT OF THEIR DESPERATE NEED FOR GOD, WHO IS SELF SUFFICIENT, AND ETERNALLY EXISTENT. GOD MADE US; WE DID NOT MAKE HIM! WE HAD TO LEARN ABOUT GOD, WHO ALREADY KNEW US; COMPLETELY!

> *But we have renounced the hidden things of dishonesty, not walking in craftyness, nor handling the word of God deceitfully; but by manifestation of the truth comending ourselves to every man's conscience in the sight of God. But if our gospel be hid, it is hid to them that are lost. In whom the god of this world hath blinded the minds of them which believe not, lest the light of the glorious gospel of Christ, who is the image of God, should shine unto them.*   II Corinthians 4:2-4

Playing In the Dark*

IT IS TO BE ASSUMED THAT WE, WHO

Darkened Perspectives

have come into the light of the Lord, would always shun the idea of being in darkness at any time for the rest of our lives. The glorious light of the Lord is so powerfully filled with joy, and enlightenment for finding the present pathways of elevated living in the newness of life in Christ.

Far too many people, who have been brought out of darkness to the power of the light, have been plagued with what I will call the "Lot's Wife" syndrome. They are driven to take another look back into the darkened places of which they were in fact delivered from.

Most have no intentions to return to the darkness to stay, often they have struggled with the reality of their change to the point they feel that they have to extrapolate back over the paths of their lives to see if things were really as sinful as they have now been revealed to have been, relative to their lifestyles.

Being saved now don't mean that we are now at a more shielded place against sin, in that now we can handle sinners and remain in the company of sinfully wicked people, feeling that we have now become the untouchables in Christ.

Hidden In the Light*

O~NCE~ S~AVE~; A~LWAYS~ S~AVED~? O~NCE~ L~IT~; A~LWAYS A~ L~IGHT~? P~EOPLE USE SOME COMMON SENSE, AND READ THE WORD AGAIN.~

J~ESUS; REOPENED A ONCE SHUT DOOR TO THE FELLOWSHIP WITH OUR~ G~OD, ALLOWING THE POWER OF~ G~OD TO FREE US FROM ALL OF THE CLAIMS OF~ S~ATAN OVER OUR LIVES, WHICH WERE STYLED AS SIN AND INIQUITY.~ O~NLY THE POWER OF~ G~OD COULD BREAK THE POWERFUL HOLD THAT SIN HAD INDEED GRIPPED OUR LIVES, HANDING US OVER TO THE OWNERSHIP OF~ S~ATAN.~

S~INCE WE HAD SOLD OURSELVES OUT TO THE WILL OF~ S~ATAN,~ G~OD HAD TO BUY US BACK. I~N WHICH H~E DID DO SO; THROUGH THE DEATH, BURIAL, AND THE RESURRECTION OF THE ONLY BEGOTTEN SON OF~ G~OD;~ J~ESUS~ C~HRIST.~ S~ALVATION AND DELIVERANCE WAS NOT AT ALL CHEAP!~ J~ESUS PAID A PRICE THAT NEITHER OF US COULD HAVE EVER PAID, EVEN A DEBT THAT~ H~E DID NOT OWE!~

J~UST BECAUSE~ G~OD DID FOR US, THAT WHICH WE COULD HAVE NEVER DONE FOR OURSELVES, IS NO REASON TO MISTREAT THE GIFT OF SALVATION AS IS OFTEN THE CASE SCENARIO IN THE LIVES OF MANY WHO HAVE COME TO THE~ L~ORD TO BE SAVED.~

I~N OTHER WORDS, JUST BECAUSE WE HAVE RECEIVED~ J~ESUS, IS NO REASON TO CONTINUE TO BE PERSONALLY ACQUAINTED WITH~ S~ATAN AND WITH ALL OF THE WORKS OF DARKNESS.~

Darkened Perspectives *

Although you have been told to never forget where the Lord brought you from, let me urge you to let go of it!

Too many people are having weekend flings with the devil, going out on the town with Satan on Saturday night, with the intentions of getting out of the bed early Sunday morning to go out to the church to meet the Lord; only if they haven't had too much to drink the night before.

You have not done God a favor, if you show up at the church on Sunday wearing dark shades to cover your swollen red eyes, eating breath mints and Peppermints to cover the smell of alcohol on your breath.

Some people have gone so far with idea of being exempted from the possibility of ever being able to offend the righteousness of Christ through sinful living now that they have confessed Christ as their Lord and savior; that they will even show at the church reeking of Marijuana and other drug smoke, and for God's sakes; cigarettes!

Something's awfully wrong, if you are still able to continue stumbling over the same things in the light, which you

Hidden In the Light*

were indeed stumbling over in the dark!

A reckless and dangerous driver is as deadly in the daylight just as they may have been while driving in the darkness of the night. They are just reckless drivers; there is no safe handling of their automobile or even safe driving about them!

Perhaps you are simply suggesting to this encompassing great cloud of witnesses, that you are just a crazy reckless soul, dangerously plowing your way through what should be righteous living in Christ?

Salvation is not insurance to sustain an individual, just in case or whenever they collide with sin and unrighteousness. If so; most people would only be like the average people that we are familiar with, they only have enough insurance to cover the cost of the other persons automobile repairs in case of an accident. They don't even acquire and maintain what is referred and known to us as Full Coverage Auto Insurance.

Many people don't have the mind to properly care for themselves in the ways that is going to be most productive and proactive for the benefit of them. Selfishness and self preservation are not

Darkened Perspectives *

at all the same things. Many people of the church have come to the Lord with selfish motives relative to the reasons they desire to be saved in the first place.

This is the reason that they enjoy the idea of having an everlasting bubble of salvation wrapped around them, they are very selfish!

God did not save us, to enable us a more sure opportunity to play around in the dark and to insure that the hidden dangers of the dark wouldn't be able to have us, now that the hand of the Lord has touch our lives, even though we might continue to play around in the dark.

Now if such thinking and teachings were actually sound and indeed the purposeful intention of the Lord, there would not be as many Clergymen, Priest, and other people who have been active members of the church in the penitentiary, and in all sorts of trouble with the Law.

The very light of an illuminated mindset is at stake whenever an individual consistently dips back and forth into the dark places of their past, before they met The Lord to be saved.

It doesn't make much sense to turn out the light on yourself knowing that

Hidden In the Light*

You were truly in the darkness of your mind relative to the righteousness of Christ and clean living, and you are not even responsible for turning the light on yourself.

Sin, and iniquity, is consistently reaching for the light switch to turn out the light for every believer. The purposeful scheme for sin and iniquity in the first place was to show you and me just how unrighteous an unlike God we are, being the fleshly human beings that we indeed are.

Salvation comes to remind us of the fact that God made us in His own likeness and even in His own image!

Through all that mankind has ever done against the knowledge of God; God never changed His mind! Therefore I am more like God than I thought! He never said that we were no longer like Him or made in His own image and likeness even though we as people persist to live contrary to the knowledge and the nature of God.

God told us who we were from the beginning; but, through the process of sinning and iniquitous living we forgot the fact that we were indeed like Him, but only in a human form.

God, first created us in the spirit,

Darkened Perspectives *

AS SPIRITUAL BEINGS; BUT IN ORDER FOR US TO INHABIT THE EARTH WE NEEDED A HUMAN FORM. THEREFORE, SECONDLY, GOD FORMED US IN THE NATURAL! HE PLACED AN HUMAN SHELL AROUND OUR GOD CREATED SPIRITS, IN AN EFFORT FOR US TO NATURALLY TOUCH AND TO ACTUALLY MANIPULATE THE TANGIBLE THINGS OF THE EARTH.

SATAN'S PLOT IS TO SEE TO IT THAT WE NEVER MAKE IT BACK TO THE PERCEPTIONS OF OUR OWN TRUE SPIRITUAL IMAGES OF GOD'S RIGHTEOUSNESS IN US, WHEREAS WE WOULD BE MORE SPIRITUALLY DOMINATING IN THE EARTH, PUTTING THE DEVIL IN HIS PLACE AND KEEPING HIM THERE UNDER OUR FEET!

THANK GOD, I HAVE COME INTO THE KNOWLEDGE MYSELF; THAT WE CANNOT WALK IN THE GLORIOUS LIGHT OF THE LORD AND SIMULTANEOUSLY PLAY IN THE DARK. WHILE WE MAY PLAYFULLY STEP AWAY FROM THE LIGHT FOR AN OCCASION OF SELF INDULGENCE THINKING THAT WE WILL RETURN SHORTLY, THE DEVIL IS NOT PLAYING AROUND IN THE DARK AND HE HAS SET TRAPS THERE FOR ALL OF THE PEOPLE WHO HAVE COME INTO THE KNOWLEDGE OF THE LORD!

HE LIVES IN THE DARK INTENTIONALLY, AND HE IS FAMILIAR WITH THOSE WHO THINK THAT THEY NEED TO RETURN TO DARKNESS FOR A LAST LOOK! EVERY HIDDEN SCHEME OF THE DEVIL IS HOUSED IN THE DARK, SO AS TO

Hidden In the Light*

BE KEPT AWAY FROM THE LIGHT OF THE LORD.

Let The Light vs. Flashing The Light!

Let your light so shine before men, that they may see your good works, and glorify your Father which is in heaven.   St. Matthew 5: 16

SO MANY PEOPLE HAVE EITHER DRIVEN THEMSELVES, OR HAVE BEEN DRIVEN INTO THE DARKNESS OF LIVING, TO THE POINT THAT THEY ARE OFTEN FOUND STRUGGLING WITH AN ATTEMPT TO MAKE THEIR LIGHTS SHINE; THAT IS IF THERE IS EVEN A LIGHT STILL ILLUMINATED ON THE INSIDE OF THEM TO SHINE FORTH.

AS SINFUL AS THE HUMAN NATURE CAN BE, THERE IS STILL SOMETHING ON THE INSIDE OF THE AVERAGE INDIVIDUAL THAT DOESN'T WANT TO BE AS SINFULLY WICKED AS THE NEXT PERSON. AND FOR CERTAIN WE WOULD NEVER WANT TO BE CITED AS BEING IN A WORSE STATE THAN ANYONE ELSE!

JESUS SAID THAT WE SHOULD LET OUR LIGHTS SHINE BEFORE MEN, AND THAT IS NEVER TO BE TRANSLATED INTO MEANING THAT AT ANYTIME ARE WE TO MAKE OUR LIGHTS SHINE.

IT IS ONE THING FOR PEOPLE TO BE IMPRESSED WITH THE FACT THAT OUR LIGHTS ARE SHINING FORTH TO GLORIFY THE LORD, BUT IT IS ALL TOGETHER A TOTALLY DIFFERENT

Darkened Perspectives *

kind of thing to posture ourselves in a manner to impress the people of our daily surroundings, as if to make them believe that we are something in the Lord that we may not in fact be.

Certain places in life can be so far away from God that there is absolutely no illumination at all; its pitch black dark in the atmosphere as it relates to the righteousness of Christ.

The average persons who dwell in those types of places don't have any desire for the light of the Lord. The light of the Lord is so powerful that it will shine forth without your consent, even. In such darkened places of living, upon your entrance into the room, as an illuminated being in Christ, the people can't help but to see your light.

Here is where many people would need to be admonished to let their lights so shine before the men of their surroundings. It is usually obvious that others might be rather uncomfortable in your presence; just don't ever forget the fact that it's not at all about you, it's all about the light of the Lord shining through you.

When people see the light of the Lord shining forth through you, respect the fact that they are able to

Hidden In the Light*

see the light.

Being in the wrong place as a child of God, it is not necessary to begin trying to make others see Christ living in you, get away from there!

Don't be pressured into participating with their wrong doings as a measure of proving to them that you really do still belong with them. Such behavior becomes an assassin to your witness of the Lord.

There were places that even our natural parents forbade us to go, and most of us obeyed out of respect to our parents.

Why would you try to disguise the illuminated reflection of the light of the Lord shining forth through you? You need to obey the word of God and stay out the wrong places.

I realize that we need to take light to the dark places in this world, but for what purpose are you found going to the darker places of your surrounding?

The excuse of witnessing has gotten to be so tired and worn out, because the same people that were in those places, who were indeed supposed to be changed, went in there, and are still there to this very day if they haven't passed away, or are not bed ridden in a hospital bed?

Darkened Perspectives *

Whether we are aware or not, when we as believers walk into those darkened places, we go in wearing the dark clothes woven from the motives and the fowl intentions that led to those places. Only, the problem is that the light of the Lord will shine through a button hole or a zipper out from underneath those clothing to expose what should be our true identity.

On the other hand, whenever we do enter those places for the purpose of sharing Christ to the lost people of the darkness of this world, the light of Christ shining will expose them!

The light is so powerful that it will illuminate the cracks and the even the hidden corners and those who dwell in them for a hiding place.

Believe in the light of the Lord and don't be ashamed of it. Don't you dare make an attempt to put a cover over the light of the Lord shining through you.

Satan, and sin will consistently try to blanket the illumination of the Lord's light over your life, with the intentions of showing those persons in observation of your walk with the Lord, that you are not as polished as you appear.

The older saints, of which most of

Hidden In the Light*

them are now sleeping in their graves, used to sing a song that said; "This Little Light of Mine, I'm Going to let it Shine!"

God has given me the light just as he has given me life. I don't have to ask God to let me live every day that I'm awaken out of my sleep, it comes natural to just go ahead and do what God has given me the right to do.

Likewise, I was a member of a church where we used to sing a song that said; "Jesus is the light of the world; He's forever shining in my soul!"

I don't have to ask the light to shine today, all I have to do is continue to submit and commit my way unto the Lord. Jesus will always do what He has come into my life to do as long as I am in agreement with Him.

> *In him was life; and the life was the light of men. And the light shineth in darkness; and the darkness comprehended it not.* St. John 1: 4-5

The darkness itself does not even argue with the power of the light; so you might as well respect the power of the light of the Lord that is shining forth in your life before all, no matter who they are.

A flash of the light is only powerful

Darkened Perspectives *

ENOUGH TO DISPEL DARKNESS FOR ONLY A VERY SHORT SPAN, SO I'M SURE THAT GOD NEVER INTENDED FOR US TO ONLY BE FLASH LIGHTS.

USUALLY FLASHLIGHTS ARE USED WHEN WE ARE LOOKING FOR SOMETHING THAT MIGHT HAVE BEEN LOST, OR WHEN WE ARE ATTEMPTING TO FIX OR REPAIR SOMETHING THAT IS IN THE DARK AWAY FROM THE LIGHT.

A FEW GOOD EXAMPLES OF SPIRITUAL FLASHLIGHTS WOULD BE THOSE INDIVIDUALS THAT ARE PRONE TO SHOW FORTH THE LIGHT OF CHRIST IN A CRISIS.

IN THE PRESENCE OF GRIEVING PEOPLE THAT MIGHT HAVE LOST A LOVE ONE, OR IN THE PRESENCE OF A MARITAL SEPARATION, OR SOMEONE HAS GONE TO JAIL FOR A CRIME.

AN INDIVIDUAL THAT HAD NOT OTHERWISE REACHED OUT AND WOULD NOT HAVE REACHED FORTH UNTO THEM OR STRETCHED FORTH THEIR HELPING HANDS ARE NOTHING MORE THAN FLASHLIGHTS.

GOD NEVER INTENDED FOR US GO AROUND SHOWING OFF AS IF WE ARE SOMETHING SPECIAL IN THE LORD, RATHER HE EXPECTS FOR US TO SHINE FORTH AND TO SHOW FORTH THE LOVE OF CHRIST WHICH IS THE EVERLASTING LIGHT OF GOD.

SHINING COMES NATURAL FOR US AS CHILDREN OF THE MOST HIGH. WE ARE NATURALLY PRONE TO SHOW LOVE AND TO SUPPORT ONE ANOTHER ON A DAILY BASIS.

Chapter 4

*Nothing!**

Behold, I am the Lord, the God of all flesh: is there anything too hard for me?
Jeremiah 32: 27

Nay, in all these things we are more than conquerors through him that loved us. For I am persuaded, that neither death, nor life, nor angels, nor principalities, nor powers, nor things present, nor things to come, nor height, nor depth, nor any other creature, shall be able to separate us from the love of God, which is in Christ Jesus our Lord.
Romans 8: 37-39

Hidden In the Light*

Though I speak with the tongues of men and of angels, and have not charity, I am become a sounding brass, or a tinkling cymbal. And though I have the gift of prophecy, and understand all mysteries, and all knowledge; and though I have all faith, so that I could remove mountains, and have not charity, I am nothing. And though I bestow all my goods to feed the poor, and though I give my body to be burned, and have not charity, it profiteth me nothing.   I Corinthians 13; 1-3

NOTHING-[no-thing] *not anything; no part, share or trace; a thing that does not exist; a thing of no importance or significance; a person of no importance: zero, naught, worthless;*

No Reason to Stay Away From the Light!

HOW WONDERFUL IT IS TO REALIZE THAT GOD IS ALL WONDERFUL, OMNIPOTENT AND AWESOMELY ABLE; TO DO EXCEEDING AND ABUNDANTLY MORE THAN WE COULD EVER EVEN FATHOM IN OUR LITTLE MINUTE BOXED-IN CAPACITORS THAT WE CALL OUR MINDS.

KNOWING AND BELIEVING THESE TRUTHS, WE AS INDIVIDUALS ARE NEVER TO

Nothing**

find ourselves at odds with God, feeling as if we are everything that we want to be and that through the process of time over the years past, that we have developed into being everything that we ought to be on our own without the help of the Lord.

I am; whatever I am; by the grace of God; and only by His grace am I whatever I am! I am not of my own righteousness, nor am I of my own source of provision.

Thank God that I realized a long time ago, that I had problems and situations that I was incapable of handling on my own. I realized, that if God don't help me that there was no one else able to help me, because no one else could.

Many people who confess to be truly walking in the glorious light of the Lord, are always in consideration of something, afraid of most everything, refuse to believe anything, and as it relates to growing in the grace of God to the intent of building up the Kingdom of God, almost all of the people are doing nothing!

People are daily in need of the Lord's help, but they will do absolutely nothing about it. My reference is to

Hidden In the Light*

those persons who are aware of the exact help that they need. They are not in the dark relative to knowing of the reality and the power of God. They just appear to be stuck on the stupidity of staying in the situations that they are in, even though they are in extreme anguish over their life's conditions.

The late recording artist "Billy Preston" wrote a song that was, and probably still is a hit to this very day, called; "Nothing; From Nothing, Leaves Nothing!" Seems to me that people would have learned to do the math by now, and come to grips with the fact that if you are going to get something out of life, you won't get it out of doing absolutely nothing!

To say nothing; is not relative to whatever an individual may not have or acquire as a personal possession only, but, it also refers gravely to an individual's inactivity relative to their desired accomplishments.

Nothing, refers to what hasn't been acquired through the years of frequently visiting the church for a service, although an individual might have been dubbed as a faithful member?

Nothing is what many people of the local churches have to offer to an

Nothing**

INDIVIDUAL THAT ASK OF A REASON OF THE FAITH THAT THEY ARE SUPPOSED TO HAVE IN GOD THROUGH JESUS CHRIST.

NOTHING, IS ACTUALLY PERCEIVABLE TO THOSE WHO ARE STANDING ON THE OPPOSITE SIDE OF THE ISSUES OF FAITH AND RIGHTEOUSNESS, BECAUSE ABSOLUTELY NOTHING IS BEING REQUIRED FOR THE SAKE OF BEING ACCOUNTABLE IN THE PRESENCE OF THEIR FAVORABLE OR MAYBE EVEN THEIR UNFAVORABLE PEERS ON A DAILY BASIS. PEOPLE ARE BEING ENCOURAGED TO EMBRACE THE IDEA MORE FREQUENTLY, THAT THEY ARE NOTHING SPECIAL JUST BECAUSE THEY HAVE BEEN SAVED.

AS WE SCAN THE AUDIENCES OVER THE TELEVISION MEDIA AND IN THE SANCTUARY OF MANY OF THE CHURCHES, WE SEE WHAT LOOKS LIKE PEOPLE LISTENING TO THE PREACHED WORD OF GOD, BUT TOO SOON, IT IS ALSO DISCOVERED THAT MANY OF THEM ACTUALLY GOT NOTHING FROM WHAT THEY HAD ACTUALLY HEARD.

THE FACT IS; IF NOTHING IS WHAT YOU ARE HEARING, FOR CERTAIN, NOTHING IS WHAT YOU ARE GOING TO BE PRONE TO DO ON A DAILY BASIS. SOMETHING HAS TO PUSH YOU FROM THE INSIDE OUT TO MOTIVATE YOU TO PUT FORTH THE EXAMPLES OF YOUR TEACHING.

HERE IN, WE ARE SEEING THE DANGERS OF ONLY ENTERTAINING THE PEOPLE OF THE

Hidden In the Light*

church, when we in fact ought to be teaching them the proper mandates for holy and righteous living. Those who oppose the teachings of the Holy bible are coming out in the open on a more frequent basis to question the reality of our faith and the lack luster lifestyles of what should be clean Christian living.

Christians, don't seem to have a desire to confront the pressures brought upon the church by the community leaders, who have rejected the deity of Christ. Many of today's leaders, have the attitude that things are better served, when left to work themselves out on their own.

The fact is; we are still dealing with many things that we were told would work themselves out several decades ago.

Often, we don't take it very seriously, that the people of the church live with and work with, and are often married to people who have not believed in the power of God.

Too many of the people from the church have been allowed to participate in the spiritual affairs of the church who are also as active with many of the street activities that are against the word of God, and righteousness.

Nothing**

We all know that sinners are watching us to see if there is an authentic spirit of integrity about us that lends to the truth of our changed character through the gospel of God.

As a result, whenever they know that a friend of their's is being allowed to participate in the church without being changed, they want to participate also, without changing their lifestyles.

Many times, it has been apparent that the ministers are still overly attracted to the women who frequent the church, which is the only reason that many of the women come out to the church in the first place. They are attracted to the ministers and don't mind showing it.

It takes all kinds of examination and evaluation skills for monitoring the behavior of men watching them up close, to get an understanding relative to the real reasons that they are frequenters of the church.

Men have many motives and intentions for being in the church that have absolutely nothing to do with Jesus. They don't want to be save, set free, and filled with the power of the Holy Ghost.

Men, want to be watchmen,

Hidden In the Light*

ACCOUNTANTS, INSTIGATORS AND INVESTIGATORS IN THE CHURCH, WATCHING THE MONEY AND THE RELATIONSHIPS BETWEEN THE PASTOR AND THE PARISHIONERS. They are consistently looking for opportunities to report any human-ness that may have been either displayed or suspected, or even cited in the pastoral leadership of the church.

As of late; the scant poise of these controverscial male figures around the churches, have proven to be beneficial to the ongoing investigations of the sexual predators, and money laundering scheme artist, in the clergy.

The media itself has reported too frequently, that there are homosexuals and lesbians in the Christian church at the helm, supposedly leading the people. Many carnally thinking people don't see a problem with them attempting to lead the church, because they don't seem to feel that anything is actually wrong with being sexually perverted and twisted.

Although many of the church leaders, who have been hidden and undercover in their twisted lifestyles, are now being exposed to the public, that doesn't mean that there has been a change in the mandates of Christian

Nothing**

LIVING, ALLOWING FOR THOSE THAT ARE TRULY UNGODLY IN ALL MANNER OF THEIR LIFESTYLES, TO STEP FORWARD AND BEGIN TO LEAD THE CHURCH OF GOD.

HOW DOES ONE WHO TRULY HATE AND DESPISE THE LIGHT OF THE LORD THEMSELVES, BUT, SUPPOSEDLY THEY ARE ABLE TO REACH UP FROM UNDERNEATH THE INIQUITOUS HEAP OF THEIR OWN LIFESTYLE TO LEAD OTHERS TO THE LIGHT OF THE LORD TO BE SAVED, SET FREE, AND DELIVERED FROM A LIFE OF SIN AND SHAME, WHEN THEY THEMSELVES DON'T EVEN HAVE A DESIRE TO WALK IN THE LIGHT OF THE LORD?

THIS IS THE REASON THAT THEY CONTINUE TO TRY AND HIDE IN THE CHURCH; SO THAT THEY WON'T BE FORCED TO CHANGE THEIR WAYS ANYTIME SOON.

HIDING OFTEN HINDERS THESE PEOPLE FROM BEING SOON DISCOVERED, AND OPENLY DISPLAYED AS THE TRUE ADVOCATES OF THE DEVIL, WHO HAVE SLITHERED THEIR WAY INTO THE INNER POPULATION OF THE CHURCH BODY. DON'T GET TOO SPIRITUAL ON ME, BECAUSE THE BIBLE TELLS US, THAT FOR A SURETY THEY ARE THERE IN THE CHURCHES.

The bible styles these people as the "tares";

> **Tares-** *zizanion* **(2215)** is a kind of darnel, the commonest of the four species, being the bearded, growing in the grain fields,

Hidden In the Light*

as tall as wheat and barley, and resembling wheat in appearance. It was credited among the Jews with being degenerate wheat. The rabbis called it "Bastard." The seeds are poisonous to man and to herbivorous animals, producing sleepiness, nausea, convulsions and even death.

The Lord describes the tares as "the sons of the evil one"; the custom as in the parable; is to leave off from separating the wheat from the tares, until harvest time. [Vines bible dictionary]

Another parable put he forth unto them, saying, The kingdom of heaven is likened unto a man which sowed good seed in his field: But while the man slept, his enemy came forth and sowed tares among the wheat, and went his way. But when the blade was sprung up, and brought forth fruit, then appeared the tares also. So the servants of the householder came and said unto him, Sir, didst not thou sow good seed in thy field? From whence then hath it tares? He said unto them, an enemy hath done this. The servants said unto him, Wilt thou then that we go and gather them up? But he said, Nay; lest while ye gather up the tares, ye root up also the wheat with them. Let both grow together until the harvest: and in the time of harvest I will say to the reapers, Gather ye together first the tares, and bind them in bundles to burn them: but gather the wheat into my barn.   St. Matthew 13:24-30

Nothing**

The Paralysis of Analysis!

Lot's of people get locked away in the prison cells of their own minds, where their own stinking thoughts have long since begun to rot away any reasonable decision to think on the righteousness of Christ, even at a base level.

Thinking that they have become wise in their own conceits, many people have actually become fools. Their constitutional strength for believing has waned, as a result of frequently welcomed doubting and unbelief, sending impotence and fearfulness to the forefront of their thought process, to extenuate any righteous thoughts that are allowed to enter their minds.

People are so busy checking every thing at the gateway of their minds ability to process thoughts, that nothing of any essence ever gets into their mind to heal the crippling sickness of their own thinking.

By the slate of their own cunning craftiness, they have become paralyzed and ineffective to even live what would be referred to as a normal life. They have spent so much of their time

Hidden In the Light*

ANALYZING EVERYTHING, PUTTING THINGS INTO A CERTAIN CATAGORY SO THAT THINGS WILL BEGIN TO MAKE SENSE TO THEM, THAT NOW NOTHING ACTUALLY MAKES SENSE TO THEM ANYMORE!

REFUSING TO SET BOUNDARIES FOR WHAT THEY ALLOW THEMSELVES TO THINK, THEIR MINDS SOAR THROUGH THE SPIRIT REALMS UNWATCHED AND UNGUARDED, VULNERABLE TO ALL OF THE WICKED SCHEMES OF THE DEVIL.

IT IS NO WONDER THAT THE PEOPLE AROUND THE CHURCH HAVE BEEN CITED FOR DOING AND HAVEN DONE MANY VERY HEINOUS THINGS, WHILE STILL CLAIMING TO BE BORN AGAIN; BLOOD WASHED; CHILDREN OF GOD.

> *But without faith it is impossible to please him: for he that cometh to God must believe that he is, and that he is a rewarder of them that diligently seek him.*
>
> *Hebrews 11:6*

MANY, WHO FINALLY COME TO THE POINT OF FAITHFULLY BELIEVING GOD THROUGH THE WORD OF GOD, ARE USUALLY REGRETFUL OF THE FACT THAT THEY THOUGHT THEY COULD FIGURE EVERYTHING OUT ON THE STRENGTH OF THEIR OWN MINDS.

EVEN THOUGH WE ARE ENCOURAGED TO THINK FOR OURSELVES, AND THIS IS EXTREMELY NECESSARY; IT HAS NEVER BEEN THE PLAN OF GOD FOR US TO BE LEFT TO OURSELVES, TO THINK OUR OWN WAYS THROUGH LIFE,

Nothing**

without the patterns of our thinking being trained to reflect on the word of God, in the midst of processing our thoughts.

That, that we hope for which establishes the balancing platform for our faith, is the object element that we truly expect for the Lord to do for us. What we expect, is definitely what we are most geared to think on consistently, without even taking a break; until we come to the point of faith.

Faith allows us to take a break from consistently meditating on our expectations of the Lord, and it allows us to enter into resting and trusting in the fact that the Lord has heard our hearts request, and as a result of believing in faith, it is determined that we will not be denied.

Thinking within ourselves, that we are thinking deeply simply because we strongly analyze everything that we allow ourselves to think on, camouflages the truth in the fact that we are not really thinking at all in a manner that will please the Lord to honor His own word concerning us!

We stop the hand of God from helping us, and the arm of the Lord from

Hidden In the Light*

REVEALING HIS STRENGTH TO KEEP US AND TO SUSTAIN US, SIMPLY BECAUSE WE CHOOSE ONLY TO LOOK AT THE WORD OF THE LORD, BUT, NEVER BRINGING OURSELVES TO BELIEVE IT!

IN THIS NEW MILLENNIUM, MANY OF THE SO CALLED SCIENTIFIC THINKERS OF OUR MODERN SOCIETY, HAVE BEGUN TO ANALYZE THE CHURCH AND THE WORD OF GOD, WITH THE INTENTIONS OF SHOWING THE ORGANIZED BODY OF CHURCHES WORLD WIDE, AND ALL OF THE FOLLOWERS OF THE TEACHINGS AND THE DOCTRINES OF THE BIBLE; THAT THE BIBLE HAS ALL BEEN A FARCE AND A WHITEWASHED BLANKET OF DECEPTION, RELATIVE TO THE TRUTH OF CHRIST JESUS.

BUT ONLY A FOOL WOULD THINK THAT SUCH CARNAL FINDINGS ARE CAPABLE OF REVEALING TO US, WHAT IS TO BE RECEIVED AND THOROUGHLY EMBRACED AS THE TRUTH.

> *Search the scriptures; for in them ye think ye have eternal life: and they are they which testify of me.*
> *St. John 5:39*

IN THIS PARTICULAR SCRIPTURE, JESUS IS TALKING TO THE JEWS ABOUT THE FACT THAT THEY THOUGHT THAT THEY ALREADY KNEW WHAT THEY SHOULD KNOW FROM THE WRITING OF THE SCRIPTURES, RELATIVE TO THEIR SALVATION AND ETERNAL LIFE.

THE JEWS OF JESUS' GENERATION HAD BEEN RAISED ON THE TEACHING AND THE

Nothing**

story of Abraham. They were determined to convince the "bread of life" that they already knew what to think about salvation.

Even though Jesus suggest to them to search the scripture, He did not leave it to their own discretion to choose which scriptures that they were going to look at. He gave them help even before they asked, because they desperately needed the Lord's help and He knew that they wouldn't ask for His help, because they were prone to think for themselves!

Mind you, the Jews had already looked at the scriptures and were led to believe that their salvation was indeed n Abraham, and in their obedience to follow Jewish customs.

Most people destroy the possibilities for the help they need, thinking that they already know it all.

They Couldn't!

He came unto his own, and his own received him not. This beginning of miracles did Jesus in Cana of Gal'i-lee, and manifested forth his glory; and his disciples believed on him. Verily, verily, I say unto thee, we speak that we do know, and testify that we have seen, and ye receive not our witness.

St. John 1:11; 2:11; 3:11

Hidden In the Light*

Passionately moved with compassion, Jesus came before His own native people, to share the message of the gospel of deliverance to an obviously lost generation of Jewish people. He went out of His way to share the mystery of His own divine deity, but, the Jews could not receive Him.

It was only obvious that others of the rabbis and teachers in the Jewish synagogues and the temples, had gotten to the Jews first, before Jesus had ever begun to move before the people showing forth the glory of His own deity. His own people were stubbornly set on seeking for a messiah, of which in their own minds, he had not yet come to the earth.

Jesus did not come to the earth adorned as, an heir to the Jewish throne, by the bloodline of any natural king on a throne, even though He is the King of kings; and the Lord of all lords.

He was not born into the wealth and the riches of the society of His own times, and neither did He come before the Jews riding in a Golden chariot followed by an entourage, even though He holds the wealth and the riches of this world in His hands.

Nothing**

He came humbly, walking into the company of the people alone, all by Himself; but, He always comes before us bearing the eternal weight of the glory of His own truth; exceeding the existence of time in His own being, yet in the natural He was younger in age than most of the Jewish men who stood by in observance of Him.

His stature may not have been as great as most of the men of His day, yet the entire realm of the cosmos are seated in the palm of His hand!

As it was; Christ came to the earth with only a limited measure of His own deity, citing back on the mountain, in the presence of Moses; "that no man could ever see the face of God and live."

God came to the earth in the expression of mercy and grace, so that the automatic sentence of mankind for looking upon the deity of God would not be pronounced upon mankind, killing them all, destroying them and removing us all from the face of the earth.

God suited Himself in the form of sinful man; and while men are so accustomed to holding one another hostage to the human state of being, and/or either dehumanizing one

Hidden In the Light*

ANOTHER IN ONE FORM OR ANOTHER, FOR THIS CAUSE ALONE, THEY COULD NOT SEE GOD IN JESUS!

THEY WERE PERCEPTIVELY HANDICAPPED AND SPIRITUALLY PARALYZED AS A RESULT OF THEIR OWN HUMANNESS OF MIND. WHENEVER WE ARE SET ON THINKING IN THE NATURAL, IT ALWAYS HINDERS US FROM SEEING GOD IN THE SPIRIT. JESUS CAME IN THE NATURAL AND IN THE SPIRIT, BOTH GOD AND MAN IN THE VERY SAME BODY.

IT NEVER MADE ANY SENSE TO THEM, JUST AS IT DOESN'T MAKE A LOT SENSE TO THE PEOPLE OF TODAY, HOW GOD WOULD COME TO THE EARTH IN THE FORM OF A SINFUL MAN; MANY PEOPLE HAVE NOT BEEN ABLE TO UNDERSTAND WHY GOD WOULD NOT CHOOSE ANY OF THEM IN THE DAYS OF OLD, OR ANY OF US TODAY, TO BE THE "ANOINTED ONE".

TOO MANY PEOPLE REALLY LIKE TO THINK OF THEMSELVES AS TRULY BEING A GOOD PERSON; EVEN BEING AS GOOD AS ANYONE ELSE ON THE FACE OF THE EARTH. IT IS NOT ABOUT THE GOODNESS OF ANY MAN, PAST OR PRESENT; IT HAS ALWAYS BEEN ALL ABOUT THE GOODNESS OF THE LORD!

JESUS DID THINGS IN THE MIDST OF THE JEWS, EVEN AS HE HAS ALSO DONE MANY MIRACLES AND WONDERFUL THINGS IN THE MIDST OF US TODAY; YET MERE MEN FIND IT IMPOSSIBLE TO WRAP JESUS AROUND THE

Nothing**

MINDS, OR TO EVEN WRAP THEIR MINDS AROUND THE REALITY OF JESUS!

IT IS AMAZING TO ME THAT SUCH GOOD PEOPLE OF THE EARTH, ARE ALWAYS FINDING IT TOO GOOD TO BE TRUE, WHEN CHALLENGED TO BELIEVE AND TO RECEIVE THE MOVE OF GOD IN THE MIDST OF THE PEOPLE.

WOULDN'T YOU BELIEVE, THAT THOSE WHO WERE INDEED DONNED AS BEING GOOD PEOPLE, WOULD ALWAYS RECEIVE THAT WHICH IS ALSO GOOD, NO MATTER WHERE IT ORIGINATED?

> *Then came the Jews round about him, and said unto him, how long dost thou make us to doubt? If thou be the Christ, tell us plainly. Jesus answered them, I told you, and ye believed not: the works that I do in my father's name, they bear witness of me. Then the Jews took up stones again to stone him. Jesus answered them, many good works have I shewed you from my father; for which of those works do ye stone me? The Jews answered him, saying, for a good work we stone thee not; but for blasphemy; and because that thou being a man, makest thyself God. If I do not the works of my Father, believe me not. But if I do, though ye believe me not, believe the works: that the Father is in me, and I in Him.*   St. John 10: 24-25, 31-33, 37-38

ALTHOUGH JESUS DID; AND HE STILL DOES THINGS THAT NO OTHER NATURAL MAN COULD EVER DO, MAN SOUGHT BACK THEN AND THEY STILL SEEK TODAY AS OF LATE, TO

Hidden In the Light*

humanize Jesus as being nothing more than a spiritually gifted man.

He is the only begotten son of God; as a gift to the fate of humanity, but, He is never at any time just a man! Jesus even works with the created things of the earth in ways that no other mere man could ever do.

The bible is chocked full of the many things that Jesus did while He walked the earth in the presence of man. Of the most remarkable things to which Jesus did while He walked the earth, was for sure the manner in which He handled the presentation of sin and temptation when it was evidently hurled at Him.

Perhaps this is the real reason that most men are angered at the idea that Jesus is the son of God?

Most people can receive Jesus as being a good man in the flesh; they just refuse to receive Him as God; in the flesh!

Good, places Jesus on an equal playing field with humanity; whereas God places Him where He belongs, which is high and lifted up above us!

Good, always seems to blind the eyes, or the seeing perception of people everywhere, while God always seeks to

Nothing[**]

OPEN THE EYES OF THE BLINDED, BOTH NATURALLY AND SPIRITUALLY, TO ALLOW THEM TO SEE AND TO PERCEIVE, THAT MEN MIGHT RECEIVE THE GOSPEL OF JESUS CHRIST, EVERYWHERE.

YOU KNOW AS I DO MYSELF, THAT PEOPLE DON'T ALWAYS HANDLE THE OPPOSITIONS OF SINFUL TEMPTATIONS, WHEN CONFRONTED WITH DECISIONS TO PLEASE OURSELVES, OR TO PLEASE THE LORD, AS A RESULT OF RESISTING THE PRESENTATION OF ANY DELIGHTSOME NUANCE.

PEOPLE ANGRILY REFUSE TO EMBRACE THE REALITY OF THE SINLESS CHRIST, WHO WALKED IN THE MIDST, AND OFTEN TOUCHED AND CAME INTO CONTACT WITH SINFUL PEOPLE.

THE AVERAGE PERSONS OF THE SOCIETY BELIEVE AND CONDUCT THEMSELVES IN THE MANNER OF SAYING, THAT IF EVERYONE ELSE IS DOING A PARTICULAR THING, THAT THERE IS PROBABLY NO ONE WHO CAN BE FOUND ABSTAINING FROM IT.

THIS TYPE OF A CONSENSUS, MIGHT ACTUALLY HAVE A PARTICULAR WEIGHT OF GRAVITY ATTACHED TO A GREAT PERCENTAGE OF THE POPULOUS, AS LONG AS WE SPEAK IN REFERENCE TO OTHER PEOPLE, BUT IT NEVER WILL EVER CARRY ANY RELEVANCE WHEN APPLIED TO THE REALITY OF CHRIST.

Seeing then that we have a great high priest, that is

Hidden In the Light*

passed into the heavens, Jesus the son of God, let us hold fast our profession. For we have not an high priest which cannot be touched with the feeling of our infirmities; but was in all points tempted like as are, yet without sin. Let us therefore come boldly unto the throne of grace, that we may obtain mercy, and find grace to help in the time of need.   Hebrews 4:14-16
For such an high priest became us, who is holy, harmless, undefiled, separate from sinners, and made higher than the heavens; Who needed not daily, as those high priest, to offer up sacrifice, first for his own sins, and then for the people's: for this did he once, when he offered up himself. For the law maketh men high priest which have infirmity; but the word of the oath, which was since the law, maketh the son, who is consecrated forever.   Hebrews 7:26-28

Nothing; Is Higher Than He Is!

It is rather remarkable that Christ being as high as He is, above all things that are created; that He stooped all of the way down to humanity, just to save us from sin and the penalty of being sinful partakers.

It's amazing that Jesus loves us beyond our human comprehension, even to the point of oblivion, relative to any human reason.

Only Jesus; could stand in the illumination of His own light and not

Nothing**

be clearly seen of the people who beheld Him. Whenever you or myself, stand or walk in the light of the Lord, people see us and recognize the light of the Lord shining through us, rather they desire to see the light of the Lord or not.

Whenever you flip the switch to turn on the lights in a dark room, is your determination to see the light bulb, or are you likely prone to see the light in the room, that replaced the darkness?

Perhaps blindness would be the only reason that you would not actually see anything in a well lighted room? The light in the room causes everything in the room that is visible to the naked eyeball to jump out at us, and to make itself available for being able to be seen of us.

This dispensation of which we are now living, we are prone to see the movement of the spirit of the Lord, and not the physical form of Jesus, as He has been lifted to the throne of God, high above the earth.

Haven't you ever noticed, that lights are of an even greater benefit, to those that are using the lights, when they have been lifted to the top of the ceiling to shine downward upon us?

Whenever the lights are shining

Hidden In the Light*

down on us from above, the light has the ability to illuminate most everything in the room underneath the glow of the bulbs in the light fixture. Jesus is now become a light fixture there at the throne of God, whereas, illumines of the glory of God; lights the pathways in the world for all men to see if they have a desire to see from God's perspective, and at times even whenever they don't.

In the natural, we don't come into physical contact with working light bulbs, and actually we do not touch the illumination of the light bulb either. However, we are usually in physical contact with the switch that is in contact with the power source which touches the light bulb and turns that light on in the room.

I know that it is awesome and a bit much for a carnal mind to fathom, but we will just have to deal with the fact that Jesus is both the power source and the light that shines down on us!

We have a high priest that is touched with our inability to light our own pathways of life. We have absolutely nothing to do with Him being the light of the world, and neither are we responsible for Him shining.

Nothing**

He is shining whether we allow Him to shine through us or not. The light of the Lord never ever goes out! Jesus is the eternal flame of Glory; so in order to come into contact with the light of the Lord, we have to actually allow the light of the Lord to come into contact with us.

The revelation of Christ, through the word of God, is the switching mechanism that allows the light to be turned on in our lives through faith and repentance, by the hand of God.

Even as the disciples and the Jews of old wanted to physically see the Father; the people of today are in constant battle within themselves striving to touch Jesus, in effect that they might know and believe that He is real.

I can guarantee you, that all you need to do is to allow the hand of the Lord to touch you instead, and you will never ever doubt that He is real ever again.

When the light in the room touches the darkness and everything under the illumination of the light bulb, there is no question as to whether or not the power is indeed on, or that the light bulb and even the light fixture is

Hidden In the Light*

in working order. We know these things by the light that is shining down all over the room.

Jesus will show you everything as a result of shining down on you and your own ways. Being highly exalted above us, is the greater benefit that we as believers have over those individuals that have rejected Jesus and have chosen other sources, as a means of supply.

It is not possible for anything to get out of the reach of the Lord, simply for the fact that everything is positioned underneath the dominion of Christ. Remember that David told us, and I state in short, that there is absolutely no where that we could ever go to flee the presence of the Lord.

The entire world sits inside of the palm of God's hand; what about the rest of Him? How big is God? How high is high? Being that God has highly exalted Jesus and given Him a name higher above every other name?

Nothing can block Jesus or even stop Him; it is only that men refuse to allow Him into their hearts to be their Lord and savior. Just because the Lord will not work for any individual under these damnable circumstances, it doesn't mean by no stretch of any imagination,

Nothing**

that God has lost His ability to do what He will do in a surrendered life.

Whatever you may be dealing with has got to be more than God is Himself, and higher that the exalted name of Jesus Christ, in order to be a problem too much for the Lord to handle!

No darkness is too dark for Him to see through it; no water is too deep or too swift in its current for Him to deliver you out of it!

No fire is too hot for God to step in to get you out of it!

For our God is a consuming fire.
Hebrews 12:29

No wind is too powerful, for Him to tame, remember that He is the Holy Ghost who came in riding on the sound of a rushing mighty wind. And we will never forget the fact that Jesus stood on the deck of the ship and commanded the wind and the sea to behave, and it was so.

Some of these Johnny-come-lately's of this latter generation have developed the idea in their minds, that the devil and demon spirits are too much for the Lord to handle.

Nothing, that God made will ever be too much for the Lord to handle.

Hidden In the Light*

Everything that is; was made by the hand of the Lord, rather you believe that or not!

In retrospect, God is too much for the devil and for demon spirits to handle! Absolutely nothing is too hard for God!

Chapter 5

The Breaking of Day!

And Jacob was left alone; and there wrestled a man with him until the breaking of day. And he said, let me go, for the day breaketh. And he said, I will not let thee go, except thou bless me.   *Genesis 32: 24, 26*

Remember ye not the former things, neither consider the things of old. Behold, I will do a new thing; now it shall spring forth; shall ye not know it? I will even make a way in the wilderness, and rivers in the desert.

         Isaiah 43:18-19

I must work the works of him that sent me while it is day: the night cometh, when no man can work.   *St. John 9:4*

Bring On the Next Day*

Even the mention of this particular topic, is as explosively captivating as it sounds!

Personally, I hear and perceive the forceful intrusion of the coming forth of another period of sunset and the timely release of the sunrise, without the consent of the eminent claim of the present day, today; of which we are standing in right now, or the previous hold of former days or any particular day, singularly.

Whatever the case scenario, either a new day has come forth or it is on the way; that depends on how you are looking at it and where you stand, respectively.

No matter how blissful, the experiences of the day might have been, it is necessary for the present day to pass on for the sake of the next chance opportunity in the new turn of events to take place in our lives on a new day.

You have got to be sensible enough to realize that everything wonderful that is going to take place in your life, is not all going to happen to you or even for you, all in one day!

If you think that what God has

The Breaking Of Day!

DONE FOR YOU TODAY HAS BEEN MAGNIFICENTLY AWESOME AND GREAT, JUST WAIT UNTIL THE NEXT MOVE OF GOD, TO COME FOR YOU ON ANOTHER DAY! HE, WILL BLOW YOUR MIND OVER, AND OVER AGAIN!

HERE'S A REALITY THAT WE AS PEOPLE OF THE AMERICAN POPULATION MIGHT NOT WANT TO FACE; THERE IS A CERTAIN PERCENTAGE OF THE PEOPLE OF OUR COMMUNITIES WHO HAVE BEEN CAUGHT UP IN THE GRINDER OF THE NEVER ENDING CYCLE OF WAKING UP, TO WHAT SEEMS TO BE THE EXACT VERY SAME DAY, EVERYDAY!

FROM DAY TO DAY; IT APPEARS THAT THE CIRCUMSTANCES SEEM TO BE SET ON A REWOUND VCR TAPE EVERY MORNING, THAT BEGINS TO PLAY BY THE POWER OF REMOTE CONTROL IN THE HAND OF A MYSTERIOUS BEING, ON THE OUTSIDE OF THEIR OWN LIVING REALITY.

OFTEN, EVEN AS MINISTERS, WE FIND OURSELVES MINISTERING TO PEOPLE WHO HAVE BOUGHT INTO THE DECEPTION, THAT THINGS WILL ALWAYS BE THE SAME AS THEY ARE RIGHT NOW! TO THEM, THEIR NEXT DAY IS ONLY GOING TO BE THE SAME AS THE OLD DAYS! THEY'RE NEVER GOING TO BE NEW!

THEY DON'T EMBRACE THE EXCITEMENT IN THE REALITY OF A NEW DAY COMING FORTH WITH BRAND NEW CIRCUMSTANCES, PRESENTING THE OPPORTUNITIES FOR POSITIVE

Hidden In the Light*

changes, in their lives. They only exist in the hum-drum reality of one extremely long, never ending dreadful day!

My point of reference, is not really to those people who are intentionally stuck on stupid, that don't even see the need for any change; I am simply speaking in reference to those individuals who have fallen prey to the undermining schemes of the devil.

They have been taken hostage to poverty, where they lack charisma in the spirit of their minds and a winning perception that would drive them to want to succeed far beyond their present circumstances!

Hollywood film producers have produced, and it seems that they continue to produce films that depict the repetition in circumstantial events, whereas the characters in the films awake to the very same day, over and over again!

I am not a fan of these types of films for the simple fact that while people are musing over these films thinking that they are being entertained, the enemy is subtly attempting to lull them into becoming drive-less, immobile, impotent beings of society.

Although the remote control has

The Breaking Of Day!

BEEN EQUIPPED WITH THE NUMBERS TO CALL UP EVERY CHANNEL ON THE NETWORK, BEING LULLED INTO BELIEVING IN A DEAD REALITY, ONE MIGHT FIND THEMSELVES ONLY REMOTELY DIALING INTO ONE CHANNEL, THE SAME CHANNEL; EVERY DAY OF THEIR LIVES!

THOUGH THEY ARE GETTING OLDER EVERYDAY, THEY ARE CONVINCED THAT NOTHING IS EVER GOING TO BE CHANGED?

MOST PEOPLE DESIRE TO DO WHATEVER THEY HAVE DONE BEFORE! BUT, THEY HAVE ALSO DISCOVERED THAT REPETIVELY DOING THOSE THINGS, CAN BE EXTREMELY BORING AND UNINTERESTING, WITHOUT SOME TYPE OF PROGRESSIVE CHANGES AND/OR SOME TYPES OF ALTERATIONS, BEING THAT THEY ARE ALREADY SO FAMILIAR WITH THOSE THINGS.

THE HUMAN MIND, AND THE HUMAN BODY, HAVE BEEN CONSTRUCTED TO PROCESS FRESH CHANGE ON A CONSISTENT BASIS. THIS; MY FRIEND IS THE REASON THAT THE WORLD TURNS AND SPINS ON THE EARTH'S AXIS, WHILE ORBITING AROUND THE SUN!

I HAVE TO MOVE THINGS AROUND IN MY HOME AND EVEN IN THE CHURCH EVERY NOW AND THEN, BECAUSE IT IS DEPRESSING AND NERVE RACKING TO SEE THINGS IN THE EXACT SAME POSITION AND STATE WITHOUT ANY CHANGE, FOR MONTHS ON END.

I DISCOVERED MANY YEARS AGO, THAT YOU DO NOT GET CHANGE UNTIL YOU MAKE

Hidden In the Light*

CHANGE! NO PROGRESS; IS SOON TO REVEAL STAGNATE, MORTAL REALITIES, THAT LEAD IN THE DIRECTION OF DYING AND EVEN TO THE ACTUAL POINT OF DEATH.

*In Forward Progression; But; Always Present**

WE ALL WANT CHANGES TO HAPPEN IN OUR LIVES, BUT, WE WANT THINGS TO CHANGE MYSTERIOUSLY WHILE WE ARE EITHER SLEEPING OR AWAY SOMEWHERE FROM THE REALITY OF THE CHANGES THAT ARE TAKING PLACE, SO THAT WE CAN WAKE UP TO THE REFRESHING NEWNESS IN EXTREME SURPRISE TO THE ACTUALITY OF THE CHANGE.

IT WILL BE OF GREAT BENEFIT TO YOU, TO EMBRACE THE UNDERSTANDING, THAT PERHAPS THE THINGS THAT YOU MAY DESIRE TO CHANGE FOR YOU, IN YOUR OWN LIFE; THE SAME THINGS ARE ACTUALLY CHANGING RIGHT BEFORE YOUR VERY EYES, WHILE YOU ARE PRESENT TO EXPERIENCE THE ALTERATIONS OF YOUR LIFE'S CIRCUMSTANCES.

IT'S GOD'S ULTIMATE DESIGN, THAT WE WOULD BE PRESENT PARTICIPATORS IN THE PROCESS OF CHANGE, IN EITHER ONE WAY OR ANOTHER.

HAVEN'T YOU EVER NOTICED THAT THE DAYS ON THE CALENDAR ALL START AT THE NUMBER ONE AND PROGRESSES ON TO THE

The Breaking Of Day!

FINAL DAY OF THAT PARTICULAR MONTH?

HOW ABOUT THE CALENDAR YEAR! AS WE EXTRAPOLATE BACK OVER THE YEARS SINCE JESUS CAME TO THE EARTH AND LEFT, EACH YEAR HAD BEGUN TO COUNT, MOVING FORWARD IN NUMERICAL, CHRONOLOGICAL ORDER, BEGINNING WITH THE NUMBER ONE, ALL OF THE WAY UP TO 2009.

ALTHOUGH TODAY HAS REARED THE AWESOMENESS OF IT'S SPLENDOR TO BLESS US WITH THE DAYLIGHT TO SPOTLIGHT AND TO HIGHLIGHT THE NEXT STAGE FOR THE PRESENTATION IN THE DRAMATICAL ESCAPADES OF HUMAN LIVING; THE FACT IS THAT TODAY ONLY CAME FORTH BECAUSE YESTERDAY RESCINDED IN AGREEMENT TO THE CHRONOLOGICLE ORDER OF DAYS, CITING THAT FACT THAT IT HAD SERVED ITS PURPOSE IN TIME AND SPACE TO THE COSMO-EDICTAL COMMAND.

IN OTHER WORDS, "TODAY"; ON YESTERDAY IT WAS AT FIRST ONLY HOPES FOR ANOTHER TOMORROW, UNTIL IT ARRIVED TO ANSWER TO THE ROLE CALL AS ANOTHER "TODAY."

TODAY IS ALWAYS PRESENT AND CURRENTLY RIGHT NOW AVAILABLE AS THE MOMENTS OF OUR LIVES ROLL ON BY THE SECOND, THE MINUTE, AND THE HOUR.

AS SOON AS THE ALLOTTED HOURLY SPAN OF THE DAY HAS EXPIRED, DRESSED IN THE

Hidden In the Light*

After 5 evening attire of the night, today slips away, as tomorrow swiftly transforms itself into the present manifestation of today.

It's a great mystery that tomorrow always shows up as today even though the day will take on the name of the next day of the week; never-the-less, it is still another day!

See; as long as we keep on living, tomorrow will never be stated as being tomorrow upon its arrival. Have you ever asked anybody what day it is, only for them to answer you by saying that it's tomorrow?

Even though I fell asleep on yesterday, I was awakened only to realize that it is another today without a doubt.

The average people of the world have been programmed to remain in constant expectation of tomorrow. We will often spend a great portion of today making plans for tomorrow, many times for the purpose of getting things done tomorrow that should actually be done today!

Too often tomorrow seems to be more accessible and powerful than today, whether that is a deception or a reality, the fact is that people desperately look

The Breaking Of Day!

TO THE COMING OF THE NEXT DAY, WHICH IS USUALLY TOMORROW.

*Quicker Than At Once; Day Breaketh**

Boast not thyself of tomorrow; for thou knowest not what a day may bring forth. Proverbs 27:1
Through the tender mercy of our God; whereby the day-spring from on high hath visited us, to give light to them that sit in darkness and in the shadow of death, to guide our feet into the way of peace. St. Luke 1:78-79

IT MAY OR IT MAY NOT BE SUCH A GOOD THING TO VOW A PARTICULAR THING BASED ON TOMORROW. IT IS SO EASY TO SAY TO ANOTHER INDIVIDUAL; "YOU JUST WAIT UNTIL TOMORROW", BELIEVING THAT THE NEXT DAY WILL BRING FOR US, WHATEVER WE FAILED TO BRING FORTH TODAY.

SOMETIMES WE HOPEFULLY EXPECT TO SUCCEED AT A PARTICULAR LEVEL THAT DID NOT AVAIL ITSELF TO US ON THE PRESENT DAY OF OUR FAILURE, OR MAYBE AT LEAST ON THE DAY WHEN WE FELL SHORT OF OUR EXPECTATIONS.

THE PRACTICE OF HOLDING TOMORROW AT BAY FOR US AS INDIVIDUALS, OFTEN DATES BACK TO OUR CHILDHOOD WHERE WE PLANNED AND EVEN VOWED TO DO BETTER, MAYBE; THE NEXT TIME, IF TOMORROW WOULD BE SO KIND TO US.

Hidden In the Light*

The little league baseball player who strikes out while up to bat, often vows to hit a homerun tomorrow.

In a classroom, certain of the students would misspell a word during a classroom assignment or even during the spelling bee, but, they would always vow to get it right tomorrow.

Whenever we went to the amusement park, or to the circus or to the state fair, and we played the games, whereas we didn't win the prize, almost always we vow that either we would never play those games again or we would vow to win all of the prizes tomorrow or the next time.

Many people have been shocked at just how soon tomorrow came upon us and caught us with our guards down and sometimes with our ability to do better than we had done before, no better than we had actually done previously.

The unfamiliar newness of the today may often find us unprepared for the unexpected events that have been ordained to take place at center stage in the run of this day.

Had it not been so that Jacob had a visit in the middle of the night while he had been left alone, he would have

The Breaking Of Day!

AWAKENED TOMORROW TO DO THE SAME THINGS THAT HE HAD DONE ALL ALONG.

He already had a plan to convince his brother Esau that he did not have all of the stuff that his brother knew that he did indeed have.

Jacob had sent his wives and servants along with the livestock and all of his possessions in separate bands, so that if one band was attacked and the stuff was lost as a result, that his brother might believe that he had destroyed all of Jacobs stuff.

Jacob was still determined to work tricks and schemes in the morning, even though he had prayed to the Lord for a change the night before. Jacob asked the Lord to deliver him from the wrath of his brother Esau.

We believe that Jacob wrestled with an angel in the mid-night hours. Just prior to finding this particular resting place, Jacob saw a band of angels following he and his entourage on their journey.

He recognized them as the Lord's host of angels, he realized that he was indeed in the presence of the Lord and he worshipped Him there in that place. Although he was assured that the Lord was with him on his journey, he still had

Hidden In the Light*

a mind to settle the matter between he and his brother in his own way. He was cunning and crafty in his dealings with people.

Most people either devise a scheme or make their plans to handle their shady affairs in the night hours before daybreak. Others, as a result of fear, they pray; though lacking faith only expecting the worse to happen to them in the morning or on the next day.

Whenever Jacob lay down for the night to sleep, he had been afraid of his brother coming to slay him, so he prayed from his own heart to ask the Lords protection.

He fell asleep in fear, but he arose the next day in confidence assured by the angel of the Lord that he had indeed prevailed as a prince before the Lord.

We always fear in darkness. Whether we are in the darkness of our understanding, or simply in the darkness of circumstantial reasoning, whereas the details of our situations have not yet been exposed to clarify the foggy blinders that hindered the ability of our minds to tunnel our way through any situation.

I can remember as if it were yesterday, in the eighth grade at

The Breaking Of Day!

Handley Middle School back in 1973, here in Fort Worth, Texas.

Myself, and a few friends auditioned for the talent show and we were accepted. However, what took me by storm, to which I had never even had a clue until, now, was a classmate who sang a choral piece for the talent show, a Hymn titled; "Morning Has Broken;"

I have always remembered the lyrics of the song. They went like so;

"Morning has broken, like the first morning; like the first sunrise, on the first bird; morning has broken, like the first morning; like the first morning on the first bird."

As she sang the song during practice for the talent show there at the school, like most of the students, I initially thought that the song was rather corny, because we were doing the popular dances of the time, to the popular radio tunes, while others were singing the most up-to-date songs.

Most of us who participated in the talent show wanted to treat her performance as if she were a failed act at show time @ the Apollo Theatre in New York. But we wouldn't dare boo her for the fear of being cut from the

Hidden In the Light*

performance of the talent show ourselves.

She sang the song with so much grace and without any fear it seemed, to the rejection of any of the other classmates who might have rejected her performance.

The faculty and the talent show staff were just overwhelmed with her choice of song for the talent show. It almost seemed as if the rest of us could have chosen to pull ourselves from the line-up of the show; they liked her song so well!

I believe that it was their liking for the song that started me to meditating on the song so heavily. I wanted to know why the teachers were so into her song selection.

For sure, they knew that we did not get the message in the song that she sang. We were still in that happy go lucky stage of living, not knowing that the time would come when indeed we would need the lyrics of that song to speak hope to us and to help us make it through the many dark nights to come, of our lives.

Perhaps if we could have understood the powerful breaking of the day, we would have been more apt to

The Breaking Of Day!

AVOID EVEN BEING LULLED TO SLEEP THROUGH THE APATHETIC HOPELESSNESS OF THE REOCCURRENCES IN OUR SURROUNDINGS.

THE POWERFUL EXCITEMENT OF THE DAY-BREAK MUST BE EXPERIENCED, IN AN EFFORT TO APPRECIATE ITS ARRIVAL.

THOSE LYRICAL EXPRESSIONS HAD ALWAYS REMAINED FRESH IN THE SPIRIT OF MY MIND, BUT WITHOUT ANY DEFINITIVE COMPREHENSION FOR MOST OF THE TIME TO STEER ME IN THE DIRECTION OF ALWAYS ANTICIPATING DAY-BREAK!

IN MOST OF THE PAST GHETTO STYLE; NEIGHBORHOOD UPBRINGINGS, THE ATMOSPHERIC SURROUNDINGS WERE USUALLY DARKENED BY UNFAVORABLE HAPPENSTANCES THAT OCCUR ON A DAILY BASIS AND ESPECIALLY IN THE DARKNESS OF THE NIGHT.

AS A RESULT, WE OFTEN, ARE STILL PRONE TO ANTICIPATE THE COMING OF THE NIGHTFALL IN FEAR, RATHER THAN TO CONTINUE IN FAITH BELIEVING GOD, AND WELCOMING THE SPLENDOR OF THE NEXT DAYBREAK.

YOU SEE WHERE THERE IS NO NIGHT, THERE IS SIMPLY NO NEED!

NO MATTER WHERE YOU MAY BE IN THE MIDST OF YOUR NIGHT, WHENEVER THE "SON" OF GOD" COMES INTO YOUR NIGHT, IT WILL IMMEDIATELY BE TURNED TO DAY. YOUR NIGHT SEASON IS CLEARLY A DEPICTION OF AN

Hidden In the Light*

area of need for you, for which you can only be in the need for whatever it may be that you need, until the supplier comes in to fix and to fulfill your need.

Jesus said; "I must work the works of Him that sent me, while it is day!" Meaning; He had everything He needed to do whatever needed to be done in the realm of all humanity. Haven't you noticed that Jesus always supplied whatever the people needed, and was never in the need of being supplied?

Even whenever it came to laying His head down for the night to sleep, He wasn't at a loss or begging for someone to supply a place for Him to rest.

Even as He divided the "Fish and Loaves" among the multitudes, notice that he did not need a butcher or a baker to separate the portions to the people, He was well endowed within Himself to not only divide the portions but, also to increase the initially limited measure that they began with from the start.

Whenever the sick were healed, Jesus never called or sent for physicians and the medical specialist of that day to assist in the healing process.

Even to this very day Jesus is the healing and the specialist. Jesus; is the light of the day!

The Breaking Of Day!

Where there is no night; there can be no need!

The only night for Jesus came on the cross of Calvary; for which He only really experienced three nights before the day of Lord broke though Eternally Chronos; in the realm of humanity!

Even in the dense darkness of the night in the midst of a raging storm; Jesus comes walking towards the ship on the water to meet the disciples out on the sea.

At night, it is extremely dark out over the ocean and the sea. There is no way to install lights out over the water so that the atmosphere would be bright enough to see as within the daylight hours.

The day in which Jesus is speaking of is also to be reckoned as to mean; an opportune period of awareness. It really should not take the balance of our days, for us to become aware of the things of God at the closing of the days of our lives.

Many people have spent their entire lives clueless and void of understanding the things that God would have for them to know relative to their on personalized destinies.

It is possible, to have the skills to

Hidden In the Light*

work with to complete a particular task, but, never be aware of it. Most people only need to be made aware of the given tools to which they themselves have been endowed.

To be made aware; is to come into the knowledge of the reality of an actual existing reality about oneself.

Nowadays, many people are enrolled into Theological Seminaries and learning institutes, who are finding themselves at awe, and in complete perplexity, as it relates to being able to exact influence and to effectively bring forth the kinds of changes to redirect the rapid courses of sin, in the lives of the people, from the paths of their own eminent destruction.

Many people are consistently looking, but they are never seeing; they are listening but, they are never hearing; they are always working but, never ever getting anything done; they are talking all of the time but, they are never really ever saying anything of any substance; they are always in school but, they are never being taught anything!

The world, as we know of it today, is actually in the night season? . . . .

The bible clearly speaks of these days. It's not pleasing the Lord, that

The Breaking Of Day!

The light has been turned on for humanity, but whether or not we as individuals choose to be in the dark, the fact is that the balance of the earths population, are forever willfully in the darkness of their own understanding.

Consistently, we are in the presence of one another, but often we are not even aware of who it is that we are even blessed to be in the company of. We are not usually aware of who it is that we are keeping company with.

Pay attention to your company and you will be made aware of whom it is that you have chosen to covenant with as a friend. The persons of whom we only prefer to casually associate ourselves with, having no substance at all to the relationship, they have a tendency to leave the debris of their own stinking lifestyles behind, clinging on to us as they pass on.

At nineteen years of age, the spirit of the Lord spoke to me and said to me in the very early hours of the morning, before the daylight; "Show Me Your Company Keeper and I Will Show You Who You Are?!"

Somehow or another, I just knew that I had read that in the scriptures. I searched the scriptures for years

Hidden In the Light*

following that time and I have never found those exact words written in the Bible!

I, now realize that what I did indeed hear, was the revelatory comprehensive instruction from the spirit of the Lord, admonishing me to take a closer look at the company that I was keeping. I needed to be aware of my friends!

There were people in my life at the time that didn't mean me any good. I have matured to realize the actuality of being in bad company, relative to the behavior of my own past choice of conduct, as a result from being attached to the wrong people.

I was forever learning about the people in my life the hard way, until I became aware of the knowledge of truth about me and all of the bad influences around me, both male and female.

Bad influences for me were both in and out of the church. It took me a while, but, thank God I came to the knowledge of the truth, though in many instances it was very painful.

The "day", broke forth for me, when I realized, that everyone that was laughing with me, while we were supposed to be having a good time in the company

The Breaking Of Day!

OF EACH OTHER, THAT MANY OF THOSE SAME PEOPLE WERE ACTUALLY LAUGHING AT ME SIMULTANEOUS!

SOMETIMES THEIR GOOD LAUGH WAS ONLY FOR THE PURPOSE OF EXAMINING ME TO SEE IF WHETHER OR NOT I HAD ACTUALLY BECOME AWARE OF THE FACT THAT THEY WERE UNDERMINING AND SETTING ME UP FOR THE BIG LET DOWN!

Ever learning, and never able to come into the knowledge of the truth.   II Timothy 3:7

PEOPLE SPEND MANY HOURS IN TEACHING SESSIONS AND CLASSROOMS, LEARNING ABOUT JESUS CHRIST. SO MUCH ERRONEOUS INFORMATION HAS BEEN PASSED TO THE BIBLE STUDENTS, THAT IT IS NO WONDER THAT SO MANY PEOPLE ARE FOREVER LEARNING BUT NEVER ABLE TO COME INTO THE KNOWLEDGE OF THE TRUTH.

THE TRUTH WILL NEVER BE FOUND IN THE MIDST OF LIES. GULLIBLE PEOPLE EAT UP EVERY THING THAT SOUNDS LIKE THE INCREDIBLE DETAILS OF THE LIFE AND TIMES OF JESUS; WHILE HE WALKED THE EARTH.

THOUGH THE ENEMY HAS BAITED THE LINE TO FISH US INTO THE FARCE OF HIS OWN LYING ATMOSPHERE, WE ARE THE ONLY RESPONSIBLE PARTIES TO TAKE THE BLAME FOR HAVEN TAKEN THE BAIT.

YOU DON'T GO LOOKING IN THE DARK

Hidden In the Light*

to find the light! At all times; you must take notice of the fact that there is no light in the darkness. If the light were there, it wouldn't be dark!

Whenever darkness falls into your own personal atmosphere, don't be so arrogant as to believe that the light is already there, though you cannot even see your way through the darkness at all!

You have got to invite the light into your situation, knowing that the light that you need to invite to dispel the darkness of your situation is Jesus; Jesus is the light of the world.

There will never be a time when it is too dark for the Lord to see through any situation. He also said; "The night cometh when no man can work."

If you will take a closer look at what He said, you will notice that He said, that no man can work in the night. It will at times get to be too dark in a situation, for you to work things out for yourself, or for anyone else.

Here's why: God in His infinite wisdom; He knows that the night must fall in the lives of every person, else we feel that as a result of always having the light available to us, we might begin to think that we have become self sufficient

The Breaking Of Day!

TO CHART THE PATH OF OUR OWN COURSE.

Naturally, people want to be in charge and in total control of their own destinies. We need always to be aware of the fact that we are in need of the Lord's help. It's a common practice, for people to blow it and to create the biggest mess of their lives, whenever they take the control, determining to leave the Lord out of the scheme of things, of their agendas.

For as long as we are in the night, we have insufficient circumstances that create atmospheric hindrances, that would not even allow us to begin to set the stage for preparing a working space.

Never forget the fact that the night bespeaks of our inability to produce or to perform any task necessary for producing favorable outcomes.

We can't be productive, because we still need that which enables us to forefront the working desires of our hearts.

Until we have Jesus in our lives, and take the initiative to step back away from the tasks that are confronting us on a consistent basis, we will always be in the night seasons of our lives.

Allow Jesus, to workout the situations that might have been holding

Hidden In the Light*

back the success from our lives, even though at times, He may work through us!......................

God did not work in the dark, being His people, we are not endowed or even purposed to work in the darkness either!

It's not at all like God, to attempt to work from the dark, to complete that which is only to be displayed in the light!................

It's sort of like dressing in the dark, only to realize that whenever you came into the light, that the clothes to which you had put on were not even suitable for wearing, for any number of reasons?

Even in a well lighted room, many women will require a lighted mirror to aid them in putting on their makeup and cosmetics. Not even a dead corpse, is dressed in the dark, for their own funerals!

We need the light; so for this reason alone God never left the entire cosmos of the world in the dark. Everybody receives the blessing of the light though we may not all receive the light at the very same rate.

One side of the earth basks in the splendor of the daylight, while the

The Breaking Of Day!

OTHER HALF OF THE EARTH IS VEILED IN THE COVER OF THE NIGHT. NEVERTHELESS, WE ALL RECEIVE THE BLESSING OF THE LIGHT, WHETHER WE ARE RESPECTFUL OF THE LIGHT AS IT SHINES ON OUR LIVES, AND/OR EVEN KNOWLEDGEABLE OF THE PURPOSE FOR OUR OWN ATMOSPHERES BEING LIGHTED FOR OUR OWN PERSONAL USAGE.

*The Sun/Son Cometh**

BE HONEST WITH ME; HAVE YOU EVER SEEN THE SUN SHINING IN THE MIDDLE OF THE NIGHT UNDER ANY <u>NORMAL</u> CIRCUMSTANCES, WHERE THE MOON AND THE STARS ARE IN THEIR SPACES TO LIGHT THE DOMINANCE OF THE SKY IN THE NIGHT? NO! AND OF COURSE YOU NEVER WILL SEE THE SUN SHINING IN THE NIGHT! AS A MATTER OF THE FACT THE QUESTION IS; HOW DO YOU SEE THE SUN?

LOTS OF DARK AND TRAGIC THINGS MAY HAPPEN TO US IN THE NIGHT SEASONS OF OUR LIVES, BUT DON'T BE DISMAYED; LOOK FOR THE RISING OF THE SUN.

MOST TRAGIC SITUATIONS, WILL HAVE OUR HEADS HUNG DOWN, WITH OUR FACE TOWARDS THE GROUND, OR THE EARTH IF YOU PREFER? ON A SIDE NOTE: EVERYONE SHOULD HAVE NOTICED THAT AFTER LOOKING DOWN FOR SO LONG NOW, THAT THE ANSWERS THAT

Hidden In the Light*

WE ARE SEEKING, ARE NOT ON THE GROUND, OR MOST TIMES, NOT EVEN IN THE EARTH!

The sun rises in the morning, or in our more common terminology, the sun comes up in the morning time. In certain geographical areas, it may even appear that the sun is actually coming up from beneath our own vantage points, from underneath us; but, as soon as the light of the day is in full measure, it is obvious that we have to look up to actually see the sun.

The sun is always up in the sky above our heads. Nothing should sit on our necks so heavy that it disallows our heads from rising upwards to view the glory of the sun.

The tragedy is; the sun has come up, and it is shining for the entire world to see it, but far too many people are failing to look up! People believe in looking out, especially for one another; perhaps they have also discovered the truth in the fact that absolutely no one can look up for you!

I have had some people to tell me that they had been so depressed that they did not even have a desire to get out of the bed in the morning! They could not bare the bourden of living another day with things as they were the

The Breaking Of Day!

DAY BEFORE.

In my own opinion, they had lost the ability to look upwards to see the blessing of a new day of sunshine. Every new day of sunshine, or even daylight that is given to us, signifies that there is a new opportunity for every circumstantial situation of our lives to change.

Even a prisoner locked away behind bars, doing a life sentence without the possibility of parole, though they may know the actuality of their own situation, as result of the crime to which they had committed, someway or another they keep looking for the possibility of a change in their own lawfully mandated and predetermined outcome.

Though the concrete walls of the prison, blocks out the visibility of the sunlight up in the sky, it only opens the way for the light of the SON of God; to shine through to their now dark place of living.

Wake Up its Daybreak

Have you ever gone to bed on the close of what might have been cited for whatever the reason, as a bad day for

Hidden In the Light*

you, with the feeling that all you needed was for the day to be over, and for another opportunity to wake up to a brand new day?

The madness of one day, is often aborted with the entrance of a brand new day, at the turn of the clock's midnight hour.

Some people have literally cried all night long until the sunlight broke forth on the next day. Few people rarely find themselves ready for the next day to actually come forth in their lives.

Whenever we allow fear to blanket our atmosphere with the unforeseen negative possibilities for terrible circumstances of terror, we also allow the darkness of our own night seasons to be extended, for much longer periods than that of which had been originally allotted for the night itself.

We created an extended version of the actuality of the night.

God's intentional period of the night was rightfully established from the beginning of the creation of the very first initial night, which was created from the woven blanket of darkness that covered the face of the earth.

Through the carefulness of being

The Breaking Of Day!

SURE THAT WE REMIND OURSELVES TO BE AFRAID OF THE DARKNESS, WE ADD MORE HOURS TO THE NIGHT, LESS HINDERING THE AWAITED ARRIVAL OF OUR OWN DAY-BREAK!

THERE ARE TIMES WHEN THE NIGHT SEEMS SO LONG, AS A RESULT OF FEAR, IT'S BEEN REPORTED, THAT IT APPEARS THE GATES OF HELL HAVE BEEN UNLOCKED, RELEASING ALL OF THE TERRORS OF THE NIGHT TO LAUNCH THEIR ATTACK IN THE DARKENED STILLNESS OF THE NIGHT.

OFTEN, WHEN FEAR IS PRESENT IN THE STALE DAMPNESS OF THE NIGHT HOURS, WHAT IS FELT UPON THE SURFACE OF THE SKIN, IS AS IF THE DARKNESS ITSELF, HAS BEGAN TO VIBRATE OR TO MOVE ABOUT IN THE ROOM.

HAS THERE EVER BEEN AN EXPERIENCE IN YOUR LIFE WHEREAS, IT APPEARED THAT THE NIGHT BROUGHT ON THE TERRORS AND THE HORRORS OF EVIL, RIGHT TO YOUR OWN BEDSIDE IN A DARK ROOM?

THE WORLD SAYS; THAT "FREAKS COME OUT AT NIGHT!"

HAVEN'T YOU EVER WONDERED WHY THE PEOPLE THAT PARTICIPATE IN TRICK-OR-TREAT, ON HALLOWEEN, DO SO IN THE NIGHT?

THE ALTRUISTIC REALITY OF THAT THAT IS REGARDED AS EVIL, IS REVEALED AND APPRECIATED ONLY IN DARKNESS. WHETHER THE DARKNESS IS OF THE STILLNESS OF THE NIGHT OR THE DARKENED UNDERSTANDING

Hidden In the Light*

of an individual's mind perception, in the way that they process thoughts; only the darkness creates a suitable atmosphere for the existence of evil.

Most horror films usually depict tragic events during a movie, as after-dark situations of evil circumstances, that take place in the darkness of the night. Even the ungodly people of the world know that it does not make sense to portray an evil event in the daylight hours?

We used to see films of evil, where Dracula would not dare be caught reeking havoc in the sunlight!

To be caught in the sun meant sudden death! Even if the room where Dracula had been, during the time of which he would be doing his evil business, it had thick dark heavy curtains to block every trace of the sun, he would be justified to continue his misdeeds.

However, the moment the curtain was rolled back, like as unto the unveiling of the early morning hours of sunlight; to reveal the rising of the sun at daybreak; right in the middle of his act, Dracula would be terminated and he would dissolve right before the very eyes of the person/persons in which he had been terrorizing.

The Breaking Of Day!

So it is with the dark atrocities that plague the lives of people, as long as it is dark, things may be allowed to remain as they are. But, be assured, that whenever the light comes in, things have to change!

Sometimes, the circumstances are demanded to change instantaneously, while others will have to follow the natural process of illimination with the passing of time.

You will be better off, to begin realizing that the light itself, bespeak of an illuminated change, in the midst of our atmosphere!

To be in denial of the fact that ligiit is shining, doesn't excuse the damnd for change, which at times, change in and of itself, may be screaming out for your attention!

You are called to come into the light; what is your problem?

Many people have discovered that by the time they came to the realization, that they were indeed tired of being in the dark, that it wasn't the darkness that was holding them hostage to the sunken state of living;

They were actually holding on to the darkness, gripping other opportunities, to continue to practice

Hidden In the Light[*]

THE WICKED SCHEMES OF THEIR OWN DEMONICALLY INFLUENSED TRADE!
Now the Light Is On!
The Day Breaketh!

Chapter 6

Mystery R' Myth ***

But if the Spirit of Him that raised up Jesus from the dead dwell in you, he that raised up Christ from the dead shall also quicken your mortal bodies by his Spirit that dwelleth in you. Therefore, brethren, we are debtors, not to the flesh, to live after the flesh. For if ye live after the flesh, ye shall die: but if ye through the Spirit do mortify the deeds of the body, ye shall live. For as many as be led by the Spirit of God, they are the sons of God. For ye have not received the spirit of bondage again to fear; but ye have receive the spirit of adoption, whereby we cry, Ab'ba, Father. The Spirit itself beareth witness with our spirit, that we are the children of God: Romans 8:11-16

Beloved, believe not every spirit, but try the spirits whether they are of God: because many false prophets

Hidden In the Light*

are gone out into the world. Hereby know ye the spirit of God: Every spirit that confesseth that Jesus Christ is come in the flesh is of God: And every spirit that confesseth not that Jesus Christ is come in the flesh is not of God: and this is that spirit of the anti-Christ, whereof ye have heard that it should come; and even now already it is in the world. Ye are of God, little children, and have overcome them: because greater is he that is in you, than he that is in the world. No man hath seen God at any time. If we love one another, God dwelleth in us, and his love is perfected in us. And we have known and believed the love that God hath to us, God is Love; and he that dwelleth in love dwelleth in God, and God in him. Herein is our love made perfect, that we may have boldness in the day of judgment: because as he is, so are we in this world.

I John 4:1-4, 12, 16-17

*Most People Are Confused***

Make no mistake about it, most people dare not even come close to approaching unto the mysteries of God, for fear of being made a fool of themselves, by those who don't believe. There are more people intrigued to try God, than there are those persons who have totally dismissed the reality of the existence of God altogether.

When truthfully examining people, you will likewise discover that there are many people desperately desiring a

Mystery R' Myth**

relationship with the Lord; though the average individual on the outside of the present kingdom of God may have been grossly deceived. They are now in a state of complex perplexity, confused, humanistically bound to miss the reality of God.

One of the more mistaken theories of the people of the church, is that everybody on the outside of the church, are totally to the left and completely turned off at the idea of God in Christ Jesus.

I don't know how it is that the people of the church feel the effectiveness to ever be successful witnesses if they believe that the people that we are supposed to witness to, are totally and completely dead from the neck up, as it relates to the spirit of God?

We are lead to believe that our actual function as members of the church, is to somehow interest people who are totally uninterested in the salvation of Christ, initially. God only comes near unto those people who have actually come near unto him!

Don't fool yourself, people are interested in knowing God!

It has become a common occurrence both in; and on the outside of the church, for people in general to question

Hidden In the Light*

THOSE THINGS THAT ARE TRULY UNQUESTIONABLE. THOSE THINGS WHEREAS THE ONLY EXPLANATION FOR THEIR EXISTENCE COULD ONLY BE GOD, REGARDLESS OF SCIENCE OR ANY OTHER SYSTEM OF BELIEVING.

AS A RESULT, MANY PEOPLE HAVE BECOME QUESTIONABLE IN THEIR OWN CHARACTER DISPOSITIONS. THEY WALK ABOUT THEIR DAILY AFFAIRS, UNSURE IN EVERY MANNER OF THEIR INDIVIDUAL DEMEANOR. NOT ONLY ARE THEY INCAPABLE OF UNDERSTANDING THEMSELVES, BUT, THEY ARE ALSO DEVOID OF ANY BENEFIT TO HUMAN COMPREHENSION AS IT RELATES TO AIDING ANOTHER INDIVIDUAL TO HAVE FAITH IN GOD.

AS WE ARE CONTINUOUSLY LEFT TO OURSELVES, TO DEVELOP AND TO MAINTAIN OUR INDIVIDUAL WAY OF THINKING ABOUT SALVATION AND OR EVEN THE NEED FOR BEING SAVED, WE ARE DANGEROUSLY DAMAGING OUR OWN ABILITY TO RECEIVE ANYTHING THAT WE MAY EVER NEED FROM GOD. THE GREATER DESTRUCTION IS WITHIN THE FACT THAT PEOPLE ARE SERIOUSLY DESIRING TO PUT ASIDE THE BIBLE, SEEKING TO FIND GOD THROUGH ANY OTHER MEANS.

IT IS A MYSTERIOUS REALITY, TO DISCOVER THAT WHENEVER WE DO COME TO THE LORD TO SURRENDER OUR LIVES TO HIM TO BE SAVED FROM OURSELVES AND FROM THE POWER OF SIN, THAT WE HAVE ALSO COME TO HIM TO RECEIVE EVERYTHING ELSE THAT WE WILL EVER NEED TO

MAKE IT THROUGH THE REST OF OUR LIVES AS A SAVED INDIVIDUAL.

GOD WILL ALWAYS GIVE TO YOU MUCH MORE THAN YOU WILL EVER BE ABLE TO ASK FOR OR TO EVEN THINK OF ASKING IN THE SPIRIT OF YOUR OWN NATURAL MIND.

PERHAPS MORE PEOPLE WOULD REFRAIN FROM LIVING SINFUL LIVES IF THEY TRULY UNDERSTOOD THE ACTUAL POWER OF SIN, IN THAT IT HAS THE PRESENT AUTHORITY TO SEPARATE EVERY SINNER FROM THE PRESENCE OF GOD. THE SEPARATING POWER OF SIN, IN MY OPINION, IS NOT WHERE THE MYSTERY LIES, IT IS HOWEVER MYSTERIOUS TO ME HOW THAT MOST PEOPLE ARE NOT EVEN WILLING TO CALL SIN WHAT IT IS, INDEED. [LEVITICUS 10:10]

PEOPLE IN GENERAL, HAVE NO DESIRE USUALLY, TO EVEN DEAL WITH THE ACTUALITY OF THE SIN WHICH THEY MAY BE PARTAKING OF IN THEIR DAILY LIVES. THEY CHOOSE TO IGNORE THE REALITY THAT THEIR PRESENT BEHAVIOR IS IN DIRECT DISOBEDIENCE TOWARDS GOD, WHICH IS A SIN.

MOST PEOPLE HAVE MASTERED THE ART OF IGNORING SIN, CALLING IT NOTHING MORE THAN A CHOICE AND THEIR RIGHT TO CHOOSE. FROM THE VANTAGE POINTS OF SINNERS, THE PEOPLE OF THE CHURCH WHO TRULY BELIEVE THAT THE BIBLE IS THE WRITTEN WORD OF GOD, ARE EXTREME IN THEIR BELIEF SYSTEMS, AND ARE OFTEN SAID TO BE DANGEROUS FOR HUMANITY.

Hidden In the Light*

Christianity and Christ; are now thought of in the light of being only one of the many religious choices that are available to the people of the society. Americans now belief that it is healthy for the people of the country to exercise the extremeties of choice, as it relates to having religion.

Many other religious schemes have now been erected as viable options of choosing relative to faith. However, absolutely nothing of a substance of hope is presented as a real benefiting alternative choice, to be received as an object for faithfully believing.

Only God had the power to start from the actuality of nothing to create everything.

As it relates to faith, there has got to be something on the other side of your own present reality, much more powerful than only your ability to choose it as an option to believe; if in fact your faith is going to ever produce anything for you.

People now believe that as long as they show up at a gathering of people, to do religious stuff, then it must be the definitive clarification of the meaning of a worship service; though the spirit of the Lord never enters, nor is even invoked to reside in the presence of the people.

Other religious persuasions, never

Mystery R' Myth**

EVEN INTEND FOR THE SPIRIT OF THE LORD TO TAKE UP RESIDENCY IN THE MIDST OF THEIR GATHERING. THEY ARE IN TOTAL REJECTION OF THE DEITY OF CHRIST FROM THE BEGINNING, FOR WHICH THEY ARE NOT IN-DISCLOSED ABOUT THEIR SYSTEMS OF DISBELIEF.

I HAVE DISCOVERED THROUGH MY OWN PERSONAL RESEARCH, THAT MOST OF THE OTHER RELIGIONS, AND THE COMPILATION OF THEIR WRITTEN RELIGIOUS MATERIAL, NEVER DEAL WITH THE IDEALISM OF WHAT IS OR IS NOT A SIN, AND NEITHER DO THEY EVEN HAVE A MEANS FOR DEALING WITH SIN ISSUES.

AS A MATTER OF THE FACT, MOST OF THE OTHER RELIGIOUS AFFILIATIONS, DO NOT EVEN REGARD HUMANISTIC MISBEHAVIOR AS SIN. AS LONG AS THEY OBSERVE THE IDEA OF THE POSSIBILITY OF A HIGHER BEING, THEY ARE FREED TO LIVE AS THEY ARE PLEASED TO DO SO, BY THEIR OWN CHOICE.

IT IS NO SURPRISE TO GOD THAT PEOPLE EVENTUALLY EMERGED IN THESE LATTER GENERATIONS TO DETERMINE WITHIN THEIR OWN MINDS, THAT THEY ARE THEIR OWN GOD! MORE AND MORE NOW, PEOPLE ARE DETERMINING THAT THEY NO LONGER NEED THE LOCAL CHURCH TO FIND GOD, AND TO DEVELOP AND MAINTAIN A RIGHTEOUS RELATIONSHIP WITH HIM.

MANY PEOPLE HAVE DETERMINED TO READ THE BIBLE FROM COVER TO COVER, ONLY, THEY HAVE REFUSED TO REGARD THE BIBLE AS BEING

Hidden In the Light*

THE WORD OF GOD.

THIS IS ONLY SO, BECAUSE THE BIBLE IS ALL ABOUT GETTING INTO OUR DAILY AFFAIRS, AND IT REQUIRES US TO CLEAN UP OUR LIFESTYLES, WHENEVER WE HAVE COME TO JESUS TO BE SAVED, SET FREE AND DELIVERED. TO THE AVERAGE PERSON, THE BIBLE IS A COMPLETED BOOK OF MYSTERIES; TO OTHERS IT IS ONLY A DARK WORK OF MYTHS; WHICH SEEKS TO AIMLESSLY CONTROL THE DAILY AFFAIRS OF THE PEOPLE THAT READ IT, WHETHER THEY BELIEVE IT OR NOT.

AMAZINGLY, PEOPLE DIVE INTO EVERY OTHER TYPICAL TOPIC OF BOOKS THERE ARE IN THE WORLD, OF WHICH MANY OF THEM ARE DANGEROUS TO ANY HUMAN WELFARE. BUT, MANY OF THE SAME PEOPLE ARE TERRIFICALLY HORRIFIED OVER THE IDEA OF LETTING THEIR MINDS GO WHILE EXPLORING THE WRITTEN WORD OF GOD.

THE MINDS OF MERE MEN AND WOMEN ARE OPENED TO EVERY OTHER FORM OF INFORMATION ALONG THE LINES OF READING MATERIALS, BUT AS THEY READ THE WORD OF GOD, SOMEHOW THEIR MINDS ARE CLOSED, AND THEIR SPIRITS ARE UNBELIEVING.

*Naturally Being Human**

AS MANY PEOPLE READ THE BIBLE, THEY ALSO DECIDE WITHIN THEMSELVES THAT THE BIBLE IS FILLED WITH CONTRADICTIONS AND

Mystery R' Myth**

MYTHS, WHICH SIMPLY EXCUSES THEM TO DECIDE AGAINST SURRENDERING THEIR WILL TO THE WILL OF GOD.

WHENEVER I HAVE BEEN ATTEMPTING TO MINISTER TO CERTAIN PEOPLE, AS IT BECOMES OBVIOUS THAT I MIGHT HAVE HIT A BRICK WALL, SEVERAL OF THOSE PEOPLE HAVE STATED TO ME, WHAT THEY BELIEVE TO BE THE FOUND FACTS ABOUT THE BIBLE?

THEY FEEL THAT THEY ARE TELLING ME SOMETHING ABOUT THE BIBLE, OF WHICH I BELIEVE TO BE THE WRITTEN WORD OF GOD, THEY BEGIN SUGGESTING TO ME THAT THE BIBLE IS FILLED WITH CONTRADICTIONS.

IT IS MYSTERIOUS TO ME THAT THEY ARE SO COMFORTABLE WITH THE BOOKS OF THE OTHER AUTHORS OF THE WORLD WHICH HAVE NO BENEFIT TO THEM OTHER THAN ENTERTAINMENT.

SEVERAL OF THE NOW SO-CALLED EDUCATED PERSONS OF THE SOCIETY, REFER TO THE BIBLE AS FICTITIOUS. SOMEHOW THEY HAVE BEEN INSTRUCTED TO BELIEVE THAT THE BIBLE IS JUST A MYTH; YET THEY HAVE NOT BEEN ABLE TO DISCONNECT THE SPIRIT OF THE LORD FROM THE WRITTEN MANUSCRIPT.

MANY OF THE SAME PEOPLE ARE REQUIRED IN COLLEGE TO PARTAKE OF GREEK MYTHOLOGY. OUR TWISTED SOCIETY, WILL HAVE US TO BELIEVE THAT PEOPLE HAVE SUCCESSFULLY ARRIVED IF THEY SHOULD GET THE OPPORTUNITY TO PERFORM IN STAGE PLAYS ON

Hidden In the Light*

Broadway, which usually highlight Greek Mythological Philosophies, many of them.

The very people that believe in myths, are the same people who would have you to believe that there is indeed something wrong with your way of thinking, because you embrace the mysteries of God.

Many of the people who stand in the pulpits, are often heard quoting Greek Philosophy in the midst of their sermons. They won't allow the movement of the spirit in their worship services, but, they spread "make believe" character's statements in the ears of the people in the audiences of the sanctuary of the churches all over the world.

Erroneously, people will embrace most things that are tangible, as long as they can either witness that other people are responsible for those things, or in light of the written record of individuals who refute the reality of the bible, and deny the actuality of Christ's deity.

Often people will say; "I Was There", usually being all that it will take to get others to embrace the matter as being accounted as true.

Mere men look to other men for the validated allowance of acceptable reasoning, as it relates to receiving evidence of proclaimed true's. Most

Mystery R' Myth**

PEOPLE ARE DETERMINED TO REQUIRE SOMEONE ELSE TO BE STANDING ON THE VERY SAME PLATFORM OF FIND OR FICTION, IF THEY ARE GOING TO STAND THERE THEMSELVES. THEY DO NOT EMBRACE THE IDEA, THE NEED, OR EVEN THE ABILITY TO STAND ALONE IN THEIR OWN SYSTEMS OF BELIEF.

MOST PEOPLE STAND IN SHEER FRIGHT AS IT RELATES TO BEING FOUND SINGLE IN ANY AREA OF BELIEF. THEY DON'T OFTEN DESIRE THE JACKET OF BEING LABELED, DIFFERENT; BIZARRE OR STRANGE; OR EVEN TOO SPIRITUAL! THEY WANT PEOPLE TO RECEIVE THEM AS ACCEPTABLE TO THE COMMON CAUSE OF WHATEVER THEIR SURROUNDING BELIEFS ARE.

PEOPLE ARE OFTEN MORE TAKEN WITH THE IDEA OF FITTING IN TO THE CROWD, MORE THAN THEY WOULD EVER BE WITH THE IDEA OF GETTING AWAY FROM THE COMMON CROWD.

SO MANY PEOPLE HAVE SHUNNED THE HIGH CALLINGS OF GOD AND THE GIFTS OF THE SPIRIT, BECAUSE THOSE AREAS OF SPIRITUAL STATUS ARE NOT NECESSARILY POPULAR WITH THE COMMON PEOPLE.

IT IS NOT COMMON, NOR OF THE GREATEST REALITY TO SEE PREACHERS ON STAGE AT THE "GRAMMY'S" TO RECEIVE AWARDS. NEITHER DO WE HEAR OF THE AVERAGE TRUE CHRISTIAN, BEING RECOGNIZED FOR BEING TRUE AND HONEST IN THEIR WALK WITH THE LORD. NATURALLY THOSE THINGS THAT ARE ACTUALLY TRUE AND HONEST ARE CONSIDERED

Hidden In the Light*

TO BE BORING AND NOT VERY EXCITING.

But, the moment one of the persons that are supposed to be true, are found in gross error, their misbehavior generates more publicity than the best good book on a New York Times, Best Sellers list.

Naturally, people are in constant search of new exciting episodes of flare in the lives of other interesting people, whether the occurrences are good or bad. That that is often presented by other human beings does not have to be good or even beneficial for other people, to be acceptable in the realm of human excitement.

So how do we get people to understand the contrastingly defined differences between what is regarded as the Mysteries of God; and the things that are truly regarded as myths, when most people are so taken in with whatever is usually false?

For a moment let's consider the extreme success of the movie making industry; movies are filled with actors who pretend to be characters that they are not in reality.

Yet, these "Professional Fakers"; cannot even walk down the street without a bodyguard, because they are so popular and so well accepted by the

GENERAL POPULOUS. BOTH IN AND ON THE OUTSIDE OF THE CHURCH, THE REGARD FOR ACTORS IS OFTEN THE SAME. PEOPLE EMBRACE THE UNTRUTH, OVER AND ABOVE THAT WHICH IS ACTUALLY TRUE.

IN EARLIER DECADES, PEOPLE WERE INQUISITIVE AND CURIOUS ABOUT CERTAIN THINGS THAT THEY WERE ACTUALLY A BIT MORE HESITANT TO EXPLORE AS A BORN AGAIN BELIEVER IN THE BODY OF CHRIST. BUT, THE PEOPLE OF THESE LATER GENERATIONS, HAVE BEEN STEERED AWAY FROM THE TRUTH OF THE WORD OF GOD, SINCE HAVING SURRENDERED TO THE SIDELINE ACTIVITIES OF THE SOCIETY, MAKING THEM ALTERNATIVE PRIORITIES TO THEIR OWN RELIGION BASED CHRISTIAN DEMEANOR.

THERE REALLY WAS A TIME WHEN THE PEOPLE OF THE CHURCH USED TO SHUN AND SHY AWAY FROM THE DEGRADING THINGS THAT WOULD SHAME THE BODY OF CHRIST, AND PLACE A STAIN ON THE LOCAL CHURCH IN THE FACE OF SOCIETY.

I'M COMPELLED TO WRITE THIS PARTICULAR CHAPTER, SIMPLY BECAUSE OF THE HIGH VOLUME OF MYTH BELIEVERS IN THE MIDST OF THE CHURCHES, THAT BECOME VIOLENTLY ENRAGED AT THE MENTION OF BEING FILLED WITH THE HOLY GHOST, WHILE THEY GO ALL OF THE WAY OUT TO OBSERVE SECULAR MYTHOLOGICAL ACTIVITIES SUCH AS HALLOWEEN, ST. PATRICK'S DAY, APRIL FOOLS DAY, AND MOST OTHER SUPPOSEDLY CHRISTIAN HOLIDAYS THAT HAVE

Hidden In the Light*

been Paganisticly donned!

Lately, I have been in churches that welcome magic shows for the young people of the churches, and fictitious cartoon characters. Even the people of the churches are now becoming too apprehensive with sharing Christ with the young people, citing an over abundance of information too mature for their younger minds.

Some may feel that I'm wired a bit too tight, for the simple reason that I sort of cringe at the mention of having a party, when spoken by born again, bible believing, saved and sanctified people of the body of Christ!

Because, I know that it is a common occurrence for partiers to get out of control. You see; people are more in tune with drinking alcohol and having something to smoke, whether legal or illegal, much more than they are aware of the ingrained benefits with taking communion in the worship service.

As it is, people of all ethnic groups want to dance; and I don't mean dancing in the spirit, I mean shaking their behinds. There is no doubt that there is going to be shaking going on at the party. People are going to get their groove on, no matter what others may think about it!

That form of dancing to which the

Mystery R' Myth**

saints of old fought vigorously to prevent it from entering into the church, has now entered, helping people to remain out of control.

There is no longer a distinction to define what is and what is not the acceptable behavioral patterns of the people of the church and the sinners who have not surrendered to the will of the Lord. Nowadays, one just might be asked to leave the church if they openly reject the display of people dancing in the aisles of the churches.

You might not be allowed to participate as a member of the choir, in many of the churches, if you refuse to perform the popular dance steps.

You could swiftly be labeled as too spiritual, or holier than Thou for refusing to conform to a lifestyle that is totally to the left of the teachings of the bible.

It's a myth that God doesn't care about the way we live whenever we exit the four walls of the church. It is also a matter of the fact that we are not at liberty to have sex with whomever we choose, whenever we choose, and however we choose to do so. Though many have had more than one sex partner in life, it is not to be received as acceptable in the eyes of God.

Hidden In the Light*

Mystery - mys-ter-y1 [míst - ree] n
1. puzzling event or situation: an event or situation that is difficult to fully understand or explain
2. unknown one: an unknown, secret, or hidden person or thing
3. strangeness: the quality of being strange, secret, or puzzling
4. story about puzzling event: a book, play, or movie about a puzzling event, especially an unsolved crime, that makes great use of suspense
5. Christianity something known by divine revelation: in Christian belief, a belief or truth that is considered to be beyond human understanding and can be made known only by divine revelation
6. Christianity incident from the life of Jesus Christ: an incident in the life of Jesus Christ that Christians believe to have special spiritual significance, especially, in Roman Catholicism, one of 15 events including the Annunciation and the Crucifixion
7. Christianity Christian sacrament: one of the Christian sacraments, especially Communion
Mysteries [plural] - (mys-ter-ies), n
1. secret knowledge: special knowledge known only to people skilled or involved in a particular activity, group, or subject
2. Christianity consecrated bread and wine: in Christianity, the consecrated bread and wine used in the sacrament of Communion

[14th century. Directly or via Anglo-Norman < Latin mysterium < Greek must-´÷"X˘"˘-rion "secret rite" < must-´÷"X˘"˘-s "initiated person" < muein "close the eyes or lips, initiate"]

Mystery R' Myth**

Encarta ® World English Dictionary © & (P) 1998-2005 Microsoft Corporation. All rights reserved.

Myth - [mith] (plural myths) n
1. ancient story: a traditional story about heroes or supernatural beings, often attempting to explain the origins of natural phenomena or aspects of human behavior
2. myths collectively: considered as a group or as a genre
3. idealized conception: a set of often idealized or glamorized ideas and stories surrounding a particular phenomenon, concept, or famous person the myth of the new man
4. false belief: a widely held but mistaken belief
5. fictitious person or thing: somebody who or something that is fictitious or nonexistent, <u>but whose existence is widely believed in</u>

[Mid-19th century. Directly or via French mythe < modern Latin mythus < Greek muthos "speech, myth"]
Encarta ® World English Dictionary © & (P) 1998-2005 Microsoft Corporation. All rights reserved.

*Too Close ; But, Not Close Enough***

THE TWO SCENARIOS, BOTH THE MYSTERIOUS AND THE MYTHYLOGICAL, REQUIRE THE ENGAGEMENT OF THE BELIEF SYSTEM.

AS IT RELATES TO THE MYSTERY; BELIEVING ONLY ALLOWS FOR THE MANIFESTATION OF THAT WHICH HAS BEEN INITIALLY HIDDEN FROM THE KNOWLEDGEABLE SCOPE OF REASONING OF THE INDIVIDUAL SEEKING TO UNDERSTAND THE SPIRITUAL PHENOMENON.

THE PHENOMENAL SPIRIT OF GOD MUST BE RECEIVED IN THE HEART AND THE MIND OF AN INDIVIDUAL, RATHER THAN BEING FIRSTLY

Hidden In the Light*

perceived and psychologically digested in the mind of the person, and totally understood in their reasonable process of thought.

Whenever we come to the point of receiving the spirit of God, we soon discover the available revelatory comprehensiveness of the spirit itself, uncovering the truth of the unseen, unknown deity and reality, in the spirit of our own mind.

But we also discover the awesome spill-over of the spirit of Christ in and throughout our entire beings. The spirit of the Lord will leave absolutely no part of our total being uncovered, neither untouched.

The greatest danger surrounding mysteries, is realized when allowing someone on the outside of your own spirit, soul and body, to make uncanny attempts at determining for you, whether or not you should or shouldn't believe the mysterious characteristics of the spirit of God.

Don't allow people or things that are gravely attributed to the natural, to define what is actually spiritual; or not! Without the help of the spirit, the things of the spirit cannot even be understood!

Other people may indeed recognize the presence of the spirit of the Lord,

Mystery R' Myth**

BUT THEY MAY ALSO POSSESS A HOSTEL SPIRIT TOWARDS THE WORD OF GOD, WHEREAS THEY MIGHT EVEN BE MORE APT TO DETER YOU FROM RESPECTING THE SPIRIT OF THE LORD, OR THEY MAY EVEN BE DETERMINED TO DECEIVE YOU RELATIVE TO RECEIVING THE SPIRIT OF THE LORD.

MANY PREACHERS WHO SAY THAT THEY TRULY BELIEVE IN THE SPIRIT OF THE LORD, ARE DETERMINED TO DISCOURAGE PEOPLE IN GENERAL FROM BEING DIAMETRICALLY OPPOSED TO SINFULLY LIVING AS A MANNER OF BEING SPIRITUAL.

> *My little children, these tings write I unto you, that ye sin not. And if any man sin, we have an advocate with the Father, Jesus Christ the righteous: And he is the propitiation for our sins: and not for our's only, but also for the sins of the whole world. And hereby we do know that we know him, if we keep his commandments. He that saith, I know him, and keepeth not his commandments, is a liar, and the truth is not in him.*   *I John 2:1-4*

I HEAR MINISTERS SAY FROM THE PULPITS OFTEN THAT WE SIN EVERYDAY, AS IF SINNING IS AN ACCEPTABLE THING IN THE SIGHT OF THE LORD. WHILE THEY ARE OVERWHELMED WITH THE GREEK LANGUAGE AND DEFINITIONS, RELATIVE TO WHAT THEY ARE DETERMINED TO BELIEVE GIVES US A MORE EXASPERATING EXHAUSTIVE UNDERSTANDING OF THE BIBLE,

Hidden In the Light*

THEY ARE LIKEWISE LULLED INTO BEING MORE HUMANISTIC AND LESS LIKE THE SPIRIT OF GOD.

THE MYSTERY IS; IF WE ARE GOING TO INDEED BE MORE LIKE GOD, OUR FOCUS HAS GOT TO BE AFFIXED ON HIM EVERY MOMENT OF OUR LIVES. AS WE SEARCH THE SCRIPTURE, IT SHOULD NOT BE OUR POSITION TO SCIENTIFICALLY DISPROVE THE REALITY OF GOD, AND THE GIFTS OF THE SPIRIT, BUT RATHER THE SCRIPTURE WILL EQUIP US TO BECOME MORE AND EVEN MORE LIKE GOD IN OUR DAILY WALK WITH HIM WHEN OUR FOCUS IS RIGHT.

THE IMAGE OF GOD IS NOT JUST SOME FREAK PHOTOGRAPHIC STROKE OF OUR IMAGINATION THAT WE HAVE CAPTURED IN OUR OWN CREATIVE THINKING CAPACITY, BASED ON WHAT WE HAD BEEN PREVIOUSLY INFORMED AND INSTRUCTED TO BELIEVE.

WE STRUGGLE WITH THE FACT OF SCRIPTURE WHICH SUGGEST TO US AS HUMAN BEINGS, THAT WE WERE MADE IN HIS IMAGE AND IN HIS OWN LIKENESS, BECAUSE OF THE LIMITED IMAGINATIVE ABILITY TO PSYCHOLOGICALLY CONSTRUCT THE PICTORIAL FOCUS OF GOD IN OUR MINDS EYE, BECAUSE WE CAN'T SEE HIM IN THE NATURAL.

THE VERY POWER OF THE SCIENTIFIC EVALUATION OF THE TOTAL CONSISTENCY IN THE MAKEUP OF MANKIND, HAS BEEN GROSSLY MISCONSTRUED, SIMPLY BECAUSE MAN HAVE TRIED TO UNDERSTAND THEMSELVES, WITHOUT THE AID OF THE ONE THAT MADE HIM.

Mystery R' Myth**

There are a few very fundamental things that must be recognized before we will ever be able to understand who we truly are. It is for sure that we were never Apes or Gorillas, that somehow evolved into a different type of being! Our existence as mankind is also very mysterious, while it is also a manifested reality.

To paint a picture in the minds of people everywhere, I would have to say to you that God is indescribably awesome in every manner of His being. The vocabulary communicative dialogue in the entire Cosmos, don't have the words to describe all that God is. Only wordless description could even come anywhere remotely close to making an adequate description of God; words as such to likeness of moaning; "HMMM!"

I know, it's a mystery; according to the 8th chapter of Romans, the spirit of God groans whenever He speaks in reference to us to the Father. Isn't that amazing! We are as awesome to God, as He is to us! The closer we get to God, and the closer that we come to His spirit, we discover through the word of God that we may not know what to say about each other, being that we love each other so much!

Likewise the spirit also helpeth our infirmities:

Hidden In the Light*

for we know not what we should pray for as we ought: but the spirit maketh intercession for us with groanings which cannot be uttered.
                                                        Romans 8:26

God knows that we don't have the words to describe Him, and neither do we have the vocabulary to adequately express our hearts desires to Him; so, He has a system of understanding us whenever we moan and groan while thinking of Him.

Whenever we attempt at sufficiently praying to Him in the words of our own limited dialogue, the spirit reinterprets our words to the Father, groaning from the heart of the spirit, to the heart of the Father, in description of the words from our hearts; all in the name of Jesus!

Even as the Father has given Jesus a name above every other name; He has also given us a language communication over and above every other language. The language of the spirit is of the most mysterious realities available in the realm of all humanity.

The language of the spirit drives men wild in their non-surrendered spirits, to the point that they tend to blaspheme the reality of the spirit. Certain denominations deny the reality of the language of the spirit all together. It is considered to be a heresy, and a totally

Mystery R' Myth**

FORBIDDEN ACTIVITY IN THEIR CHURCHES.

For he that speaketh in an unknown tongue speaketh not unto men, but unto God: for no man understand him; howbeit in the spirit he speaketh mysteries.   I Corinthians 14:2

WE DO UNDERSTAND THAT GOD IS NOT THE AUTHOR OF CONFUSION; SO I WOULD URGE YOU AS AN INDIVIDUAL NOT TO TRY TO UNDERSTAND OTHER INDIVIDUALS WHENEVER THEY BEGIN TO SPEAK IN THE LANGUAGE OF THE SPIRIT OF THE LORD.

IF YOU HAVE NOT BEEN GIFTED TO INTERPRET THE LANGUAGE BY THE VERY UNCTION OF THE HOLY SPIRIT, YOU NEED NOT TO CONCERN YOURSELF WITH WHAT ANOTHER INDIVIDUAL MIGHT HAVE TO SAY TO THE SPIRIT OF THE LORD OUT OF THEIR OWN SPIRIT.

ALWAYS REMEMBER THAT THE SCRIPTURE SAYS THAT THAT OTHER INDIVIDUAL IS SPEAKING UNTO GOD, AND NO MAN UNDERSTAND HIM. THE LANGUAGE ITSELF MAY SOUND A BIT CONFUSING, BUT DON'T YOU BE TOO CONCERNED WITH THAT; IT'S A LANGUAGE THAT GOD UNDERSTANDS WELL.

THE SPIRIT OF THE LORD, HAS HIS OWN LANGUAGE, AND IT IS NOT GOING TO DISAPPEAR SIMPLY BECAUSE SOME PEOPLE CAN'T STAND TO HEAR THE LANGUAGE SPOKEN IN THEIR EARS. HOW DO YOU KNOW THAT YOU ARE BORN OF THE SPIRIT OF GOD, WHEN YOU CAN NOT EVEN STAND TO HEAR HIM SPEAKING?

On The Other Hand*

For what if some did not believe? Shall their unbelief make the faith of God without effect? God forbid: yea, let God be true, but every man a liar; as it is written, that thou mightest be justified in thy sayings, and mightest overcome when thou art judged.   Romans 3:3-4

As relating to a Myth; the myth needs the system of belief to even exist!

Without anyone to believe the myths, a myth only becomes a fading lie! Although a myth is make believe from the beginning, and at best it is a total lie; those who choose to believe in the myth, give life to the myth only for as long they are willing to continuously adhere to the matter. Such as to when certain persons keep superstitious sayings as rules and mandates for the benefit of their own well being.

Many people in the churches, while they never adhere to the word of the Lord, or the language of the spirit, they foolishly embrace the language of demonic enchantments and the wicked dialogue of incantations, to cast spells, and to frustrate the work of the hands of the people of the Lord because they are jealous and demonically driven.

They have the nerve to study the

Mystery R' Myth**

LANGUAGE OF WIZARDS AND WARLOCKS, WITCHES AND SORCERERS. Whatever you put on the inside of yourself, is what you are most apt to practice.

It is more than mysterious to me, how that people can stand in front of the mirror and practice lying through their teeth. It really doesn't matter where they might be or to whom they may be speaking to, they intend to lie.

They are often baffled at the fact that they can never lie to the Holy Ghost. The spirit in the belly of the spirit filled believer will expose a liar every time, and He will also reveal the lies that have been breathed out of the mouth of the liars. [Acts 5:]

Prideful gossipers around the church, often project themselves as special people, because they always appear to know every bodies business. They are usually adamant about telling other people's affairs, and very headstrong when challenged to consider the feelings of the people that they are talking about, and when asked to refrain from such destructive behavior.

It is also quite mysterious how that most gossipers are shattered to pieces and totally destroyed whenever they discover that somebody else is telling their business.

Hidden In the Light*

Believing in a myth, never makes it to be true or real! Believing only takes up space in the heart and the spirit of an individual, making it impossible for the person to house the truth doubtless, and with the integrity of their own true spirit.

It is not possible to doubt and to believe simultaneously; as one will cancel out the other, vigorously defeating the lesser of the two.

HERE'S A GREATER MYSTERY:

Many people seriously believe in their doubts! We often refer to them as pessimistic, or negative; whatever the case, they have convinced themselves that they have doubts about certain things, that they are just not willing to concede. Likewise, such people also doubt that they actually believe in the spirit of the Lord!

Being a former fan of the discovery channel, I had been a consistant viewer, when they introduced a show entitled; "Myth Busters." Many of the more worldly ideological myths relative to old wives tales, and superstitions, were often exposed for the fear of breeding the lies that they are. Other myths; the average American prided themselves on, to follow as necessities were also proven to be falsified rumors.

I was really disturb when my mother

Mystery R' Myth**

and my oldest brother finally told me that Santa Clause; having eight tiny Reindeer and a sleigh, who could come down the chimney to bring us gifts on Christmas day, even though we didn't have a chimney, that it was all a myth. I struggled over the idea that I had been lied to all of those years for the sake of being made happy by receiving gifts under the Christmas tree.

Most of us would have to admit, that the so-called Santa Clause; brought to us good gifts, but, **GOD IS GOOD! TO! US!** Far too many people prefer a mythological excitement about what we receive and where we get those things from, over and above the mystery of God loving us beyond the realistic fact that we don't even deserve His love. As unlovable as we are as mankind, it is unfathomable to understand how God could love us beyond our human comprehension.

Make no mistake about it, God loves us right now in spite of us! However, it's a myth to believe that we are at liberty to remain as we are, as sinful as possible, while never changing our natural behavior to mirror the image of God, through the spirit of Christ.

Just because we believe in the articles of Christmas celebrations, it doesn't mean

Hidden In the Light*

THAT THOSE THINGS THAT LEND CREDENCE TO THE MYTHOLOGICAL SIDE OF CELEBRATING THE HOLIDAY ARE ACCEPTABLE TO GOD. TO BE HONEST; MOST PEOPLE DO NOT EVEN KNOW THE MEANINGS OF THE THINGS THAT WE PLACE AROUND OUR HOUSES TO CELEBRATE THE HOLIDAY, WE JUST USE THEM CONTINUOUSLY, YEAR AFTER YEAR.

THE COLORFUL LIGHTS PLACE US IN SUCH A SPIRITUAL MOOD TO GIVE TO OTHER PEOPLE, EVEN WHEN WE DO NOT EVEN KNOW THEM, OR EVEN LIKE THEM VERY WELL. THE BEAUTIFUL GIFT WRAP, CAUSES US TO DESIRE TO SEE THE COUNTENANCE OF OTHERS LIGHT UP AS THEY RECEIVE THE REMARKABLE PACKAGES.

AS I MATURED IN THE SPIRIT OF CHRIST; I EVEN BEGIN TO QUESTION AND TO DISCOUNT THE TOTAL NECESSITY OF THE DECORATED TREE, ON CHRISTMAS DAY. OF COURSE YOU SHOULD UNDERSTAND THAT I DO ENJOY THE IDEA OF A BEAUTIFUL TREE DURING THE HOLIDAY SEASON, MY FAMILY PUT THAT IN ME WHEN I WAS VERY YOUNG. NOW MY OWN CHILDREN ENJOY THE BEAUTIFULLY DECORATED TREE; BUT, THEY KNOW THE REAL TRUTH ABOUT THE NON-EXISTENCE OF GOOD OLE' SAINT NICHOLAS.

YET, I WAS MADE AWARE OF THE PAGANISM ASSOCIATION, ATTACHED TO THE TREE, WHICH WAS DESIGNED TO STEAL THE GLORY OF THE LORD JESUS; FROM THE CHRISTMAS HOLIDAY.

IN THIS NEW MILLENNIUM, MANY PEOPLE

Mystery R' Myth**

ARE DIVIDED FIFTY/FIFTY, RIGHT UP THE MIDDLE, THINKING AND FURTHER BELIEVING FOR FACT, THAT IT IS A SPIRITUAL THING TO PLACE A NATIVITY SCENE OUT ON OPEN DISPLAY, DURING THE CHRISTMAS SEASON. ONE HALF OF THE PEOPLE WELCOME THE SCENERY, WHILE THE OTHER HALF STRUGGLES TO HAVE IT REMOVED FROM THE VISIBILITY OF THE PEOPLE. THEY HAVE MADE THE MEANING OF THE HOLIDAY SOMETHING OTHER THAN WHAT IT REALLY REPRESENTS.

THE WORLD IS RATHER TWISTED, IN THAT THEY HAVE TRIED TO COMBINE FACT WITH FICTION, AND MYSTERY WITH A MYTH, SIMULTANEOUSLY SCRUNCHING THE OPPOSING SCENARIOS INTO ONE EXISTENCE, AND CALLING IT ACCEPTABLE. TRUE; NEVER MIXES WITH THE UNTRUE; BEING MESHED TOGETHER NEVER TO REVEAL IT'S ACTUALITY. THE VERY SAME AS THE FACT THAT THE LIGHT NEVER EVER MIXES WITH DARKNESS, ALLOWING THE BOTH TO REMAIN IN TACT SHOWING THEIR OWN INDIVIDUAL TRUE SHADES.

AS I FIND MYSELF TALKING TO MORE PEOPLE NOWADAYS, I FIND THAT MANY OF THE PEOPLE NOW BELIEVE THAT THEY CAN ACTUALLY BE BOTH RIGHTEOUS AND SINFUL, GODLY AND UNGODLY, AND RIGHT AND WRONG WHILE CONFESSING TO BE CHILDREN OF THE MOST HIGH GOD!

SOME PEOPLE MAKE THE UNSUCCESSFUL ATTEMPTS OF HAVING JESUS IN THEIR LIVES

Hidden In the Light*

right along the side of Buddha, Muhammad, Moon and other mythological beings. The churches of today's generations, want to "Hip Hop", and praise God all at the same time; only the one is diametrically opposed to the other.

We have got to choose whom we will serve, and the choice has to be one or the other, the benefit of our choices is never the award of choosing one and the other.

I will never understand how so many people nowadays claim to enjoy the twisted idea of desiring to be both male and female alike! Genetically; we can be made up of two or more races of people; alike the Apostle Paul, we may even have dual citizenships, but, we have only been given the award of being one person!

It is only an inflated myth that transgender surgeries can actually change an individuals identity. Others may respect or bring themselves to accept the fact that you have altered your body, but those who had known you best in the past, they will always know who you were initially. God always knows who you are; He made You!

Many, who have added titles to their names, as it relates to the ministry, often they desire that their former

Mystery R' Myth**

IDENTITY, AS KNOWN OF OTHERS, THAT IT WOULD BE AMASKED, HAVING THE POWER TO TRANSFORM THEIR TRUE CHARACTER.

But to the dismay of many who have stepped into the ministry for the purpose of hiding from themselves, they have all collided head on, into the shocking reality of the fact that they did not have the power to transform themselves, no matter how slick they might have thought they were.

Whenever we are all desperately confronted to deal with the reality of ourselves, only the real you will be able to come forth to answer the demand of the call.

False or fake identities can never respond to a true request for the real person on the inside of you to come forth. Whatever we call ourselves respectively, does not necessarily stand up under the pressure of exposure. But who we are truly, will stand even in the face of death!

He Is Who He Says That He is**

Multiples, upon multiples of people by the scores, over the past millenniums, have tried to unmask the true deity of Christ, trying to convince multitudes of nations that He is not the Christ. They

Hidden In the Light*

have tried desperately to prove that Jesus is someone other than who He truly is, but to no avail. As always, they have failed in their attempts to disrobe the kingly glorified attire of Christ.

The Jews seemingly had no problem receiving Him as one of the children of the neighborhood society, but they were not accepting that He could be anything or anyone more than what they could see with their natural eye sight.

They knew His parents in the natural, although Joseph and Mary knew and believed the report of the angels of the Lord. People in the natural will normally see you just as another person, even in the church, but they will often refuse to believe that there is a spiritual connection between yourself and the Lord; God.

Even in light of the fact that in the midst of going forth in the ministry to which you have been endowed, whereas signs and wonders may be manifested, others still will not believe that it was the Spirit of the Lord working through you, although they witness you giving the glory to God for the wonderful works of the Spirit of God.

People will watch you worship God with all brokenness and observe the change in the atmosphere, as the glory

Mystery R' Myth**

of God fills the place, but, they still won't believe!

To all of the skeptics of today, you probably would have passed out to see Jesus raise the dead, and even call Lazarus from the grave. It was not the rumors that angered the leaders of the Jewish community; it was however, the manifested evidence of miracles that He worked in the cities and in the fields among the people.

John The Baptist; who knew that Jesus was coming, even as he, himself prophesied the fact to be so; began to ask unnecessary questions!

He knew exactly who Jesus was by the aid of the spirit, when He showed up coming down the hillside, as John was baptizing in the river of Jordon. As John saw Jesus approaching, he stopped what he was doing and immediately announced; "Behold the lamb of God, Which taketh away the sins of the world."

Upon recognizing Jesus, as that promised one, John baptized Him with water, even though he had promised the people that Jesus would baptize them with fire; the Holy Ghost; The Spirit of Truth!

As the two of them came up out of the water, the spirit lit upon the shoulder of Jesus in the form of a dove, and the

Hidden In the Light*

VOICE OF GOD SPOKE OUT OF THE CLOUDS AND SAID; "THIS IS MY BELOVED SON, IN WHOM I AM WELL PLEASED!" JOHN HEARD THIS PERSONALLY AND WAS A WITNESS OF THE DEITY OF CHRIST, YET HE FOUND IT NECESSARY TO QUESTION HIM.

THE BIRTHS OF BOTH JOHN AND JESUS WERE ON THE SIMILAR MANNER, MARY; THEN MOTHER OF JESUS; WAS A VIRGIN FAVORED OF GOD; ELIZABETH; THE MOTHER OF JOHN; WAS INITIALLY A BARREN WOMAN WITH A HUSBAND NAMED ZACHARIAS; BUT SHE COULD NOT BEAR CHILDREN.

GOD BLESSED THEM BOTH TO BE PREGNANT AND TO BRING FORTH CHILDREN. THE BOYS WERE ONLY SIX MONTHS APART IN BIRTH. ELIZABETH AND MARY WERE COUSINS, OF WHICH MARY CONFIDED IN ELIZABETH, OF THE WONDERFUL WORKS OF GOD IN HER LIFE. AS MARY SPOKE WITH ELIZABETH THE BABE JOHN, LEAPED IN HER WOMB. JOHN AND JESUS, WERE BOTH BORN OF THE SPIRIT AND IN THE NATURAL SIMULTANEOUSLY, FOR WHICH THEY WERE CONNECTED IN ALL MANNER OF THEIR BEINGS.

JOHN; KNEW JESUS; EVEN IN THE WOMBS OF THEIR MOTHERS; BUT AS OTHER UNFAVORABLE CIRCUMSTANCES PLAGUED BOTH THE LIFE AND THE MINISTRY OF JOHN THE BAPTIST; WHEREAS, JOHN WAS PUT IN PRISON FOR HIS MINISTRY, JOHN STARTED QUESTIONING THE UNQUESTIONABLE.

Mystery R' Myth**

Now when John had heard in the prison the works of Christ, he sent two of his disciples, And said unto him, Art thou he that should come, or do we look for another? Jesus answered and said unto them, Go and shew John again those things which ye do hear and see: The blind receive their sight, and the lame walk, the lepers are cleansed, and the deaf hear, the dead are raised up, and the poor have the gospel preached to them. And blessed is he, whosoever shall not be offended in me.   St. Matthew 11: 2-6

John always reminded the people and his own disciples, that he was not the Messiah! He spoke highly favorably of the coming ministry of Christ, and he appeared to have no shame or a display of the spirit of jealously, whenever he said to them that he, himself was of no comparison to the coming Christ.

Most everyone likes what Jesus can do, but they have problems with excepting who He is! Had Jesus done all of the miracles anonymously, never revealing the true deity of His own existence, most of the people would never have had any problems.

This is often true among us today as people in the body of Christ, as we follow Jesus Closely! Many people want whatever we can do, while they are not particularly interested in who we are.

Hidden In the Light*

You would be amazed, at the volume of people who have called me on the telephone, showed up at my house, or either they called and showed up at the church I pastored for prayer and counseling, who have never even mentioned it to anyone else!

The same people would not even support my ministry, even though they had been blessed as a result of my ministry.

The more specially endowed an individual may appear to be, others, more vigorously endeavor to convince that same individual, as well as those that might appear to be well wishers of that person, that they are not that special after all!

Many people will stamp you as a myth at any given chance to do so. Of course, Jesus had already informed us that we would be hated and despised without a cause, but, he also said for us to remember that the world hated Him first! [St. John 15:18]

Maybe you hadn't read in the scripture, but the Jews desired to get rid of Jesus long before the actual crucifixion on the cross.

Had it not been for the fact that Jesus is the Messiah; "The Anointed One"; the Jews might have been successful at their futile attempts to take the life of

Jesus, further discouraging the people from believing in Him.

> *Believest thou not that I am in the Father, and the Father in me? The words that I speak unto you I speak not of myself; but the Father that dwelleth in me, he doeth the works. Believe me that I am in the Father, and the Father in me: or else believe me for the very works' sake. Verily, Verily, I say unto you, He that believeth on me, the works that I do shall he do also; and greater works than these shall he do; because I go unto my Father. And whatsoever ye shall ask in my name, that will I do, that the Father may be glorified in the son. If ye shall ask anything in my name, I will do it.* St. John 14:10-14

God comes into our presence, bearing the consent of the perfect sacrifice of Christ, and the ability to do whatever we ask of Him in Jesus name. He is, His own counselor; should it be necessary for the Lord to meet with anyone concerning you and your needs, He will have already met with Himself before any question could ever arise concerning you.

He is already ahead of the situational crises which showed up in our lives, even before we have had the ability to examine the circumstances, to evaluate the level of need that we may have.

Everything that we have ever been

Hidden In the Light*

TOLD THAT GOD CAN DO, HE CAN DO ALL OF THAT AND THEN SO MUCH MORE! GOD CAN DO THINGS THAT NO ONE EVER ON THE FACE OF THE EARTH HAS EVER HAD THE MINDFUL ABILITY TO THINK TO ASK HIM TO DO FOR THEM.

GOD'S GOT NUMBERS THE NO HUMAN BEING IN THE EARTH COULD EVER GIVE A NAME TO, OR EVEN HAVE THE SKILL TO EDIT IN TO THE NUMERICAL SCHEME OF COUNTING.

> *After this I beheld, and lo, a great multitude, which no man could number, of all nations, and kindreds, and people, and tongues, stood before the throne, and before the Lamb, clothed with white robes, and palms in their hands.*
>
> *Revelation 7:9*

IT IS A MYSTERY THAT THE PRESENCE OF GOD IS AT THE POINT OF THE COMMANDED RELEASE, WHERE THE MOVEMENT OF THE WIND IS LAUNCHED TO PASS OVER THE FACE OF THE EARTH, AND SIMULTANEOUSLY, HE IS ALSO SEATED AT THE DESTINATION AWAITING THE ARRIVAL OF THE WIND AFTER IT WILL HAVE FINISHED ITS COURSE OF TRAVEL.

GOD; COMES FROM WHERE HE IS GOING; WERE IT NOT FOR THE FACT THAT HE IS OMNIPRESENT, EVERYWHERE ALL OF THE TIME, HE WOULD BE CONSISTENTLY PASSING HIMSELF, COMING AND GOING, AS HE MOVED THROUGHOUT THE LAND. HE HAS REMAINED WHERE HE HAS COME FROM, WHILE BEING HERE

Mystery R' Myth**

where we are, without anyone being able to document that God had been in motion, moving and traveling throughout the land.

Before you could ever truly understand that God is always everywhere that you are, you need to understand that God is always everywhere that He is!

In every land and country where people are calling on the name of the Lord in the name of Jesus Christ, God is there! And He is here right now! I call Him savior, and Master, I recognize Him to be the Lord of the Universe; Creator of all Heaven and Earth. He is the mighty God!

He is so masterful at being who He is, and very great at remaining who He is, and never changing who He is; even though He became who we are!

God is totally matchless at doing everything that He does. Many people have not as of yet, embraced God because they have chosen other sources. We serve the incomparable God of the Universe; the maker and the creator of Heaven and Earth.

Perhaps, someone should show me one of the trees, or the grass, the land, or another sea, and any of the other creations that are in the earth, that was

Hidden In the Light*

created and formed by the other gods?

God, is a loving God for real; He loves the people of the earth even when they choose to worship another dead God. Suppose God; said to those who chose to worship other gods; "you may do so, but not with my breath that I breathed into your body! Ask your god for more breath to worship them!"

I tell you that many people would be devastated, and dead! Suppose God took back the eyesight of those who look in every other book other than the bible; can you imagine the number of blind people in the land?

What if God asked for the return of the vocal chords and the tongues to be given back to Him, by those people that won't talk to Him, or sing His songs; the earth would be a very silent place. All other conversations would cease immediately!

I could only imagine that the suicide rate all over the world would increase very quickly. Suppose all of the opposers of God lost all of their speaking ability, and their manipulative skills to write and to publish countering messages to the written word of God?

God is more powerful than many people have the mind to investigate, or the patience to explore. Don't be so easily

Mystery R' Myth**

taken in by people who talk so big about God not really being God. They are more afraid that He really is God, than they may desire for you to know.

I have heard testimonies of people who had made up in their own minds not to reverence God, how that they almost lost it when God sent only an angel to them to assure them that God is indeed the God of this Universe. They were terrified!

Those that I have spoken to, have changed their attitude and their minds relative to what they thought about God. I often wonder what they would have done other than to have died, had it been God who showed up in their presence.

People make a lot of noise because they really are afraid of the spirit of the Lord. Being great pretenders at best, they sway the attention of the people onto themselves, thinking that they might be successful at hindering others from thinking on the Lord.

People are not afraid of myths because they know for a fact that they are not real or even true! But, the mysteries of God, bespeak of the reality of a greater being, higher than all of the earth.

The apprehensive spirits of the people

Hidden In the Light*

that fail to embrace the reality of God, often bespeak of the unspoken, but, fearful recognition of the awesomely terrific spirit of God.

They are not really fooling anyone, in their own trembling fear, they believe that He is God, and they know that He is not a myth. They just refuse to surrender their will to the spirit of the Lord. They feel that the Lord's will might interfere with their own plans to live as they choose to do so.

Everything in the present atmospheric realm of mankind all over the earth, and in the entire cosmopolitan scope of the Universe, bespeaks of the reality that God is; and that God can!

Now you decide; is this yet a mystery; or is it a myth?

Chapter 7

Feet & Paths **

Thy word is a lamp unto my feet, a light unto my path.   Psalms 119 : 105
How beautiful are the feet of them that preach the gospel,
                Isaiah 52 : 7; Romans 10 : 15

Walk In The Light Of The Lord

My friend, if God can't have your feet, truth is that He will never have your heart! Contrary to erroneous teachings, God wants more than just our hearts, He wants our whole spirit, soul and body, which definitely includes our feet.

From this point onward, throughout your walk with the Lord, you need to understand literarily, according to written biblical dialogue, that your feet, both feet, must be under arrest to the will of God, if you are going to successfully live the Christian life.

You ever hear the statement, they've got one foot in and one foot out? The actuality is that they have both feet still walking in the sinful influences outside of the will of God, while yet confessing to be presently walking in the ways of God!

It is also common and very familiar to hear people of the churches making statements about others who have not quite completely walked in true Christianity, like; "They are stratling the fence!" Which is an indication that there is a foot placed on each side of the fence of living, relative to the saved and the

Feet & Paths**

UNSAVED LIFESTYLES.

Most people, who attempt to take a stand on each side, refusing to choose a side, from paupers to the president, both sinners and saints, they often find themselves ripped right up the middle! They soon realize the very painful discovery of the fence and the reason that it had been installed in the first place.

What is even more painful, is the piercing realization that the fence has pricked them in the most sensitively intimate part of their being. That place of the body that is least tolerant to the infliction of pain.

Obstructions, in the middle of your walk, impedes the necessary forward progress of anyone that has determined to go on straight ahead.

Naturally speaking; the fence is often to tall to allow anyone to walk with one foot on each side of the fence. Now it is not impossible to stand stratled of the fence, or even to sit on the fence, of course that is if you have no intentions to move from where it is that you are.

This statement may be the answer to the stagnation of many people in the local churches, they're satisfied to stay where they are! We have got to walk on one side of the fence or the other.

Hidden In the Light*

Stratling the fence, even prevent sinners from being good sinners; if there is such a thing as good sinners? Not that I would be interested in teaching a sinner how to be better at sinning.

Such an attempt to stay outside while proposing to come on the inside, certainly hinders the progressive maturation process of the Christian walk. It is impossible to grow in the understanding of the ways of the Lord, staying on the outside away from the teachings of the bible, when we should willingly come in, just as it is impossible to be educated in school, skipping class.

Too many of the pastors today can't can't seem to determine within themselves, whether to be a politician; or a preacher?

They consistently stand at the fork in the road disconcerted; perplexed with caring for the spiritual aspect of the people of their congregations, or if whether to be more concerned with the natural, sociable status of people in the neighboring communities, of which most of those people do not even attend church at all.

The greater determinations are to ensure that the people of the larger mile radius, more than that of which surrounds their churches, that those people become acquainted with their names

Feet & Paths**

AND THE AUTHORITATIVE RESONANCE OF THEIR VOICES!

ON EITHER SIDE OF THE REALITY OF WHERE IT IS THAT WE AS PEOPLE OF THE CHURCH ARE WALKING, THE FACT IS THAT THE PATHS IN WHICH OUR FEET ARE TREADING CONSISTENTLY, IS THE DETERMINATE FACTOR THAT ESTABLISHES OUR CONVICTIONS, WHETHER OR NOT WE ARE TRUE ABOUT WHERE IT IS THAT WE ARE WALKING.

OBSERVATIONS HAVE REVEALED THAT MANY PEOPLE OF THE CHURCHES DON'T APPEAR TO BE HAVING A GOOD TIME WALKING WITH THE LORD? WE HAVE THE ABILITY TO ROB OURSELVES OF THE JOY OF WALKING IN THE LIGHT OF THE LORD, ALLOWING OUR FEET TO EXPLORE THE SLIPPERY SLOPES OF SINNING, OVER ON TO THE OTHER SIDE.

OUR FEET ARE THE NATURAL INSTRUMENTS OF OUR SPIRITUAL WALK WITH THE LORD. OUR FEET HAVE THE GRASP OF GOD'S ATTENTION EVEN MORE SO THAN OUR HANDS AND OUR MOUTHS, WHICH WE USE TO SPEAK FORTH OUR CONFESSIONS OF FAITH.

IT REALLY WON'T MATTER WHAT YOU SAY OUT YOUR MOUTH, AS MUCH AS WHERE YOU INTENTIONALLY PLACE YOUR FEET ON A DAILY BASIS, WE HAVE GOT TO WALK OUT THE EXACT THINGS AS THAT OF WHICH WE TALK ON A CONSISTENT BASIS, WHICH BESPEAK OF THE ACTUALITY OF THE RELATIONSHIP OR NON-RELATIONSHIP THAT WE EITHER HAVE OR DO NOT HAVE WITH GOD.

Hidden In the Light*

God is requiring clean, nurtured feet, feet that can be trained to seek out clean paths to dwell in. God is seeking feet that are geared towards climbing, reaching for the higher places in the Lord, not feet that are consistently digging deeper into the dirty situations of which they are presently entrenched, looking to go deeper than they are already.

> *He maketh my feet like hinds feet: and setteth me upon my high places.*
> *II Samuel 22: 34*

Perhaps your question is, why the feet?

"Hinds feet;" are the feet of the sheep that live in the high places of the hills, for which their feet are constructed to climb latching on to the clefts of the rocks.

It doesn't get to be too rugged for the hinds feet; the rockier the better! The jagged edges of the rocks are what the sheep use to climb to the tops of the hills, even to safety away from the predators in the wild.

The hind don't struggle to get up the hillside, they are equipped to move up the hills swiftly, with precise footing, often leaving their predators at the foot of the hills.

Feet & Paths**

Take notice of the fact that David said the Hinds feet, and not the Swine's feet! Swine; most recognized as Hogs, have pens and enclosures only when in captivity.

Otherwise, they move about through the filthy muddy swamps of the wild, treading in and throughout their own dung. It seems, the nastier it gets, the better the swine appear to be getting along.

They hurry to get their feet in the slime and the filth of the swamp. Alike the sinner and the saint who have feet naturally alike in appearance and structure, the hind and the swine have similar feet in structure and nature.

Both set of feet look alike, but they don't travel along the same paths. One set of the feet climb and go up higher, while the other set of feet dig deeper into the mud and slime of the swamps.

Figuratively speaking, whenever we come before the Lord to surrender to Him, according to the manner of the lifestyles of many people, some come bearing the resemblance of swine's feet, yet desiring to immediately walk with Him.

The Lord knows the difference between the two scenarios, being both the maker and creator, and the redeemer of

Hidden In the Light*

ALL MAN KIND. JESUS, MUST ALSO LAY HIS HANDS ON OUR FEET BECAUSE WE NEVER WILL BE ABLE TO WALK RIGHT WITHOUT THE HELP OF THE LORD.

WE COME TO THE LORD OFTEN WALKING CROOKED, AND WE WILL REMAIN CROOKED UNTIL HE STRAIGHTENS US OUT.

WHY THE FEET?...............

JESUS WASHED THE FEET OF THE APOSTLES! (ST. JOHN 13:) JESUS LOVED THE APOSTLES AND HE WAS ASSURED OF EVERYONE THAT HE HAD CHOSEN, EVEN JUDAS; BUT HE WAS ALSO AWARE OF WHAT THEY EACH NEEDED IN AN EFFORT TO BE LIVING EXAMPLES OF THE CHRISTIAN TEACHINGS OF CHRIST.

JESUS LOVES US, BUT HE ALSO KNOWS WHAT WE NEED WHENEVER WE COME TO HIM. BEING SAVED FROM OUR SINS, IS ONLY THE INITIAL STEP TO ESTABLISHING OUR RELATIONSHIP WITH THE LORD. WALKING ABOUT OUR JOURNEY WITH THE LORD WILL REQUIRE THE HELP OF THE LORD.

PETER HIMSELF, THOUGHT THAT SUCH AN HUMILIATING ACT OF CONTRITION WAS BENEATH THE SAVIOR OF THE WORLD, WHEREAS HE OPENLY REFUSED INITIALLY TO ALLOW THE LORD TO WASH HIS FEET IN THE PRESENCE OF THE OTHER APOSTLES.

BUT, JESUS SPONTANEOUSLY REPLIED TO PETER, "IF I DON'T WASH YOUR FEET PETER, YOU ARE NONE OF MINE!" PETER, HEARING THESE WORDS, KNOWING THAT HE DESPERATELY

Feet & Paths

desired the relationship with the Lord, turned and said to Jesus, not just my feet, but wash me all over!

Jesus knew that of all of the things that He would share with the Apostles, most of it would indeed be spiritual things from the Father. The shared information would seat the Apostles in heavenly places, right here on the earth; allowing them to see right into the present kingdom of the Lord, whereas others would yet be in the dark.

The Apostles needed to have their feet spiritually placed, by the washing of the water of the word of God, for which Jesus was the word made manifest to us in the earth, walking in the flesh; else they would continue walking in the carnal places of the earth's realm. They had been walking as natural mere men of the earth, before being chosen Apostles of Christ.

God has never been stomped at the fact that we are natural men on the face of this earth whenever He called us. He already knew that we were mere men, by the grace of God, we had been given the provisions of God's grace, to get us past out natural propensities to continually commit sin.

The sin nature of mankind, consistently pulls at us to run after mischief and to seek the paths of sin.

Hidden In the Light*

Without God, naturally we desire to do wrong without remorse or any guilt, it comes naturally!

Look very realistically at the fact that our feet is what actually connects us with the surface of the earth here where we live, according to the physical laws of nature and gravity.

Just imagine what the earth would appear to look like, had it been that the laws of gravity pulled our faces to the surface of the ground?

And of course, God knows that we would definitely be stuck had it been that our bodies were forced to the surface of the ground, in the way that trees are affixed to the ground.

> *Blessed is the man, that walketh not in the counsel of the ungodly, nor standeth in the way of sinners.*   Psalms 1:1

We could neither walk nor stand anywhere, without feet! Shoes mean absolutely nothing to us if we have no feet for shoes!

Can you see how that even we as the people of the Lord have overlooked the awesome gift of our feet?

We often bless the Lord for our hands, our eyes, our ears, our nose and mouth, arms, legs; but seldom do we thank the Lord for our feet. We do complain

Feet & Paths**

ABOUT OUR FEET WHEN THEY HURT US, YET WE SELDOM APPRECIATE OUR FEET, MUCH LESS THANK GOD FOR THEM.

WHILE LOOKING IN THE DICTIONARY FOR A DEFINITION OF FEET, THE DICTIONARY HAS LITTLE TO OFFER DEFINITIVELY IN EXPLANATION, OTHER THAN TO SAY THAT FEET IS THE PLURAL FORM OF THE SINGULAR FOOT.

TAKE INTO CONSIDERATION WITHOUT PREJUDICE, THAT GOD INITIALLY CREATED AND FORMED 2 FEET, FOR THE MAN AND THE WOMAN. THEREFORE, FEET COULD BE CITED AS OUR NATURAL VEHICULAR METHOD OF TRAVEL, OF WHICH USED TO BE THE CASE. MEN TRAVELED ON FOOT; OR ON THEIR OWN TWO FEET.

EVEN BEFORE MEN DISCOVERED, THAT IT WAS BETTER TO TRAVEL ON THE BACKS OF FOUR FOOTED BEAST, THEY TRAVELED ON THEIR OWN TWO FEET.

IN THE BEGINNING GOD CREATED A VAST GREAT EARTH FOR MAN TO INHABIT, WITH THE MANDATES FOR MAN TO SUBDUE, TO CONQUER, AND TO MULTIPLY. HOW FAIR WOULD IT HAVE BEEN, HAD GOD NOT MADE IT POSSIBLE FOR MAN TO MANEUVER THROUGHOUT THE EARTH, WITH NO FEET FOR MOBILIZATION, FOLLOWING THE DESIGNED PLAN OF GOD?

GOD NEVER GIVES US PLANS WITHOUT A WAY TO CARRYOUT THOSE PLANS.

GOD IS NOT UNJUST TO SAY TO US, GO; KNOWING THAT WE COULD NEVER EVEN MOVE

Hidden In the Light*

out in the first place!

To listen to most people in the world today, you would think that God is some type of an idiot, in that He has given mankind all types of unrealistic rules and mandates to follow, knowing that the laws and the rules were impossible for mankind to carry out?

Such a statement is only an excuse for the fact that mere men don't have a desire to live according to the rules and the laws of God.

Most people both saved and unsaved, conduct themselves as if they just happened to wake up one day to realize that they had been traveling in paths of life, that they did not even know that they had been on?

They're enraged and outraged at the very ideas of haven been dealt a hand most unfair to their own choices of living. You would think that most people were literally living n the twilight zone for real!

It is common and only natural that we as people consistently focus on the paths of life that we have traveled. The greater significance has been placed on the existence of the path, while we don't really regard the fact that paths would be totally insignificant were there no feet to walk in them.

Feet & Paths**

The intelligence of God is so excellent that He would never have ever created either feet nor paths to dwell in, without the existence of the other, knowing that either one would have been unnecessary to living and life, being alone!

It is my belief that the root of bitterness is planted in the spirit of most people, due to the fact that they have not been appreciative to the given paths they have been required to travel, in this life?

Alike most people who will not even seek the Lord for a reasonable explanation of their given paths, they have no understanding for having had such places of unfavorable circumstances spread out right in front of them to travel on, with no other options.

Others have had to travel very significant paths in their own lives, but without what we would refer to as instructional manuals; it seems that they were just thrown in the ring with the wrestler having no personal training as a wrestler themselves?

What's more grievous, is that whenever they have inquired of others who should have been better able to see into the realm of the spirit, solely based on their own spiritual status, no one seemed to have an adequate answer, or

Hidden In the Light*

even the interest to hear the story of the person/persons talking.

During my own plight, whenever I would begin to enquire about the lonely path to which I had been required to travel, though I always made an attempt to walk along with others, I was usually told to just suck it up, and be quiet about it, and to recognize that I was only self absorbed!

Make no mistake about it, although they were right in that I had become a bit self absorbed, they still never offered me an explanation! Neither did they say anything to me that would soothe the aching pains in my soul.

Well, they left me at the mercy of the Lord, whereas it was later revealed to me that God has a plan for those of us that will be used of Him. There are times when God actually need for us to walk through dark places, relative to our understanding of where it is that we are walking, or why it is that we are even walking in those places in the beginning?

What God never wants, is for us to look for and find our own darkened paths to place our beautiful feet, to walk in, on our own.

Most of us, who spend even the least quality time in the word of God, we have heard about how God told Abraham to

Feet & Paths

walk in the darkness of his own understanding, literally and figuratively speaking.

First and foremost, he had to walk away from his own family, and the home of his earthly father who raised him as a lad, and learn all over again to trust in another Father, though it was a spiritual Father with promises that would never be broken.

There is a purpose; and a reward; for obediently walking where we have been led to walk.

Often, others can't give an explanation for where it is that you are walking, or even the reason that you have been required to walk there, because they were never ordained to see your final destination in the anointing of the Lord.

Many times other people will not even have an appreciation for where you walk, they will often judge you untimely, and even disconnect themselves from you. It is not even those people that God is most intent on revealing your purpose to, you will be the one to reap that benefit.

It wasn't until I begin to ask the Lord about the painful places that I had been forced to walk through, that I was able to hear the Lord speaking to me revealing the reasons that I had to walk through those grievous places.

Hidden In the Light*

Being all self absorbed and pitiful of myself, feeling that it was indeed unfair to have to walk in places that were obvious to me that others were not being required to walk in those similar places.

God said to me; that He was going to use me where many others were not going to be used, therefore I had to walk where many others had never walked!

Abraham walked where others never had to walk, and as a result, he was blessed in ways that others were never blessed! I wanted to try to get God to understand that the people who knew me best, that they judged me, they left me, they even judged me according to their own understanding of the written word of God! God assured me that their judgment of me did not matter, because He ordered my steps.

It is very easy for religious people to count another individual as being out of the will of God according to the structured mandates for living, which they are taught over the pulpits in the churches.

There are more religious people in all of the churches, than there are of those who are walking in the spirit of the Lord. Even those who are walking in the spirit of the Lord daily, they won't know what God is doing with you, unless He reveals

Feet & Paths**

it to them.

There are some things about you that God will tell no one! Your purpose is actually that unique to Him; God has got a way of walking us through our journeys in this life with hands on training, whereas no one would ever be able to take the credit for us being who, and where we are in the Lord!

Even those who love us best, they wont be given the option of shaping us into the God ordained persons of faith in God that we are supposed to be.

The Same Path For Forty Years*

Yea, forty years didst thou sustain them in the wilderness, so that they lacked nothing; their clothes waxed not old, and their feet swelled not.   Nehemiah 9: 21

Has anyone ever questioned your walk?

Have you ever been held suspect to a life of ungodliness, based on the fact that your walk with the Lord doesn't look very glamorous to those who are around you?

It doesn't appear that your life is prospering and adding up to the projections of the teachings of the local churches, that aspire to the philosophy of most modern Charismatic's, anyway!

Hidden In the Light*

You may not be going up, but by the same token you're not going down either, you appear to be in a hold, just staying steady? To the onlookers, things appear to only be the same, always?

Has anyone ever made an attempt to convince you that God was not in the midst of your trials with you, because according to the studied calculations of their own teaching; only, any thing that is prosperous or prospering is of God?

They would have you to believe that there is just no way that God could ever be in the midst those situations that have gone belly up on you?

Don't forget the fact that Jobs friends thought for sure that God had left Job to the desire of the devil, all by himself. They thought that sin was for sure in the camp, even that it lieth at the door of Job.

Just take a look at the Children of Israel, on too many occasions to mention, they took it upon themselves to leave off from following the leading of the Lord, to take control of their own journey, simply because they felt they had been forsaken by God.

How about the three Hebrew boys, who were led into a fiery furnace for worshipping the one and the only true God; but, to the amazement of the people

Feet & Paths**

who stood around, whenever the furnace was opened, they all walked out the fire the same way that they had each walked into the fire.

Look at Daniel, how that his prayer life suffered him to be thrown into the lions den. But, when the king cried out in lament for Daniel, Daniel's voice took the king by surprise! Daniel was yet alive, and unharmed; no evil had befallen him.

The children of Israel themselves, being led out of Egypt, through the desert right up to the seashore of the Red Sea, across the Red Sea dry shod, and into the wilderness on the other side of the sea, had only an eight days journey to the heart of the promised land.

But, because they murmured and complained and charged God foolishly, and were not thankful for being delivered from the bondage of the Egyptians, they wondered in the same path for Forty years.

The Children of Israel, wondered in the same path for so long, that they eventually developed neighbors. In stead of embracing the fact that they were on their way to the promised land, they allowed their minds to believe that they had been led out into the wilderness to be abandoned, and to suffer.

They were forced to set up residence,

Hidden In the Light*

where they should have only been passing through. Had it not been that God was in the midst of the Children of Israel, they would have become very settled and satisfied.

God was not going to allow them to become comfortable and set in the wilderness. The wilderness was not even their originally intended destination to begin with.

The established paths that are ordained of God, all lead to destinations, for specifically intended purposes. You can never be on a path that God has assigned to you that leads to no where. In God there is no such thing as purposeless traveling and sojourning. If ever you are on a path that leads to no where, be assured that it is not a path that has been ordered by the Lord.

Even the Children of Israel, as they wondered through the wilderness, they were blessed to pass through very different portions of the same wilderness to which they had been traveling for years.

Such a scenery of seeing only the exact same thing day in and day out, can drive a person insane, out of their mind, and even into areas of complacency, whereas they would never expect to experience anything other than what they

Feet & Paths**

HAD ALREADY EXPERIENCED.

So, even though God taught them, by leading them through the wilderness, His purpose was never to destroy them, or even to deliver them finally to the promised land mentally deranged, psychologically fragmented, to the point that they would not even know who was indeed responsible for delivering them.

They would never know who to worship; in such a case as this, they could never even be thankful for finding their intended destination; God is all too wise for that.

Whenever I say to you that they traveled the same path for forty years, let it be known by reason of your understanding, that the actual pathway to which they were traveling, was the God given, intended purpose of reaching the promised land, not the sand dragged paths trodden under the feet of the people.

Their purpose, was not just the reason for them to be traveling the path of the wilderness, but, their purpose was actually their path!

Each day they were in forward progress, moving towards their intended goal, although most of the time it didn't appear that they were moving in the right direction of their destination.

Hidden In the Light*

So often, as we travel through this life, it will appear that we might have gotten off of our course. Just because we don't know where we are traveling to, doesn't mean that God has also lost His way with us?

God knows our destiny, even when we don't! We always know where it is that we want to be, but, we are not always aware of where it is, that we actually belong!

God leads us where He knows that He has purposed, disregarding the fact that we have plans of being in places of our own choosing and desires.

One the greater reasons that we struggle so hard when we are in a place that is totally unfamiliar to us, is for reason of the fact that we won't know what to tell others when they ask us where we are!

We don't want to become the laughing stock of the neighborhood, or the church community, we want people to know that we are yet in control; while God is wanting everyone to know that He is in control of our lives.

It is of course, not at all about what people are saying about you or what they say about how you behave while you walk daily, it is about what God knows about you while you walk daily among

Feet & Paths

YOUR PEERS IN THEIR PRESENCE, AND WHILE YOU WALK IN HIDDEN PATHS WHERE NO ONE ELSE IS AROUND!

*A True Sole Surrender*****

TO BE REALLY FAIR ABOUT THE WHOLE SCENARIO OF THE SOLE OF THE FEET; MANY OF OUR FORMER LEADERS FAILED TO TEACH CONCERNING THE FEET, AND OF COURSE THE AVERAGE CHURCHMEN, THEY SIMPLY COULD NOT TOUCH THE SUBJECT, FOR THE SINCERE LACK OF COMPREHENSION TO THE NECESSITY OF RECOGNIZING THE IMPORTANCE OF THE FEET.

AS I MOVED MY WORSHIP EXPERIENCE FROM THE BAPTIST CHURCH TO THE PENTECOSTAL EXPERIENCE, I NOTICED THAT A FEET WASHING CEREMONY WOULD TAKE PLACE IN THE CHURCH, EVER SO OFTEN. ABOUT TWICE A YEAR.

AS A CHILD / TEENAGER, I COULD NOT GRASP THE SPIRITUAL SIGNIFICANCE, NOR COULD I RELATE TO THE EXCITEMENT AMONG THE PEOPLE, OVER HAVING THE LEADERSHIP TO WASH THEIR FEET.

HOWEVER, I TRULY THANK GOD FOR ALLOWING THAT EXPERIENCE TO HAVE BEEN EMBEDDED INTO MY OWN PERSONAL EXPERIENCE OF WORSHIP, FROM THE PAST IN THE CHURCH OF GOD IN CHRIST. FOOT WASHING SERVICES, ARE STILL HEARD OF IN THE CHURCH, BUT IT IS EVEN MUCH LESS PRACTICED THESE DAYS, THAN

Hidden In the Light*

before in the past.

Perhaps our former patriarchs of the faith, internalized the depths in the significance of our feet, and the true relevance of how it is that our feet play an indelible part of our relationship with God, but were inadequate to verbalize the true essence and the urgency to the people of the congregation, for having their feet washed, and for having the placement of their feet established into living the truth; proof; of a life of righteousness in Christ.

Most people on the outside of life in Christ, have problems with many of the people who confess Christ, simply because they have noticed that there seems to be no difference anymore, relative to where the sinner and the believers place their feet to walk on a daily basis.

Sinners, and the ungodly, they see the confessing members of the church in the same places that they go, partaking and participating in the very same sinful things that they partake of, for the very same reasons.

The strength of the "I'm Human" excuse has waned so deeply and intensely, that no one wants to even hear it any more. Even sinners know now that that statement is only an excuse for disobeying the word of God, because they use the

Feet & Paths

excuse themselves! They know at best, that it's only a lie!

What is the true power of our feet?

When our feet are consistently set in the right places of the righteousness of Christ, on purpose by design, the cloud of witnesses which also scrutinize every move that we make as a believer, they will not have to question where your heart is, before the Lord.

People know the difference, not just in our conversations, but in what we do as a result of what we have said out of our mouths. The powerful connection of the soles of our feet, and our tongues and cheeks; is the explosive definition of the truth of our true status as a child of God.

Whether we are walking or standing in the word of God, the actual placement of our feet reveals the ring of truth in the confessions of our faith. I know that you have often heard even as I have, the statement which says; "You talk the talk, but can you walk the walk?"

The issue raised here, is not at all brand new, although it might have been spoken in a new pattern of word recognition. God has been saying the very same thing all of the time, to those of us who desire to belong to Him. God

Hidden In the Light*

IS SAYING; WALK WITH ME NOW IN FAITH THROUGH REPENTANCE, AND YOU CAN DEFINITELY BE MINE IN EVERY MANNER OF YOUR BEING.

MOST PEOPLE OF THE CHURCH WHO ARE TRULY SEEKING TO FIND A RELATIONSHIP WITH GOD, THEY ARE WITNESSES OF LEADERS WHO ARE LIVING EXAMPLES OF THE MESSAGES THAT COMES FORTH OUT OF THEIR MOUTHS. THOSE LEADERS ARE RESPONSIBLE FOR INTRODUCING THE PEOPLE TO THE PRESENCE OF GOD.

THE RELIGIOUS MAJORITY ARE JUST NOT OFTEN ACQUAINTED WITH LAYMEN WHO ARE ALSO LIVING EXAMPLES OF THE CONFESSIONS OF THEIR FAITH. MANY PROFESSING LAYMEN ARE PRONE TO SAY THAT THEY HAVE A DESIRE TO WALK WITH THE LORD DAILY, BUT THEY SHOW A TOTALLY DIFFERENT ASPECT OF LIVING, IN THEIR WALK, WHICH DOESN'T LINE UP WITH THE TALKING THAT COMES OUT OF THEIR MOUTHS. MANY OF US HAVE BEEN THERE!

FOR WHATEVER THE REASON OR THE PURPOSE, PEOPLE ARE OVERWHELMED IN THE SERVICES, AND THEY CHOOSE TO MAKE VERBAL CONFESSION OF CHRISTIANITY IN THE CONGREGATION OF THE CHURCHES, DURING THE DECISION PERIODS OF THE SERVICES.

IT REALLY DOES EXTENUATE THE CAUSE OF CHRIST, THAT SO MANY OF THE CHURCHES ARE SATISFIED TO KEEP THE PEOPLE BELIEVING THAT THEIR COMMITMENT DURING THOSE DECISION MAKING PERIODS OF THE SERVICE, WHICH IS

Feet & Paths**

often only for the purpose to bolster the membership base of that same local congregation;

They lead the people to believe that coming on board as a tithing member, simultaneously amass the decision to turn to Christ, and to begin to walk in His ways?

The only problem is that during decision time, many of the people are not having the true spiritual experiences which activates the power to change from the inside out. They emerge from the designated places in the ministries for the new member process, having never met Christ!

They have never repented for the sinful lifestyles that they had been living before walking the aisles of the church. They were never made acquainted with the power of the presence of God; they met the pastor of the church and their charismatic spirit, and the welcoming presence of the membership committee.

If you are going to walk in the newness of life with Christ, you have got to come all of the way to Christ; first!

It is imperative that we should know what it is that we are surrendering, before we ever make the commitment to release and let go!

The secret of a successful walk in the

Hidden In the Light*

LORD, IS HIDDEN IN THE LIGHT OF THE LORD, WHEREAS, WE MUST BE SPIRITUALLY ENLIGHTENED TO REALIZE THE REALITY OF THE STATUS OF OUR LIVES THROUGH THE WORD OF GOD, WILLING TO RELEASE THE SOLES OF OUR FEET TO WALK IN THE PERFECT WILL OF GOD.

> *Wherefore seeing we also are compassed about with so great cloud of witnesses, let us lay aside every weight, and the sin which doth so easily beset us, and let us run with patience the race that is set before us, looking unto Jesus the author and finisher of our faith; who for the joy that was set before him endured the cross, despising the shame, and is set down at the right hand of the throne of God. And make straight paths for your feet, lest that which is lame be turned out of the way; but let it rather be healed.*   Romans 12:1-2, 13

IT IS OFTEN ESTIMATED OF THE PEOPLE WHO MAKE CONFESSIONS, THAT ONLY ABOUT 15 OUT OF 100 PEOPLE%OR LESS, EVEN HOLD TO THOSE CONFESSIONS OF FAITH UPON EXITING THE DOORS OF THE SANCTUARY.

AS THEY WALKED THE AISLES OF THE SANCTUARY, THEY HAVE DONE SO WITHOUT ANY COGNIZANT AWARENESS IN THE TOTALITY OF WHAT IT IS THAT THEY ARE SUPPOSEDLY SURRENDERING TO.

THERE IS NO FAILURE ON THE PART OF THE SPIRIT OF GOD, THAT SO MANY ARE NOT EVEN BEING MADE ALIVE THROUGH THE QUICKENING POWER OF THE SPIRIT OF THE LORD. PEOPLE ARE DETERMINED TO BRING

Feet & Paths

Christ into their own ways of walking, rather than to walk in the ways of the Lord!

Just because you say I surrender all; doesn't mean that you will actually release everything. I have come to wonder in my own mind, if the average person would have come forward to surrender their soul, if they had actually realized that it meant giving up the determined will of where they choose to place the soles of their feet?

The one thing that I do know for sure is that there would not have been as much backsliding and turning away from the Lord. It appears to me that only in the Christian churches, is it that the people have the twisted mentality to believe that it is acceptable to walk down the aisles of the churches to walk into Christ, and no sooner than the benediction of the services, the same people walk out of the arc of the safety of Christian living, to walk again in the troubled mentality, as an unbeliever.

Only the same people who are walking outwardly, seem to feel as if they are simultaneously walking inwardly in the will of God.

Erroneous teachings have allowed people to think that they are still walking

Hidden In the Light*

in the newness of their life in Christ Jesus, as long as they continue to show up at the church on the scheduled service times, whereas, it used to be that they never attended hardly.

My wife has one of the more powerful and true testimonies that I had ever heard. Her testimony was that she felt that she had to come to the church first, before going out to the clubs to party, especially on holidays, like New Years Eve, whereas the church is often geared to pray out of the old year, and into the new year.

She thought that coming to the church first, protected her from the kinds of things that naturally occurred in the club atmospheres. She recognized that just because she went to the church first before going out to the clubs, that it didn't keep her from sinning even to the point of shame and disappointment.

Neither did it prevent her from taking in the consumption of her favorite alcoholic beverage, and partying for twice as long as she had been at the church.

Committed Soles***

Commit thy way unto the Lord ; trust also in Him ; and He shall bring it to pass.   Psalms 37 : 5

Feet & Paths**

Of the greater blessings from the past memories that I have from being in the church as a youth, are the songs that ministered to us, both back then and even today as I reflect back on those old songs. We use to sing a song that said;

"His yoke is easy, burdens are light; WALK WHERE HE LEADS ME, always be right; Cherish the race, Running with Haste; And by His Grace, I know I'll make it Home some day!"

The key phrase in this song is "WALK WHERE HE LEADS ME", of which is the turning point in the message of the song; though it is often to be taken metaphorically, as an admonishment to adhere to the will of God, it is also to be taken very seriously, in the most literary state of our actions towards God.

Even, a deaf mute, who could not hear the audible lyrics of the song, have the understanding that in order to walk anywhere, for any purpose, involves the necessary usage of our feet.

No matter what we are endeavoring to do in this life, our truest level of success will be realized only when we have literally surrendered to place our feet in the pathway of the will of God.

An actual surrender becomes a reality once we have placed our feet at the behest of the word of God, to walk, to stand,

Hidden In the Light*

and to be in motion and on the move of our assigned ministries, according to the will of God.

Many people have no problem walking where they have chosen to walk themselves, believing that they are doing the will of God, because of the religious connotations attached to the reasons they chose to do the performance of their deed.

There is no such thing as walking where I lead the Lord, the only acceptable order is to walk where the Lord leads me daily, for His own purpose, and for His glory.

The detriment to this spiritual walk is in the fact that so many people say that they have done this at one time, before, in their lives. They don't mind saying that they have been good, and possibly pleasing in the sight of the Lord at a time prior to the present time of their lives.

Then out of the blue, for reasons that make since to themselves only, they convince themselves that they have graduated, and finished the work of the Lord.

Their attitude is to the likes of saying; WOW! I really accomplished that task, now I can move on in life and do as I please with the rest of my life! Sort of to the likes of saying; I've got bigger fish

Feet & Paths**

to fry now!

Many feel satisfied to have visited the will of God, as if to have done a taste test of the things of God? They feel that they have done their part, having once come forward to see for themselves, like participating in the mandatory Jury Duty?

Their convictions ought to be along the lines of saying; "I'll serve Him for the rest of my life!"

I have fought a good fight, I have finished my course, I have kept the faith.   II Timothy 4 : 7

My friends, if you will just keep your feet, you will also find it much easier to keep your faith. The failing decline of the visible ability to reach humanity through the church, is by reason of the fact that the people of the churches have put off to do the things of Christ, according to where He wants their feet to walk, and they have involved themselves with a lot of stuff that any common individual could do without any leading of the Lord, or without an unction of the Holy Ghost to enable them to function in effort to do it.

Common carnal individuals of the society, find themselves turned off, and totally uninterested, often even angered that the people of the churches are so

Hidden In the Light*

WILLING TO SHOW THAT THERE IS NO REAL CONNECTION TO THE GOD WHO SAVES, AND SET PEOPLE FREE FROM A LIFE OF SIN, THROUGH THEIR OWN UNWILLINGNESS TO PLACE THEIR FEET AT THE MERCY OF GOD, TO WALK IN HIS WAYS.

WE WANT THE WORLD TO KNOW THAT HE'S ALIVE AND WELL, AND THAT HE IS LIVING IN US! IT IS IMPERATIVE THAT WE CHOOSE NOT TO WALK WHERE SELF AND SATAN LEADS US TO WALK IN SIN AND SELFISHNESS, CONTRARY TO THE WORD OF GOD, WHICH IS HIS WILL!

THE WORLD WILL NEVER SEE JESUS IN PEOPLE WHO WALK WHERE THEY WANT TO WALK, AND PLACE THEIR FEET WHERE THEY CHOOSE TO PLACE THEIR FEET, AND SAY TO THOSE THAT INQUIRE OF THE DISORDERLY DISPLAY IN WHICH THEY ARE CONDUCTING THEMSELVES ACCORDING TO THEIR WALK; "THE LORD KNOWS MY HEART!" "YOU CAN'T JUDGE ME!" "THIS IS MY LIFE, AND I DO WHAT I PLEASE WITH IT!" ALWAYS REMEMBER THAT "I", IS ALWAYS IN THE MIDDLE OF S-I-N!

IT REALLY DOESN'T AMOUNT TO VERY MUCH AT ALL, TO KNOW A LOT THINGS INTELLECTUALLY, AND TO BE AN ASTUTE AND DISCIPLINED LEARNER, DEDICATED TO STUDYING THE WRITTEN WORD OF GOD, IF THERE IS NO GUT WRENCHED DESIRE TO PLACE OUR FEET ALIVE AND WHOLE, RIGHT THERE, ACCORDING TO WHERE WE HAVE BEEN READING.

Feet & Paths**

All the commandments which I command thee this day shall ye observe to do, that ye may live, and multiply, and go in and possess the land which the Lord sware unto your fathers. And thou shalt remember all of the way which the Lord thy God led thee these forty years in the wilderness, to humble thee, and to prove thee, to know what was in thine heart, whether thou wouldest keep His commandments, or no. And he humbled thee, and suffered thee to hunger, and fed thee with manna, which thou knewest not, neither did thy fathers know; that He might make thee know that man doth not live by bread only, but by every word that proceeded out of the mouth of the Lord doth man live.

Deuteronomy 8 : 1-3

The commitment of our feet is what is going to tell the true story of the transformation in our spiritual status. Most people are hung up on their verbal confessions, highlighting the change in their discussions, but often they have left off to walk where they talk!

The resistance to transform the inner desire to take control of the placement of our feet, speaks in contrary to what we have been trying to convey to our well wishers, relative to being changed now.

The benefit in the greater grace of God, is neither discovered nor taken advantaged of for every individual who consistently walks on the outside of the

Hidden In the Light*

GRACEFUL REALMS OF THE SAFETY OF GOD'S PROVISIONS.

RELATIVE TO THE AWESOME BENEFITS OF BEING AN ACTUAL BELIEVER, TO THOSE WHO ARE DETERMINED TO WALK ON THE OUTSIDE OF BELIEF IN GOD, THEY WILL ALSO REMAIN ON THE OUTSIDE OF KNOWING GOD'S ESSENTIAL BENEFIT TO US AS A REWARD FOR LIVING ACCORDING TO HIS WORD.

SO MANY PEOPLE WANT THE BENEFIT OF THE BELIEVERS, BUT THEY DON'T WALK IN THE PATHS OF RIGHTEOUSNESS, THAT ARE REQUIRED FOR THOSE OF US WHO HAVE CONFESSED CHRIST IN THE PARDONING OF OUR PAST SINS. GOD DOES HEAR WHAT WE ARE SAYING OUT OF OUR MOUTHS, BUT HE IS REQUIRING US TO ALIGN OUR FEET WITH OUR TONGUE AND CHEEKS.

> *And it shall come to pass, if thou shall hearken diligently unto the voice of the Lord thy God, to observe and to do all His commandments which I command thee this day, that the Lord thy God will set thee on high above all nations of the earth : And all these blessings shall come on thee, and over take thee, if thou shalt hearken unto the voice of the Lord thy God. The Lord shall establish thee an holy people unto himself, as he hath sworn unto thee, if thou shall keep the commandments of the Lord thy God and walk in His ways. And all the people of the earth shall see that thou art called by the name of the Lord ; and they shall be afraid of thee. And the Lord shall make thee plenteous in goods, in the fruit of thy body, and in the fruit of thy cattle, and in the*

Feet & Paths[**]

fruit of thy ground, and in the land which the Lord sware unto thy fathers to give thee.

Deuteronomy 28 : 1-2, 9-11

Every place that the sole of your foot shall tread upon, that have I given unto you, as I said unto Moses. Only thou be strong and very courageous, that thou mayest observe to do according to all the law, which Moses my servant command thee : turn not from it to the right hand or to the left, that thou mayest prosper whithersoever thou goest. This book of the law shall not depart out of thy mouth; but thou shalt meditate therein day and night, that thou mayest observe to do according to all that is written therein : for then thou shalt make thy way prosperous, and then thou shalt have good success.

Joshua 1 : 3, 7-8

Chapter 8

Urgency of Emergency **

Awake, awake; put on thy strength, O Zion; put on thy beautiful garments, O Jerusalem, the holy city: for henceforth there shall no more come into thee the uncircumcised and the unclean. Shake thyself from the dust; arise, and sit down, O Jerusalem: loose thyself from the bands of thy neck, O captive daughter of Zion.
Isaiah 52:1-2

And that, knowing the time, that now it is high time to awake out of sleep: for now is our salvation nearer that when we first believed. The night is far spent, the day is at hand: let us therefore cast off the works of darkness, and let us put on the armour of light.
Romans 13:11-12

Hidden In the Light*

Church ; State of Emergency

Long since before now, the church should have managed to shake off the residue of evil dumped on it by certain people randomly, who took hold of the leadership reigns, but refused to be delivered and set free themselves, thus somewhat deafening the resounding messages of salvation and deliverance, from the pulpit.

The filthy dust of dirty secrets aired throughout the congregation and the unclean spiritual residue from iniquitous off-road living, which followed those into the worship service, that participate having no true desire of real worship, have contaminated the inner-atmosphere of the sanctuary.

Many of the saints have involuntarily inhaled that same dust of compromise, having the sharpness of their own spiritual sensitivity to God's holiness relative to the word of God, dulled, and in some instances, it has been deadened, completely!

Sinners are now questioning where to find the true freedom of salvation and deliverance, because they say that they can no longer witness the power of God, to free them from the death-

Urgency of Emergency

GRIP OF SIN AND SHAME, IN MANY OF THE CHURCHES.

Many church leaders are catagorized as only mere men and women of the communities, because they live as though they've never had any real connection to the power of God that makes the difference in the lives of people, transforming them from sinner to saint.

Nowadays; many leaders no longer desire the responsibility of walking circumspectly before the church and the people of their immediate communities. Spiritual abortion and still born Christians in the churches, are the result. The body can never live when the head itself, is dead!

Here is what I mean; people are consistently coming into the church, but they are only coming in as adjoining members with no spiritual charge, change, or experience. They know church; but they have never met Christ, they have never been baptised into the living power of Jesus that flows through the lives of the believers that repent and turn to Christ.

Should the spirit fill the atmosphere and take control as the people worship God, many don't even

Hidden In the Light*

have a clue as what to do with or in the presence of the awesome spirit of God.

Christians are supposed to be alive in Christ. Too many can only acknowledge the spiritually explosive occurrence taking place in the service, but they're at a loss to describe it according to the word of God.

Consistently chasing what appear to be the move of God, when if they knew the spirit of the Lord for themselves, they would never be caught up in the religious scandals that will at times rip through the reputiated credibility of the churches.

These same people are being fooled and tricked into believing that they can tithe and pay their way to peace and tranquility, while they continue to live in greater fellowship with sin and Satan!

Peace comes from obeying God! To those who keep their minds stayed on the Lord, and not necessarily to those who visit the idea of God in their minds every now and then. To the likes of going to church on Sunday morning, only.

To look in the eyes and on the countenance of many people of the churches, it becomes obviously apparent that people are war riddled in the spirit of their minds, without any remedies to

Urgency of Emergency

CEASE THE BATTLE IN THEIR HEADS.

Most have no desire to divulge their inner struggles to the leadership of the church, because they would never entertain the notion of being challenged to change the things that are indeed wrong and truly responsible for causing the pains that they are experiencing.

They are of the belief that they will eventually fix things on their own, though they have been unsuccessful at handling their own problems through the years in past times.

The people of the communities are praying, in the local congregations that are overrun with corruption in the leadership, but it seems to no avail!

They are sometimes faithfully, calling on the name of the Lord, seeking deliverance from the waywardness of sin and the shameful residue that is borne and bread, as a result of iniquitous living.

Many leading people of the churches now are living out loud, in sinful wickedness! They no longer feel that it is any of the churches business how they choose live, and of whom it may be that they choose to share their choices of living with.

Hidden In the Light*

Be it someone else's spouse, same sex partner, some underage youth, or an outright criminal?

Determined that no one is better than anyone else, since all people sin and make mistakes, they feel that they ought to be able to do whatever they want to do, and come to church just like the other people. It's about Him, not them!

The current church members, believe that they ought to be able to go into the devil's den a Christian, and come out still a Christian, all on their own will and agenda. Here's the truth; they do go in to those places and come out of those same places just as they were whenever they went in! The same as they were the last time they even went to church; undelivered!

They were never led into those places for the glory of God, they don't have the mind nor the will to stay away from those places. They've never been lifted from beneath the power of the world's influence.

Those same unrestrained people of the churches are constantly flooding the altars every time the invitation is given, and the pastor's offices for counseling and instruction. Crying large crocodile tears, and sometimes

Urgency of Emergency

WAILING LOUDLY IN REGRET OF THE PENALTY OF THEIR BEHAVIOR; BUT NEVER FOR THE ACTUAL BEHAVIOR ITSELF.

EVEN AFTER THE TEARS AND THE HOURS OF ADVISE GIVEN TO THEM, THEY ARE STILL NEVER ABLE TO FIND RELIEF FROM THEIR DILEMMAS.

> *Behold, the Lord's hand is not shortened, that it cannot save; neither his ear heavy, that it cannot hear: But your iniquities have separated between you and your God, and your sins have hid his face from you, that he will not hear. For your hands are defiled with blood, and your fingers with iniquity; your lips have spoken lies, and your tongue hath muttered perverseness. None calleth for justice, nor any pleadeth for truth: they trust in vanity, and speak lies; they conceive mischief, and bring forth iniquity. They hatch cockatrice eggs, and weave a spiders web: he that eateth of their eggs dieth, and that which is crushed breaketh out into a viper.*
>
> *Isaiah 59:1-5*

IT IS FAR BEYOND MY UNDERSTANDING, THAT THE LEADERS OF THE CHURCHES ARE APPREHENSIVE TO BRING TO THE ATTENTION OF THE PEOPLE, THE FACT THAT THEY HAVE BROUGHT SPIRITUAL DAMNATION UPON THEMSELVES AS A RESULT OF THEIR OWN SINFULLY DETERMINATE CHOICES OF LIVING CONTRARY TO THE WORD OF GOD.

I THINK THAT IT IS ABSOLUTELY CRAZY ON MY PART AS A LEADER, TO TRY AND COVER UP THE FACT THAT IT IS GOD IN THE DETAILS

Hidden In the Light*

causing the situations to remain as they are with no reprieve! Since God already sees us in our own present state of living.

People need to know that they are possibly living under the power of sin's most awful grip! Whenever we take hold of sin, it is not immediately apparent to us, that sin in retrospect have likewise taken hold of us.

What is eventually obvious, is the out-breaking attack on everything that is personal to us. Soon you realize that sin has sold you out to the devil and to every form of evil, giving the ownership of your goods to the destruction of demons and decay.

God is saying; if you make a move towards living righteous and holy, and repent, I will move towards your situation to deliver you from the clutches of sin and shame.

The past leadership of the churches, were rather thick skinned. They were never moved by the feelings and emotions of the people, because they knew people needed the truth more than they needed someone to identify with their struggles, being careful not to brush up against their already battered and bruised egos.

Call me old fashion, out dated, out

OF TOUCH WITH THE TIMES, OR WHATEVER YOU CHOOSE TO SAY; PEOPLE HAVE NEVER EXPERIENCED PAIN AND SUFFERING WHILE LIVING HERE ON THIS EARTH, LIKE THEY WILL IF THEY MISS HEAVEN AND GO TO HELL!

LEADERS HAVE BECOME MASTERS AT MINISTERING RETROACTIVELY IN PASSIVITY TO THE ACTUAL SINFULNESS OF THE PEOPLE. THEY FEEL THAT YOU CANNOT CHANGE THE FACT THAT PEOPLE HAVE SINNED, AND I AGREE;

BUT, WE MUST OBEY THE BIBLE TO SOUND THE TRUMPET NOW, TO SHOW PEOPLE WHERE AND EVEN HOW THEY MIGHT HAVE SINNED AGAINST GOD. SOME MAY NOT BE AWARE THAT THEY HAVE SINNED AGAINST GOD WITH THEIR ACTIONS.

IT IS OUR POSITIONS AS MINISTERS OF THE GOSPEL, TO SHOW PEOPLE IN THE WORD OF GOD THAT THEIR ACTIONS ARE IN OFFENSE TO THE WRITTEN WORD OF GOD. PEOPLE NEED TO KNOW THE TRUTH, WHICH MANY TIMES, THOSE WHO STAND IN THE PULPITS OF THE CHURCHES, REFUSE TO TELL THEM.

Silencing The Alarm **

THE PULPITS IN AMERICA AND AROUND THE WORLD, WERE ALWAYS USED TO SOUND THE ALARM, ALERTING THE PEOPLE OF THE FACT THAT GOD DOESN'T LIKE FOR US TO BEHAVE OURSELVES UGLY IN WICKEDNESS, IDOLATRY, AND SIN.

Hidden In the Light*

Many of the former pastorial leaders who are now asleep in their graves, have faced the barrel of guns, angry mobs, and acts of vandalism upon their churches and their homes, they never backed down from Holiness and admonishment to live godly!

It is perhaps fair, to say that the initial angry opposition to the sermonic alarms, were from people who couldn't appreciate being called out for their ungodly behavior. People have tried everything, in an attempt to persuade preachers to shut their mouths, and to conform to delivering messages considered less judgmental.

There are nations that forbid preaching the gospel of Jesus Christ, with deadly resistance, simply for the fact that they did want their marriages and all sexually deviant behavioral patterns, to be ruled and governed according to holiness.

According to what the bible declares to be sinful, man has always come along to rebuttal the claims of truth in the word of God.

In past centuries, certain religious people who refuse to acknowledge the deity of Christ, have reserved the very same humanistic idealisms, as of these

MORE MODERN ATHEIST.

AT BEST, BECAUSE OF THE EXTREME CARNAL GULLIBILITY TO ACQUIRE SECULAR KNOWLEDGE, DISREGARDING THE KNOWLEDGE OF THE WRITTEN WORD OF GOD, THE ATTITUDE OF REJECTION HAS ONLY BEEN BENEFICIAL FOR THE ACTUALITY OF A HEATHENISTIC DISPOSITION OF CHARACTER.

PEOPLE HAVE BEGUN TO PROGRESSIVELY RAGE, IN RESPONSE TO THEIR OWN WAYS OF THINKING. THEY TEAR THROUGH THE LIVES OF OTHER PEOPLE LIKE RAVENOUS BEASTS, DOING WHATEVER THEY FEEL THAT THEY ARE BIG ENOUGH TO DO, REFUSING TO HELD ACCOUNTABLE TO THE HOLISTIC STANDARDS OF BIBLE TEACHINGS.

FOR A WHILE IT SEEMED AS IF I COULD STILL HEAR THE ALARM OF THE PULPITS, THOUGH FAINTLY FADING AWAY WITH THE TIMES; AS MANY OF THOSE INDIVIDUALS WHO HAD BEEN RESPONSIBLE FOR SOUNDING THE ALARMS HAD BEGUN GRACEFULLY, TO AGE.

CERTAIN OF THE SELECT LEADERS WERE NOW PREOCCUPIED WITH PASSING THE TORCH TO A YOUNGER, PERHAPS STRONGER PERSON TO TAKE THE HELM FOR THESE YOUNGER GENERATIONS OF PEOPLE WHO HAD ALREADY BEGUN TO REBEL AGAINST THE SOUND OF THE ALARM FROM THESE PREACHING GENERALS.

THE DANGER OF THE TRANSFERENCE OF LEADERSHIP IN THE CHURCHES, IS THAT THOSE

Hidden In the Light*

WHO HAVE STEPPED FORWARD TO TAKE THE HELM, WERE POSSIBLY VITAL PARTNERS IN THE PRIOR REVOLT TO RESIST THE STERN STRIKING OF THE BELL, SOUNDING IT'S AWESOMELY FRIGHTENING ALARM IN THE SPIRITS OF THE PEOPLE.

THEIR TRUE FOCUS, WAS TO INFLUENCE PEOPLE TO FOLLOW THEM, GIVING THEM WHAT THEY DESIRED TO HEAR OVER THE PULPIT, RATHER THAN SPEAKING THE WORD OF TRUTH, UNCOMPROMISINGLY, BY THE DIRECTION OF THE HOLY GHOST.

IN EVERY GENERATION, MOST PEOPLE ARE GENERALLY THE SAME, IN THAT IF YOU GIVE THEM WHAT THEY WANT, THEY WILL OFTEN IN RETURN GIVE YOU WHATEVER YOU WANT FROM THEM. DON'T CONDEMN THE SIN IN MY LIFE THROUGH THE WORD OF GOD, AND I WILL GIVE YOU MY MONEY AND MY TIME AND SUPPORT IN THE MINISTRY OF THE CHURCH.

BUT IF YOU CHOOSE TO PREACH HOLINESS, THEY WILL FIND SOMEWHERE ELSE TO GO FOR A CHURCH SERVICE, AND A SERVANT; THAT WILL OBEY THEM, NOT THE BIBLE OR THE SPIRIT OF LORD!

AS A WHOLE, THE VISIBLE CHURCH HAS ALMOST COMPROMISED IT'S POSITIONS OF AUTHORITY. THROUGH BRIBERY AND SCANDALS, MOST CHURCHES HAVE ALLOWED THE FIRE TO GO OUT!

OFTEN, ALL WE HAVE NOW ARE

Urgency of Emergency

decorated candle sticks, with absolutely no flames burning atop of the candle. Everything looks good, but it is to no avail as it relates to the power to effect change and to breed conviction in the hearts of the people to adhere to the will and to the word of the Lord.

The beauty of the edifice, may at times bespeak of the excellency of the knowledge of God in the presence of a spirit filled church, other-wise, it is just another big beautiful building of the city, along with other newly constructed Court Houses, Shopping Malls, Movie Theatres, Houses, and etc…

Many leaders, of the smaller churches have been strung up by the competitive noose, swinging from the neighboring opinionated gallows, nothing more than inadequate building fund programs, social status to lobby for the communities downtown, and their willingness to rally around the social injustices of inequality and the unfair treatment of racial indifferences among the cities, and the states, while struggling to hold on as a viable organized church in the community.

Many of the larger churches, and even the Megs-churches; are totally

Hidden In the Light*

sold away on the messages of prosperity and sociable progressive status in the communities over and above that of pure holiness and righteousness. Not All of Them!

They often lack the fruit of the spirit, and the spirit! In truth; the mega churches are gaining momentum on what makes them more of a formidable entity in the community, conforming to the wealth of society, however, they are swiftly decreasing in becoming more powerful as a church, being connected to God of the universe.

More frequently now, Jesus is spoken of as He, Him, and even as a female! The average person of the churches cannot even see Jesus as the savior of the world anymore. They do embrace the idea of Christ, and the cross.

Society won't allow the total erasure of the religious idea, in that the holiday seasons bespeak idealy of the person of Christ, and partially of the sacrifice of the cross of Calvary. But there is no actual presentation of the deified reality in the spirit of the alive, and the living Christ.

I hear people say, that God is whatever you think that He; or it; is in your own mind. If I were to try and convince them that the air is whatever you think that it is in your own mind, the same people would argue with that idea!

I imagine their initial argument would be that the air is indeed the air, without a doubt! Some may arguably attempt to explain how that science has discovered that there are air molecules which can be examined in the laboratory, by whatever scientific method possible.

Aside from the fact of breathing in air, the ultimate proof of the air being a reality has been determined in a laboratory of science..........................

Somehow, though there are fowl scents, the stench of death of rotting carcasses along the roadside, and in a field that take to the air polluting the flow of the wind, traveling wherever the air will take the scents, people still embrace the air as still being the air.

Though the smell is quite vile in the nostrils of intelligent human beings, they still have the minds to separate the smell in the air, from the actual movement of the air itself, in the wind.

Pollution does not change the reality of the air, but rather the movement of the air in the wind,

Hidden In the Light*

HIGHLIGHTS THE ACTUALITY OF SOMETHING FOUL IN CLOSE PROXIMITY TO OUR IMMEDIATE SURROUNDING.

As we breathe in what is supposed to be a pure breath of air, we are often mystified and vilified by the intrusion of deadly gasses and fumes that are unpleasant to our natural sense of smell, and to the natural process of breathing.

Even the most illiterate people around us, understand that the same air that is blowing all around our atmosphere, is the same air that we are breathing every second of our lives, and they don't have to be taught that fact.

The reality of the church is true and sound; though, there are some things that have latched onto the church by way of the people, for the sake of attaching themselves to others that may already be distracted and totally disinterested in the true spirit of God.

As those certain people begin to exemplify the behavior and the spirit that is opposite from the spirit of God, though they are presently in fellowship with the gathering of the church, they do not have the power to nullify or to disqualify the reality of the church from being that which can only belong to God.

Urgency of Emergency

The church without the spirit of God; is as a body without the blood flowing through it! It's dead! There is absolutely no life flowing through the body to give it the upright posture, allowing it to stand up erect on its feet, as a living being moving through the earth in control of itself.

I have reckoned within myself to believe, that there are many people that are extremely unsettled over the fact that God can't be examined in a laboratory anywhere!

Its been my observation, that anytime people begin to feel as if they have gotten God boxed up into a container of thinking, that God makes a move outside of their own box to nullify their findings, and to detach the people from believing in the deceptive lies about God.

Chapter 9

Blind Sight**

And the disciples came, and said unto Him, Why speakest thou unto them in parables? He answered and said unto them, Because it is given unto you to know the mysteries of the kingdom of heaven, but to them it is not given. For whosoever hath, to him shall be given, and he shall have more abundance : but whosoever hath not, from him shall be taken away even that he hath. Therefore speak I to them in parables : because they seeing see not; and hearing they hear not, neither do they understand. And unto them is fulfilled the prophecy of Esaias, which saith, By hearing ye shall hear, and shall not understand; and seeing ye shall see, and shall not perceive : For this people's heart is waxed gross, and their ears are dull of hearing, and their eyes

Hidden In the Light*

they have closed; lest at anytime they should see with their eyes, and hear with their ears, and should understand with their heart, and should be converted, and I should heal them. But blessed are your eyes, for they see, and your ears for they hear.

St. Matthew 13 : 10-16

Now the disciples had forgotten to take bread, neither had they in the ship with them more than one loaf. And he charged them, saying, Take heed, beware of the leaven of the Pharisees, and of the leaven of Herod. And the reasoning among themselves, saying, It is because we have no bread. And when Jesus knew it, he saith unto them, Why reason ye, because ye have no bread? Perceive ye not yet, neither understand? Have ye your heart yet darkened? Having eyes, see ye not? And having ears, hear ye not? And do ye not remember? When I break the five loaves among the five thousand, how many baskets full of fragments took ye up? They say unto him twelve. And when the seven among four thousand, how many baskets full of fragments took ye up? And they said seven. And he said unto them, How is it that ye do not understand? And he cometh to Bethsaida; and they bring a blind man unto him, and besought him to touch him. And he took the blind man by the hand, and led him out of the town; and when he had spit on his eyes, and put his hands upon him, he asked him if he saw ought. And he looked up and said, I see men as trees walking. After that he put his hands again upon his eyes, and made him look up : and he was restored, and saw every man clearly.

St. Mark 8 : 14-25

Blind Sight

Eye-Sight; But No In-Sight

I HOPE TO SHOW YOU THAT GOD'S CONCERN RELATIVE TO OUR EYESIGHT HAS TO DO WITH MORE THAN JUST BEING ABLE TO VISUALIZE. GOD KNOWS THAT A TRUE WITNESS IS AS RESPONSIBLE FOR KNOWING WHAT IT IS THAT THEY HAVE WITNESSED ON DISPLAY, ACCORDING TO THE MENTAL PERCEPTION OF THE MIND, WITH THE PIN-POINT ACCURACY OF EYESIGHT RECOGNITION.

OFTEN, OTHERS OF PURSUASIVE AUTHORITY WILL HAVE A TENDENCY TO INFLUENCE THE PERCEPTION OF WHATEVER YOU MIGHT HAVE SEEN.

IT IS AMAZING TO ME THAT A CROWD BROUGHT A BLIND MAN TO JESUS TO HAVE HIS SIGHT HEALED, BUT INSTEAD OF HEALING THE BLIND MAN, RIGHT THEN AND THERE, HE LED HIM AWAY FROM THE SAME CROWD THAT INITIALLY BROUGHT HIM TO THE LORD TO BE HEALED!

AS WE LOOK INTO THE SCRIPTURAL ACCOUNT OF THE BLIND MAN BEING HEALED IN THE 8TH CHAPTER OF ST. MARK; WE GLEAM A GREATER INSIGHT TO THE REASONING AS TO WHY THE LORD MOVED THE MAN WAY FROM THE CROWD.

MANY MIRACLES DON'T TAKE PLACE IN LARGE CROWDS, SIMPLY FOR THE FACT THAT THE GRATER PERCENTAGES OF THE CROWDS, ARE EXTREMELY DOUBTFUL AND UNBELIEVING.

Hidden In the Light*

Jesus; already knew that the man was perceptively off, and out of sync. Upon having his eyesight restored, he saw men as trees walking. WOW!

That is frightening; could you imagine the trouble that the people of his surrounding might been subject to, had the Lord left him to his own twisted perception?

Suppose someone told him to go chop down the tree with an ax, you'd better be far away from a man who sees men as trees!

In order to get along with other people, you have got to at least see them as people equal to yourself in recognition. You're a human being, so you have got to see other people as human beings also.

Mankind had been given the most beautiful array of the earthly domain to dwell in, it would have been a tragedy to be depraved of viewing it.

Ever since I first began studying the word of God, I notice that of the miracles that Jesus performed, most often it was reported that He restored the sight to the blind.

God in heaven, is smarter than we are in the earth. He knows that it is impossible to follow the given paths to dwell in if we could never see them.

Blind Sight

God knew that He could not command us to see as He sees in the earth, if He had not given us the eyesight to do so.

It would have been unfair to Adam and to Eve, had they never been given eyesight, to blindly approached the trees in the midst of the garden; firstly not even knowing that they were in the midst of the garden, nor had they not been able to recognize the difference in all of the trees.

Many commandments had been given in the garden, to conquer and to subdue, and to have dominion over everything in the earth.

We could never corral the animals of the wild, being blind, and neither would we have a defense for their wild attacks, and counter-defensive actions against us in retaliation to being captured and taken prey.

But, now, let's submerge beneath the fact-line of the general obvious to most mankind, to evaluate the extreme depths in the missing insight that is often overlooked, passed up, or even purposefully ignored.

For an instance : what is it that you actually see whenever you look at another individual? Alike the man who had indeed been blind, do you see men as

Hidden In the Light*

TREES?

Do you see the evolutionary prognostication of the apes now mysteriously turned human?

Do you see some freak of nature uprightened to walk on two feet, while most other creatures walk on four feet?

Do you see the most intelligently created being on the face of the planet earth, of which reflect the God who created them?

In most instances, the questions are; what are you seeing, and why are you seeing it?

Is the insight of your eyesight dormant, under-working, inadequate or is it in over-drive?

In either case scenario there is an insight working right in the middle of your eyesight!

It was obvious to Jesus that the eyes of the blind man were now working according to the gift of sight; he could see!

But what this now seeing man revealed, was that he had other problems that would hinder and even alter whatever it was that he saw. These particular problems, he had developed long before coming into contact with Jesus.

Blind Sight

You have got to understand that if the blind man could not see men for the lack of eyesight, it is for certain, that neither could he see trees!

At the very beginning of creation, God had distinctively given an exact image to every thing that He created. Men have never looked like trees, and trees have never looked like mankind.

Take into consideration the fact that Jesus was also God in the form of a man; although Jesus had healed this man's sight, he would never see the Lord right, seeing that he had an obscured image of mankind to begin with.

There is a grave possibility that this blind man had even begun to recognize himself as something other than a human being. Perhaps he never even thought of himself as a man, being that he lacked one of the more needed physical character attributes that were indeed common to all mankind?

The blind man who received his sight was also in need of a savior! Would he be able to see that the same man who was indeed his healer, would also be his savior?

Many people of today don't see the Lord for who He is, for the sake of having an obscured vision of the people of God.

Hidden In the Light*

Whether it is the fault in the examples of the misbehaved people of the church that discourage other people from turning to Christ, or if it is simply for the sake of total unbelief, whereas the people are never even seen as belonging to any God of Heaven?

For too long, we as people have been left to think and to feel as if God is simply satisfied with the fact that we as mankind have a working eyesight.

So often in giving a testimony, we may be apt to thank God for the eyes that we have that can indeed see. There is absolutely nothing wrong with being thankful for eyesight.

Blind men to the likes of singer/ songwriters/ composers / artist, the late Ray Charles, and the very renowned blind genius; Stevie Wonder, have as much insight, if not even more, as to that to those of us that have working, visible eyesight!

They cannot see the things that we see naturally everyday, or even keep with the sight recognition of the vastly changing things in the earth, for the lack of eyesight.

Somehow, it may appear that their insight had never been obscured to the point that they had assigned an alienated form of recognition to the

Blind Sight

HUMAN REALM, AS DID THIS BLIND MAN OF THE SCRIPTURE. MAYBE SOMEONE HELPED THEM ALONG THE WAY? I DON'T KNOW THE ANSWER TO THAT QUESTION!

BUT WHAT I DO KNOW IS THAT SINCE WE HAVE A WORKING EYESIGHT, IT HAS TO BE COUPLED WITH THE GIVEN POWER OF INSIGHT ON THE INSIDE OF US, IN AN EFFORT TO BRING INTO TOTAL FRUITION THAT IN WHICH WE ARE SEEING RIGHT BEFORE OUR EYES.

EYESIGHT HELPS US TO SEE THE CAR, EVEN THAT IT MAY BE RED, WHITE, OR BLACK AND THAT THE CAR IS EVEN IN MOTION; BUT INSIGHTFUL INSTINCT TELLS US TO RECOGNIZE HOW FAST THE CAR IS MOVING, AND THAT IT WOULD BE WISE IF WE WAIT UNTIL THE CAR PASSES, TO CROSS THE STREET, NEVER TAKING A CHANCE ON STEPPING INTO IT'S PATH.

INSIGHT SHOULD ALSO ENABLE US TO SEE OUR SOON FUNERAL RITES OBSERVED, IN RECOGNITION TO THE LOSS OF OUR LIFE, AS RESULT OF STEPPING INTO THE PATHWAY OF THE HIGH-SPEED AUTOMOBILE.

EYESIGHT SHOWS US THAT THE SUN IS SHINING AND THAT IT IS A BEAUTIFUL DAY; BUT INSIGHT HELPS US TO DETERMINE THAT THE SUN IS INDEED SHINING FORTH ON A VERY COLD DAY AS WELL AND THAT WE NEED TO PROTECT OUR BODIES FROM THE ELEMENT OF THE COLD.

WERE IT THAT WE DEPENDED ON THE ENGAGEMENT OF VISIBILITY ALONE, WE WOULD walk out into the frigid atmosphere unprotected from the cold temperature and catch pneumonia.

As simple as it may be, whether the operation of our insight is the result of a learned behavior, or simply inherited from the spiritual nature of the creator; insight is necessary.

If that which is necessary can't be realized and taken advantage of in it's simplest form, then it is no wonder that we are so indigent to recognize the powerful necessity to engage the absolute essentials of our lives, on a daily basis.

Too often, we are clueless to the need to apply the transmission-like shift of our insight to purify, to rectify, or even to transmogrify what we are seeing with our eyesight.

Installed Obstructions

The actual benefits of change are realized at the point of recognition of which often depends on our insight, however blind sight can't see it.

We know that we are changed before others could ever realize that there has been a change in our lives. As our change matures to the point of

Blind Sight

MANIFESTING OUTWARDLY, OTHERS WILL ALSO REALIZE IT WHEN THEY CAN SEE IT, MINUS ANY OBSTRUCTING ELEMENT IN THE WAY OF THEIR OWN VISUAL PERCEPTION.

SIGHT RECOGNITION IS IMPORTANT AND ORDAINED OF GOD, BECAUSE IN THE REALM OF HUMANITY WE HAVE BEEN GIVEN SO MANY THINGS, VASTLY DIVERSIFIED AND UNIQUE TO LOOK UPON.

IT IS PARAMOUNT THAT WE VISUALLY DISTINGUISH THE VASTNESS OF THE THINGS THAT ARE AVAILABLE TO US UPON THE SIGHT RECOGNITION OF THOSE THINGS.

BUT, ALIKE THE TARES, THAT GROW UP IN THE WHEAT FIELDS, LOOKING EXACTLY LIKE THE WHEAT IN COLOR AND IN IMAGE; THE TARES CREATE AN OBSTRUCTION TO TRULY SEEING THE WHEAT IN THE FIELDS, WITHOUT PRIOR KNOWLEDGE OF THE APPEARANCE OF THE TARES, THEMSELVES.

> *Thou hypocrite, first cast out the beam out of thine own eyes, and then shalt thou see clearly to cast out the mote of thy brother's eye.   St. Matthew 7 : 5*
>
> *Unto the pure all things are pure; but unto them that are defiled and unbelieving is nothing pure; but even their mind and conscience is defiled. They profess that they know God; but in works they deny him, being abominable, and disobedient, and unto every good work reproachable.   Titus 1: 15-16*

Hidden In the Light*

So often it is assumed that we are sure of the things that we are looking at in the lives of those that are closest to us.

There may be something on the inside of us, that hinders us from seeing past any identifiable negative trait of the people that we have affixed into our own line of focus, that we cannot see the true spirit and character of the person of our focused interest.

Whenever we believe that we are seeing people for who they really are, it doesn't signify that we are judgmentally accurate and even sound, as far as the other person is concerned, as many of us have been led to believe. That, which obscures the focus, is often the erected mental screen of the mind.

Erroneous teachings, judgmental belief systems, self righteousness, and lack of understanding, causes many to feel they have the right to subjugate others. We are truly in need of Christ's help!

We may have a tendency to believe that it is of God, whenever we determine the necessity to deny others the same

God given right to walk in the glorious light of the Lord.

Many man-made reasons are given for behaving ourselves as if we are Military Police watching over the very secretive place of the Army Generals of the War; instead of being Soldiers in the Army of the Lord.

People act as if God is inadequate of knowing about the people that He has allowed in to the body of Christ! The real problem is that we really don't know the presence of God; He's with the others, just as He is with us.

We have no monopoly on the graceful presence of God, we can't tell God whomever He can or cannot be with.

The Apostles Peter; would have been biased against the men-servants of Cornelius, simply because they were not Jews. But, God took hold of Peter, while up on the house top, before the men could even arrive at Peter's place of residence.

This learned and practiced behavior of Peter was an instructional command in behavior from the superiors of the Jewish nation, perhaps even from the

Hidden In the Light*

leaders and the High-Priest of the Synagogues, the Temple, but definitely not of God.

Such a determination was to be assessed upon visually observing the nationality, diversity, by way of skin color, physical attributes, and any other trait that would lend definition to visible characteristics, to further determine a cause for distinction.

While most people believe only what they are able to see, and to naturally reason in their minds, they have become blinded to their own limited abilities to understand what they are seeing.

Sort of seems like someone has turned out the light of the spirit, and have left the people of these modern times to find their own ways to the throne of God, in the dark. Even those who stand in the stead of the leaders of the churches, have also lost their way, yet they remain in front. They have no where to lead because they are lost themselves.

As I listen to sermons of many of the preachers today, it has become apparent that not even most of those who preach are even able to see God in the bible.

Blind Sight

In this case, the blinded skills of visibly recognizing diversities would always indelibly hamper the ability to resist being a first rate, Jerk! But never a Saint of God; or more commonly recognized, a Christian.

Alike the blind man who had been blind as a result of the lack of sight, there are so many others by the scores that are blinded having sight, with their eyes wide open, but they have had their perception darkened by the foolishness of their hearts, therefore alleviating the very necessary power of perspective insight.

In the vision that God showed Peter on the housetop, Peter looked upon that which God had created and called it both common and unclean!

We are just like Peter, in that we have the nerve to tell God that what He has made, and the people that He has called are too common and unclean, even too sinful to be used of Him! Somehow we get it twisted, and think that God is asking for our approval, before He calls certain individuals from the darkness into the light!

Certain teachers of the past, have caused the church to be in dangerous positions before the Lord!

Hidden In the Light*

Those who taught such erroneous things, appeared to prosper in their own way before the people of the congregations. The people of the churches accepted the erroneous teaching and the foul behavior of those leaders, as a result of their prosperity, as if it were signification of God's own ordinance for the people of the churches.

World history, both of the past and the present, have often revealed and manifested to us, the degradable relations among people of diverse groups of ethnicity, financial status, national acclaim, etc., whenever one group has viewed the other as sub-human or inhumane?

The blinding reality is in the fact that this behavior is definitely prevalent in the church community, among all religions, racial barriers, and financial groups of people.

Many times one side is willing to omit or to ignore the judgmental standards of one group against them, while the other group of projected superiority will have no such relenting of their own negligible rights for the

Blind Sight

degradable observation of others.

Come on now; this is not new behavior among people. Somebody always emerges to project themselves as being better than someone else!

Of the more dreaded dialogue among the American population, would definitely be that concerning racial bigotry and out-right hatred.

I could stay all day on that topic alone; because there is such a greater urgency to discuss the issues concerning the racial tensions among the American people. However, I would much rather stay with the more enlightening matters of my dialogue.

I know that you remember the story of the Samaritans; how that Jesus said that it was a must to go through the town of Samaria?

The people of Samaria, were a people of interracial marriage unions, whereas they were no longer identifiable as being people of any particular original race of people, much to the likes of the interracial marriages of today.

The Jews thought of this type of mixing of the races as detestable; sounds familiar doesn't it?

It was in Samaria where Jesus met the woman at the well, who had become

Hidden In the Light*

somewhat sociably outcasted, in that most people of town probably knew all of her business. The scripture states that she had been with five different men before the man that she was living with at the time of meeting Christ?

This same sinful woman, being a Samaritan, recognized that Jesus was indeed a Jew, but she was yet willing to give Him a drink; only she noticed that He had no physical water pot to draw water out of the well. I'm sure that this woman alike many of us today began to reason within her own mind, questioning, what is this guy up to?

It would be obvious, according to the history of this woman's behavior, that she might have been well acquainted with being approached by men.............

But, here's where the story gets to be a bit more interesting; she said to Him; "How is it that you being a Jew, ask of me for a drink from the well? You know that the Jews have no dealings with the people of Samaria!" They're Prejudice! They're Ugly Towards us! Bottom Line is; They Don't Like Us!

Blind Sight

The Light of First Sight Recognition

WE CAN NEVER AFFORD OURSELVES TO FORGET THE FACT THAT JESUS IS THE WALKING, TALKING, LIVING WORD OF GOD MADE FLESH, AMONG HUMANITY.

HE IS THE WORD OF GOD; LIVING AND ALIVE, AT THIS TIME OF THE SCRIPTURAL ACCOUNT; HE IS EMANUEL (GOD WITH US). HERE WE SEE THAT JESUS WAS NOT A PLAYER OR A PIMP; HAD IT BEEN SO, PERHAPS HE WOULD HAVE HAD THIS EASY WOMAN FOR TIME OF SINFUL PLEASURE; BUT, THANK GOD, JESUS IS THE LIGHT OF THE WORLD. HE CAME TO FREE HER, AND ALL OF SAMARIA................

THIS WOMAN WAS WELL AWARE OF THE INSTALLED OBSTRUCTIONS AMONG THE SOCIABLE SOCIETY OF THE JEWS, RELATIVE TO THEIR DEALINGS WITH THE SAMARITANS.

JESUS TOOK HER MIND BY STORM; WHEN HE OPENED HIS MOUTH, THE LIGHT OF CHRIST LEAPED INTO HER MIND, AND ALL OF A SUDDEN SHE BEGAN THE THINK DIFFERENTLY ABOUT THE GENTLEMAN WHICH HAD HER ATTENTION.

THE JOY OF THE LORD, LEAPED INTO HER BELLY, AND SHE BURNED WITH CONVICTION AS JESUS SPOKE WITH HER.

HAD THE WOMAN OF SAMARIA, RECOGNIZED JESUS THE CHRIST SITTING ON

Hidden In the Light*

THE WELL, SHE WOULD HAVE BEEN FIRST TO ASK FOR A DRINK; HER INSIGHT WOULD HAVE ALLOWED HER TO REALIZE THAT JESUS IS THE LIVING WATER OF SALVATION FOR ALL MANKIND.

THE INFINITE LOVE OF GOD, BEING ALL OMNISCIENT; HE ALREADY KNEW THE DESIRES OF HER HEART, AND EVEN THAT PERHAPS SHE DID NOT KNOW HOW TO ASK, OR THAT SHE EVEN NEEDED TO ASK THE LORD TO FILL THE LONGING OF HER THIRSTY SOUL.

JESUS BEING THE LIGHT OF THE WORLD, COULD SEE THAT THIS DARKENED INDIVIDUAL NEEDED DESPERATELY TO BE ILLUMINATED IN THE ANNALS OF HER MIND. HE CHOSE NOT TO LEAVE HER IN THE DARKNESS OF HER OWN MIND; AND THANK GOD, HE TURNED THE LIGHT ON IN HER SPIRIT, SOUL AND BODY, OF WHICH IMMEDIATELY REACHED THE INNER-CHAMBERS OF HER MIND.

AS JESUS BEGAN TO TELL THIS WOMAN ABOUT HERSELF AND HER PAST BEHAVIOR, IT WASN'T FOR THE PURPOSE OF DEGRADING HER, NOR WAS IT FOR THE PURPOSE TO FURTHER CONDEMN HER! SHE WAS ALREADY CONDEMNED, AND IN NEED FOR THE SAVIOR OF THE WORLD TO CHANGE HER LIFE BY SAVING HER SOUL.

I LIKE THE WAY THAT JESUS TOLD THE SAMARITAN WOMAN THE QUESTION THAT SHE

Blind Sight

SHOULD HAVE BEEN ASKING HIM, BY WAY OF ASKING HER THE EXACT SAME QUESTION.

HE EVEN SAYS TO HER, IF YOU KNEW THE GIFT OF GOD AND THE SAVIOR WHO STANDS BEFORE YOU NOW, YOU WOULD ASK OF ME FOR A DRINK! WE AS PEOPLE ARE OFTEN COMING BEFORE THE LORD THINKING THAT WE HAVE THE ANSWERS. WE EVEN FEEL AS THOUGH WE KNOW EXACTLY WHAT TO SAY IN THE PRESENCE OF THE LORD; BUT WE ONLY KNOW WHAT TO SAY WHENEVER THE LORD GIVE US THE WORDS.

THE 8TH CHAPTER OF ROMANS, EVEN TELLS US THAT WE DON'T EVEN KNOW WHAT TO PRAY FOR AS WE REALLY OUGHT TO KNOW. BUT, HE WHO KNOWS ALL THINGS, KNOW AT ALL TIME WHAT IS THE MIND OF THE SPIRIT OF THE LORD; AS A RESULT HE MAKES AN INTERCESSION FOR US WITH A DIALOGUE OF HEAVEN THAT COULD NEVER BE UTTERED IN ANY OF THE INADEQUATE WORDS OF OUR OWN FAMILIAR SPEECH. HE HAS TO SPEAK TO THE FATHER FOR US, ON OUR OWN BEHALF. THAT'S AWESOME!

JESUS INFORMS THE SAMARITAN, THAT THE DRINK THAT SHE WAS INDEED OFFERING TO GIVE AS A RESULT OF THE LORD'S REQUEST, THAT IT WAS INDEED INSUFFICIENT TO THE ACTUAL ETERNAL NEEDS OF OUR SOUL'S THIRST. HE DID NOT LEAVE HER THERE BASKING IN

Hidden In the Light*

the fact that her offering was inadequate, even at His request. His true purpose was to inform her of His true offering and purpose for even being in Samaria.

Notice that Jesus was standing before both the blind man whose eyes were healed, and the Samaritan woman. They both received miracle blessings from the Lord Jesus Christ.

When the blind mans eyes were opened, it was not even Jesus that he was trying to see, nor even desiring others to see; he was still trying to see the other men of his own equal comparison, the initial description of his seeing experience was of men. Perhaps it was because men brought him to Jesus?

The Samaritan woman's seeing experience of the same savior of the world, sent her running, in a hurry to tell other men to come and see a man, who told me everything that I have ever done!

Her desire was for other men to see Jesus, who could change their lives forever. She brought other men to Jesus!

She actually stood alone, by herself

whenever she met the Lord Jesus. On the other hand, Jesus separated the blind man from the crowd of people, and took him to be alone with Jesus.

The crowd can often hinder you from seeing the light of the Lord, but being alone with the Lord, you can often cause the crowd to see the light of the Lord.

See For Yourself *****

We that are attuned to the spirit of the Lord, encounter people everyday that are blindly obstructed by the crowds of people in certain denominations and churches, who cannot see the Lord for adherence to the installed systems of the churches or the church's denomination.

I am even hearing too often, that the churches are allowing the marriages in the congregations to fall apart, without any necessary efforts to see those who have been joined together by God, that their relationships never be put asunder. Blind sight says that perhaps you just married the wrong person, and all it is that you need to do

Hidden In the Light*

is to just get rid of them and get a new spouse.

In such situations as these, it is obvious that the light of the candle stick in the house if God has been extinguished! Those who came together in marriage, did so seeking the Lord for an approval of the person of which they were intent on marrying.

Many of the married couples were not even originally members of the churches where they eventually split up as a couple, they happen to move their worship experience to those certain ministries.

Never allow any particular church or denomination to take hold of you, to the point that you no longer have the same respect for your spouse that you have always observed!

Even if the both of you were unsaved when you got married, don't get it twisted, God would rather see the both of you be saved, sanctified, and filled with the Holy Ghost, rather than to see the both of you in divorce court, dissolving your marriage, because one of you have gotten saved, and your church thinks that your unsaved spouse is holding you back.

Blind Sight

Don't be so easily blinded by what you think that you see in the relationship of someone else in the church.

The truth is that, you really don't know as much about the other couple as you might think! Many have learned to respect each other, as a result of haven been so disrespectful to one another in past times.

I know that it looks like the other couple have such a better relationship than your own, but what you can't see is the hard work that they each had to put into the relationship, to keep it from falling apart. You don't know the personal temptations that they each may have had to overcome, in an effort to be true to one another.

You don't even know the many times that they have had to forgive one another. In the natural recourse of a marriage relationship, somebody will get offended at one time or another, whether the offense was intended or unintentional.

Most couples would have been split

Hidden In the Light*

right up the middle had they focused on the offenses of their spouses, and had not kept their focus on the love and the commitment of their marriage.

Most of us who have been married for 25 years and more, have to tell you that we are still together by the grace of God.

It's a blessing to have others look at your relationship, and desire to model their own relationship after your own, but, how about flipping the switch to your insight, to see that perhaps if you give the wrong advice, or allow yourself to be put on a pedal stool as if to be the king and the queen of marriage, you just might be allowing the younger couple to fall apart.

You know the truth about your marriage, and your ability to stay together, through all of the ups and the downs of life.

Married couples don't think and act just alike right off, it takes at least the first 15 years of living together consistently, studying one another, serving one another and simply desiring

Blind Sight

and admiring one another in spite of the flaws, and any disappointments.

No two people are exactly alike anyway, so you have to understand that there will be differences in a marriage relationship, but you have to be determined to turn your bumps into bricks and build on your marriage.

God, in His infinite wisdom, He loves us too much to give us a spouse that is exactly just like us! Opposites attract for a purpose, and for a reason that will not be immediately understood or realized, until the undivided attentive time has been spent together, bonding and knitting yourselves together.

Sometimes there are others that can see that your spouse has a visible error attached to themselves, but never allow what someone else sees in your spouse to be the defining factor of the strength of your relationship.

A cunning spirit will tell you all of the things that they may see in your spouse that they don't like, but, they won't tell you all of things that they see in your spouse that they like very well!

Hidden In the Light*

Never let anyone see more good in your own spouse than you, because they really don't know about your lover like you do.

Sometimes, it may even be your own family members that are blasting your spouse; open your own eyes and see them for yourself.

Everybody did not go to the alter with you to make your marriage commitment, so all of the others, with the exception of the marriage counselors, should be left on the outside of your marriage relationship. All pastors are not equipped to counsel your marriage, especially whenever they are leaving their own spouses for a member of the congregation.

You need even to see clearly into the lives of those persons of which you enquire of counsel. I have fallen in love with Psalms 1:, whenever we read in between the lines of the Psalm, it is clearly admonishing us to see into the lives of those who offer to give us counsel.

Those of us who choose to see for our selves will be happier a greater percentage of the time over those who have taken faulty and erroneous advice

Blind Sight

FROM SOURCES THAT HAVE NEVER BEEN ORDAINED BY GOD.

> *Blessed is the man that walketh not in the counsel of the ungodly, nor standeth in the way of sinners, nor sitteth in the seat of the scornful. But his delight is in the law of the Lord; and in his law doth he meditate day and night. And he shall be like a tree planted by the rivers of water, that bringeth forth his fruit in his season; his leaf also shall not wither; and whatsoever he doeth shall prosper.*   *Psalms 1: 1-3*

NOW WOULD BE A GOOD TIME TO MAKE UP IN YOUR MIND WHETHER OR NOT YOU ARE WILLING TO BE IN THE POSITION OF THE BLIND MAN, OR THE SAMARITAN WOMAN AT THE WELL. EVERYBODY BROUGHT THE BLIND MAN TO JESUS, BECAUSE HE COULD NOT SEE THE LORD FOR HIMSELF, AND NEITHER COULD HE HAVE COME TO THE LORD ALL BY HIMSELF.

AS A RESULT, THERE WAS STILL OBSTRUCTIONS IN THE WAY THAT KEPT THE BLIND MAN, BLIND STILL; EVEN THOUGH JESUS HAD HEALED HIS SIGHT. THE LORD TOUCHED HIM THE SECOND TIME! UPON THE SECOND TOUCH, THE BLIND MAN CAME FORTH NOW SEEING FOR HIMSELF!

ALTHOUGH THE BLIND MAN CAME FORTH SEEING THE SECOND TIME, WE NEVER HEAR OF HIM BRINGING OTHERS TO THE LORD, TO RECEIVE THE HEALING THAT HE, HIMSELF HAD RECEIVED!

Hidden In the Light*

Even upon receiving his sight, we don't read where he acknowledge Jesus, or that he either worshipped Him. Jesus, eventually sent him away, back to his own home, and even charged him that he tell no one of the miracle that he had received.

The Samaritan woman, respectively, she caught the vision of Jesus, and determined that He was too wonderful to be kept in the secret seclusion of her own personal discovery.

She knew that Jesus would better serve the need of the Samaritan community, if she shared the news of Him among the people.

You must be able to see for your own self, before you will ever be successful sharing the blessing of the Gospel of Christ to any people.

Chapter 10

*But; I See Me***

Really Me, You See?

OVER THE LAST 20 YEARS, I HAVE BECOME AWARE OF JUST HOW UNNECESSARY IT IS TO ANSWER TO RUMORS AND OPINIONATED REPORTS WHENEVER THE PERSON TALKING TO ME, HAD ALREADY BELIEVED THE PRECEDING REPORT GIVEN BY ANOTHER PERSON.

I'VE BEEN CONFRONTED WITH PEOPLE WHO UPON THEIR FIRST TIME EVER EVEN SPEAKING TO ME, THEY HAD THE NERVE TO LOOK ME IN THE FACE AND TO SAY TO ME, "I KNOW YOU!"

UPON SHAKING HANDS WITH SOME

Hidden In the Light*

PEOPLE, THEY WANT YOU TO KNOW THAT THEY ALREADY KNOW ALL ABOUT YOU. IF YOU STOP TO LISTEN TO THEM FOR A MOMENT OR TWO, THEY WILL EVEN GIVE UP THEIR INFORMANT, AND THE DETAILS ABOUT YOU THAT THEY BELIEVE THAT THEY HAVE LEARNED. SOMETIMES PEOPLE ARE SO MISINFORMED THAT THEY ARE NOT GOING TO ALLOW YOU TO CORRECT ANY MISINFORMATION THAT THEY HAVE RECEIVED.

THOSE PERSONS HAD NEVER BEEN GIVEN THE OPPORTUNITY TO BE PERSONALLY ACQUAINTED WITH ME, NOT EVEN FOR TEN MINUTES! YET THEY FELT THAT THEY KNEW ME AND WERE ABLE TO GIVE AN ACCOUNT OF SOME CIRCUMSTANCE OR EVENT THAT HAD TAKEN PLACE IN MY LIFE.

PERHAPS THEY HEARD SOMETHING THAT HAD TAKEN PLACE WITH ME, BUT THAT DID NOT GIVE THEM THE RIGHT TO SAY THAT THEY KNEW ME, FOR WHO I AM!

CERTAIN PEOPLE WHO RECOGNIZED MY FACE, MISINTERPRETED MY PURPOSE, AND HAVE GIVEN INACCURATE ACCOUNTS OF MY PRESENCE, BY THE SLEIGHT OF THEIR OWN MISGUIDED PERCEPTIONS!

PEOPLE YET OBLIVIOUS TO THEIR OWN BEHAVIORAL PROTOTYPE, SPEND COUNTLESS

But, I See Me

HOURS TRYING TO GIVE CREDIBILE DEFINITION TO SOMEONE ELSE'S CHARACTER. WHEN CALLED INTO QUESTION, THEY ARE INDIGENT TO SPEAK-UP FOR THEMSELVES, YET THEY ARE PREOCCUPIED WITH THE CHRONICLED, DELINEATE BEHAVIOR OF SOMEONE ELSES.

SADLY, PEOPLE TAKE THE GOSSIPPING ACCOUNTS OF THOSE WHO ARE SPREADING OTHER PEOPLES BUSINESS IN THE BODY OF CHRIST AND IN THE STREETS, TO BE AN INTRODUCTORY ACCOUNT, THAT MAKES THEM PERSONALLY ACQUAINTED WITH THE PEOPLE BEING TALKED ABOUT.

IT'S NOT GODLY, OR CHRIST-LIKE TO ONLY THINK THAT YOU SEE, OR THAT YOU KNOW, OR TO EVEN BELIEVE THAT YOU PROBABLY HAVE AN ACCURATE ACCOUNT OF A PARTICULAR EVENT OR CIRCUMSTANCE, WHILE NEVER HAVING FOUND ANY OF THE KNOWLEDGE THAT YOU DO HAVE TO ACTUALLY BE FOUND PROVEN.

How do you know?

HOW DO YOU KNOW THAT WHAT YOU MIGHT HAVE SEEN, IS ACTUALLY WHAT YOU SAW?

Hidden In the Light*

Truly seeing requires reliable character traits, skills of visibility, and of course conversational integrity, that all work together consegatively within the one who reports to haven seen.

These proper elements are necessary for the purpose of lending credible validation to the establishment of trust, laying a knowledgeable foundation to authenticate knowing for sure.

People have come to the point of understanding that a much more thorough evaluation and careful analysis should be given to the cited matter if they are going to be accurate reporting what they porported to have witnessed.

Carefully viewing alone, does not lend a reason of explanation, but knowing what you really did see will aid in evaluating the given reasons for the action, or event when they are given. Anyone as intelligent as yourself would want to be for certain that you were not being deceptive or deceived, even on an accident.

If you were ever called into

But, I See Me

questioned to give a deposition of you own witnessed account, you would find the examination by the police or a judge to be extensive and thorough.

Looking or Seeing?

I went to renew my driver's license, where I was given an eye exam for the purpose of accurately judging distances and being able to communicate with other drivers. I was asked to look into a viewing machine, and to describe what I saw. What I was looking at was really not what I was actually seeing! Ha Ha!.........

Either my mind or my eyes were playing tricks on me, which in turn did not allow me to actually see the things that I was supposed to be seeing.

Whenever I finished viewing the screen, I felt as if the letters and the numbers on the screen were laughing at me, as if to suggest that I had not been educated to definitively comprehend.

I could not even give the slightest definition of what I saw. It happens to the very best of individuals, for any

Hidden In the Light*

UNCERTAIN NUMBER OF REASONS.

Good intentions just will not do, when you should have gone all of the way to see the necessary things that actually yield the defining qualities in the life of an individual.

Maybe you didn't mean to be judgmental or degrading of another individual based on whatever you might have seen, but how often have things come out that way whenever you rush to verbally divulge what you thought you might have seen?

In middle school, we did an experiment in a science class. The teacher flashed a picture of an automobile, but only for a chance to glance at it. Some said the car was red, while others said that it was orange, a third color might have been in the family of fusia, or pink.

We soon discovered that the color of the automobile strongly depended upon the person viewing the photo.

Everybody looking, don't always see the very same thing at any given time. The cause may very well be that everyone

But, I See Me

is not even looking for the very same thing, or that everyone has a different level of viewing comprehensiveness.

I preached a message once about 25 ago, titled "Looking Too Hard To See"! You know some people look at a half glass of water, and call if only half full, while the other person looks at the glass and right away pronounces the glass to be half empty.

Some people see the color of black, while others only see the absence of any white or bright colors. One person sees darkness, while another person sees the absence of any light as a result of the presence of the darkness.

Lookers and watchers!

Looker-*1 A person who looks at.*
2 U.S. Slang-For good looking;
an attractive person.

Look not thou upon the wine when it is red, when it giveth his colour in the cup, when it moveth itself aright.
PROVERBS 23:31

A looker is defined on both sides of seeing, as being one who is looked at,

Hidden In the Light*

and one who takes the time to look. A good-looking person, doesn't necessarily take the time to look good, or even to take a good look!

Looking, only requires a very minimal shallow effort to glance or to bring into focus the thing to be visualized. You can actually look but never see, lacking the determinate desire to scan the surface of a matter, to evaluate the projected image.

Most lookers, go with whatever they see at a glance. We are too tolerant of mistakes made when looking, because we fail to apply the excellence of God, our Father; being human.

The written admonition of the scripture, does not suggest that red is a bad color, or that it is not a good color for wine. The hidden wisdom advises against being deceived by the beauty of the color itself, thus rendering ourselves vulnerable to the fully deceptive intoxicating power of the wine.

There is usually more to actually see, than whatever you might be looking at.

But the Lord said unto Samuel, Look not on the countenance, or on the height of his stature; for the Lord seeth not as man seeth; for man looketh on the outward appearance, but the Lord looketh on the heart.

I SAMUEL 16:7

Look Like God***

GOD HAS SHOWED US THROUGH THE BIBLE, HOW TO ACQUIRE THE PROPER ACCURACY OF EXCELLENCE. IT IS BENEFICIAL TO TAKE ADVANTAGE OF UNDERSTANDING, THAT GOD KNOWS WHAT IT TAKES FOR US TO OPERATE AT OPTIMUM SPIRITUALITY, DISCERNING WHAT WE MAY SEE IN THE LIVES OF OTHERS.

YOU HAVE THE ABILITY TO LOOK LIKE GOD, BEING SURRENDERED TO THE WILL OF THE LORD, ALLOWING THE LORD TO BE THE HEAD OF YOUR LIFE!

GOD LOOKS PAST THE SURFACE EXTERIOR, STRAIGHT TO THE CORE DRIVING FORCE THAT GENERATES THE MOTIVATIONAL PULL ON THE INSIDE OF YOU. GOD DESIRES THE DRIVING FORCE OF EVERY INDIVIDUAL TO BE WORD OF GOD, AND THE INDWELLING POWER OF THE HOLY GHOST!

GOD HAS FIRSTLY, TO PUT HIMSELF INTO EVERYONE OF US. THERE IS NO WAY TO BE LIKE GOD, WITHOUT GOD. SEEING LIKE

Hidden In the Light*

God requires the acquisition and maintainance of godly characteristics, to properly handle what is seen.

Based on the characteristics of Saul, Samuel, would have made a judgment of what he felt God would see in a king, whenever he looked at the sons of Jesse.

Saul was head and shoulders above everybody in the camp of the tribes of Israel and Judah. He was also a very handsome man, which might have given indication to Samuel, that he knew exactly what God would be looking for in a replacement for king.

God looks through the eternal presence of an individual, although that individual may not have reached the desired potential development for whatever God sees in their life.

God sees whatever He has already fashioned and made of our lives, and never does God only see in the realm of a desire for an individual's future. Whatever God desired, He said; "Let There Be", and it was so, even to this very day! Our purpose was also included in God's desires, so He has already said

LIKEWISE; "IT IS SO!"

GOD'S FUTURE, IS, HIS PRESENCE! WHATEVER WE WILL BE IN THE LORD, IS ALREADY SO BECAUSE, EVERYTHING IS ALREADY IN THE LORD, RIGHT NOW! GOD IS NEVER IN THE POSITION OF GOING BACK TO REDO WHATEVER HE HAD ALREADY DONE.

SINCE GOD DOES IT RIGHT FROM THE BEGINNING, YOU CAN NEVER BE TRAPPED INTO BEING SOMETHING YOU WERE NEVER CREATED OR INTENDED TO BE FROM THE BEGINNING OF GOD'S INITIAL PLAN, UNLESS YOU WILL IT TO BE SO.

SO WHENEVER SAMUEL FINALLY LOOKED UPON DAVID, HE KNEW THAT THIS WAS THE ONE INDEED CHOSEN TO BE THE KING OF ALL OF ISRAEL AND JUDAH.

SAMUEL, SAW THE RADIANT ANOINTED PURPOSE EMANATING FROM THE RUDDY LITTLE SHEPPARD BOY. THE LAD WAS ALREADY THE KING, BECAUSE THE KING WAS ALREADY IN THE LAD!

THE MAN IS ALREADY IN THE LITTLE BOY, EVEN AS THE WOMAN IS ALREADY IN THE LITTLE GIRL. BOYS AND GIRLS WOULD NEVER DEVELOP INTO ADULT MEN AND WOMEN, AND PRODUCE OTHER LITTLE BOYS AND GIRLS, WHENEVER THEY COME TOGETHER AS ONE IN MARRIAGE.

Hidden In the Light*

The big tree is already in the little sapling because the little sapling is already in the seed of the big tree! It only takes a span of time for the one to develope and to manifest into the other.

It may appear that God looks from a reversal perspective, or maybe even from the rear?

If you feel that God's way is backwards, then my friend you do not look like God at all. God starts from the finished end, back to the ignited start.

Do you really believe that God could chance anyone us developing into whatever He purposed for us, further allowing us to discover our way through divine intervention, without His initial input?

We see tragedies developed daily, as a result of our own humanistic input into the developmental schemes of things that we desire, because of failure to ask God to show us what He's already made, first!

Not even the Lord can change the minds of certain people, relative of what they might think about you. Because whenever they look into your direction they look through the shades that have been installed and pulled down ever since the time they saw you sin. They refuse to ever see you clearly, again!

A Broken Reflection!

To reflect- is to go back to the original source to acknowledge that which has already taken place. God designed us to be reflective to the original composite structure and spiritual portrait of His creation. He's our Father..............

Our earthly parents expect to see the like images and features of themselves in the behavior patterns of their children. It is necessary to see the likeness of themselves in the portrait image of the lives that they have given birth to.

Parents can expect to see the family resemblence and likeness relative to the genetic code on either side of the family. Now, when the father of the child is not who it is suppose to be, it is evident at the time of the birth of the child.

Hidden In the Light*

The expected reflection of who the child should have been is broken, leaving the desired hopes for the father of the child, shattered to pieces!

What we present whenever we look into a mirror, is the exact projection to be sent right back to us immediately, without any obscurity.

Unless there is something wrong with the mirror itself, the projection of the object has to obey the mirrored command and respond with the reciprocated reposition, to the lighted image.

Mirrors have the power to redirect the image back in the very direction of which it originally came from. The creator of the mirror had to understand the return of a projected image in its exact original likeness, for the purpose of sending it back to the projector.

Mirrors don't work properly in the dark, and they don't even work at all where there is no illumination. No one can see the likeness of an image if there is no light to thrust the likeness of the image with the speed of the light into

But, I See Me

THE MIRROR, FOR THE PROJECTED IMAGE TO BE VISIBLY RETURNED?

There are many contributing factors to be taken into consideration that might possibly render a broken reflection! A cracked mirror does not have the power to stop the image from being reflected or even reposed.

Let's suppose that a mirror has been broken into many pieces, even a small fragment of the mirror still has the power of reflection. If you pick up the fragmented piece of the mirror, you would yet be able to view a projected image.

Should the entire glass of the mirror remain in tact, but removing the shiny surface of the mirror behind the glass, the power to reflect an image will also be removed.

Light passes right through glass, as water passes through a screen, being fill with many tiny little holes. The power to trap and to reflect the light, would be alleviated from the mirror, thus creating a broken reflection.

Should there be an obscurity in front of the mirror, blocking the image

Hidden In the Light*

TO BE REFLECTED THERE IS NO REPOSITION OF THE IMAGE EVEN IN THE SLIGHTEST. BEFORE BEING COMPELLED TO LOOK INTO THE MIRROR FOR THE PURPOSE OF CAPTURING AN IMAGE, THERE MUST BE A WORKING REFLECTION.

HAVE YOU EVER ENTERED A BUILDING OR A HOME, ONLY TO NOTICE A MIRROR RIGHT IN FRONT OF YOU? DID YOU REALIZE THAT YOUR AUTOMATIC RESPONSE WAS TO LOOK INTO THE MIRROR?

YOU CAN NEVER PRESENT WHAT YOU WANT TO BE ONE DAY, OR A MAKE BELIEVE IMAGE OF YOURSELF, AND SEE THAT HYPOTHETICAL IMAGE REPOSED.

Perhaps A Broken Image ?

NATURALLY THINKING WITH OUR CARNAL MINDS, WE MIGHT BE MOST APT TO BELIEVE THAT WHAT WAS INDEED MARRED, BROKEN, OR EVEN DISTORTED WAS THE MIRROR, BECAUSE THERE COULD JUST BE NOTHING WRONG WITH OUR REFLECTED IMAGE, WE LIKE TO PROJECT THAT WE ARE FLAWLESS.

For the wrath of God is revealed from Heaven against all ungodliness and unrighteousness of men, who hold the truth in unrighteousness; Because that which may be known of God is manifest in them; for God hath

But, I See Me

showed it unto them. For the invisible things of him from the creation of the world are clearly seen, being understood by the things that are made, even his eternal power and Godhead; so that they are without excuse: Because that, when they knew God, they glorified him not as God, neither were thankful; but became vain in their imaginations, and their foolish heart were darkened.   Romans 1:18-21

GOD, PROJECTED HIMSELF IN TRUTH TO THESE MEN OF UNRIGHTEOUSNESS, BUT THEY CHOSE TO IGNORE THE PROJECTED IMAGE OF CHRIST, SO THAT THEY WOULD NOT HAVE TO REPOSE THE CHRISTIAN LIKENESS IN THEIR BEHAVIOR.

COMMON SENSE, TELLS US THAT THE ORIGINAL CONDITION OF THE PROJECTED IMAGE CAN NEVER BE REFLECTED IN ANY OTHER MANNER OTHER THAN ITS ACTUAL CONDITION. THE IMAGE COMMANDS AND DEMANDS THE EXACT REPOSED IMMEDIATELY FOLLOWING IT'S INSTANTANEOUS PROJECTION.

MIRROR, AND CAMERA LENSES, DON'T EVER LIE! WHATEVER THE MIRROR OR THE CAMERA SEES, IS WHAT THEY SHOW IN REFLECTION OF THE MIRROR OR THE AFFIXED IMAGE OF THE PICTURE.

CAMERAS NEVER FIX PICTURES, JUST LIKE MIRRORS DON'T FIX ANY IMAGES.

Hidden In the Light*

Photographers fix photos sometimes to remove scars and blotches, bumps and bruises, and even to alter the size and the shape of an individual or an object.

70's comedian, "Flip Wilson" used to say; "What Cha See Is What Cha Get!" People say the same thing today, but without the integrity to mean those words!

They're well aware that they don't mean what they are saying, but in an attempt to be reticent, they still utter those words.

You can never dispise God, both figuratively and literally speaking. In order to develop the likeness of seeing things the way that God sees them, there has be a true love and reverence for God.

Sometimes, we look into the mirror and simply choose to forget what the mirror actually revealed. This is the reason that we will rush to correct what may have been deemed as being wrong with us, as if we have the power to do so.

Many things, which may be beyond the scope of our control, are usually the

THINGS THAT WE HURRY TO IGNORE OR TO ALTOGETHER DENY THE REALITY OF THOSE THINGS, AND THE NEED FOR REPARATIONS!

Who Turned Out The Lights?

DO YOU REMEMBER WHENEVER YOU WERE STANDING IN THE FRONT OF THE MIRROR PREPARING YOURSELF SO THAT EVERYTHING WOULD BE IN PLACE, AND ALL OF A SUDDEN, SOMEBODY TURNED OUT THE LIGHTS?

CAN YOU REMEMBER HOW QUICKLY THE IMAGE OF YOURSELF FADED, EVEN THOUGH YOU MAY HAVE BEEN STANDING THERE BEFORE THE MIRROR FOR A WHILE?

WHENEVER THE LIGHTS WERE TURNED OUT, YOU IMMEDIATELY DEMANDED FOR THE LIGHT SWITCH TO BE TURNED ON AGAIN SO THAT YOU COULD SEE. DON'T REMAIN IN DARKNESS JUST BECAUSE SOMEONE HAS TURNED OUT THE LIGHTS, IN ONE WAY OR ANOTHER, MAYBE EVEN CAUSING A MOMENTARY SENSE OF BLINDNESS.

CAN YOU REMEMBER WHEN SOMEONE CREPT UP BEHIND YOU AND PLACED THEIR HANDS OVER YOUR EYES, TO BLOCK OUT BOTH THE LIGHT AND THE MIRROR?

IN EL PASO, TEXAS, WHENEVER A

Hidden In the Light*

BIRTHDAY CELEBRATION FOR A CHILD WAS GIVEN, THE CHILD WOULD BE BLINDFOLDED AND SPUN AROUND FOR SEVERAL ROTATIONS, THEN RELEASED TO SWING WITH A STICK AT A HANGING PINNATTE.

BEING BLINDFOLDED AND SPUN AROUND CERTAINLY HAMPERED THE ABILITY TO SEE AND TO HIT THE TARGET. NO ONE COULD NOT EXPECT IMMEDIATE RESULTS IN THAT CONDITION!

IN EITHER, OF THE THREE SITUATIONS, THE LIGHTS WERE TURNED OUT MOMENTARILY, DEBILITATING THE ABILITY TO SEE RIGHT THEN AND THERE. BUT THAT DID NOT ENSURE THAT SEEING WOULD BE PERMANENTLY LOST AS RESULT OF HAVING BEEN MOMENTARILY OBSCURED.

IN THE PRESENCE OF WHAT IS BELIEVED TO BE A TWO-SIDED MIRROR, THERE ARE TWO MIRRORS, PLACED BACK-TO-BACK, AFFIXED TO EACH OTHER, TO PROVIDE A REFLECTION ON EITHER SIDE. WE ARE NOT ABLE TO SEE ON BOTH SIDES OF THE MIRROR.

YOU CAN WALK FROM ONE SIDE TO THE NEXT AND SEE YOUR REFLECTION ON EITHER SIDE OF THE TWO CONJOINED MIRRORS, AS LONG AS EITHER MIRROR IS IN WORKING ORDER.

Seeing On Both Sides!

Samson was a Nazarene champion, who could at times, see his enemies coming from afar off. Samson recognized a challenge and clearly discerned the times for battle with the Philistines.

Samson, also paid attention to good looking women, but his problem was that he looked in both camps. He looked within the camp of his own people and he wondered into the camp of the Philistines, to look at those beautiful women, also.

Samson often found himself in the middle of a skirmish with his enemies, not always being aware that he had been spotted off of his gaurd, whenever they caught him looking over on their side.

Consistently looking in the direction of others, failing to be watchful of oneself, has the ability to expose the vulnerability on the inside of you, yourselves, being preoccupied with seeing a side other than your own.

The people you're looking at, have the equal advantage to look right back

Hidden In the Light*

AT YOU. DEPENDING ON YOUR VANTAGE POINT, THEIR OBSERVATION OF YOU MAY BE CLEARER, AND MORE TELLING, THAN THE WATCHFUL SCOPE OF YOUR AFFIXED, JUDGMENTAL SIGHT!

SAMSON TRAVELED FOR MILES INTO THE ENEMY'S TERRITORY, BECAUSE DELILAH CAUGHT HIS EYE! DELILAH WAS QUITE BEAUTIFUL AND WELL PUT TOGETHER. ANY MAN WOULD STARE AND DESIRE THE COMPANY OF SUCH A FINE SISTER.

SHE LOOKED GOOD ENOUGH TO CAUSE THE NAZARITE CHAMPION WARRIOR, TO RELAX IN THE LAP OF THIS DECEITFUL LUSCIOUS BEAUTY, ONLY TO DISCOVER THAT THE VISION OF HIS OWN STARE HAD BEEN OBSCOURED. HE DIDN'T SEE WHAT HE SHOULD HAVE SEEN AND IT COST HIM DEARLY!

SAMSON TAUGHT US A VALUABLE LESSON ABOUT BEING TAKEN IN BY WHAT WE RECOGNIZE AS BEING ATTRACTIVE, AS THE ATTRACTIVENESS IS ONLY ON THE SURFACE AND SKIN DEEP!

SAMSON LIKED WHAT HE SAW AND RELAXED A BIT TOO MUCH, LETTING HIS GUARD DOWN (FIGURATIVELY SPEAKING), ON THE ENEMY'S BATTLEFIELD. HE ACTUALLY LAID DOWN ONLY TO BE AWAKENED BY THE THREAT of the Philistines being upon him.

This woman, was an enemy in disguise..........................

Looking To Trust!

You can never relax in the arms of the enemy because the enemy will never be at ease concerning you. Your enemy will always be on alert, waiting on the right moment to do you in.

Delilah knew that Samson was taken by her beauty and that his love for her had created an obscurity in his vision, allowing him to think that he had a comfort zone in her presence, leaving him dangerously vulnerable to his enemies.

She coaxed and beguiled Samson until the concealed covenant of his strength was disclosed to her, a divine secret she should never have known.

He un-doubtingly denied the prompting of the spirit of the Lord telling him to flee the youthful lust for this beautiful woman. He was too busy looking to actually see that she was dangerous.

Hidden In the Light*

I'm sure that Samson believed that Delilah could be trusted to forsake the fact that she was indeed a Philistine, forgetting the fact the he had destroyed the Philistines on many occasions. Well she could not be trusted, in spite of her innocent face and her beautiful physique.

The Philistines hurried to put out the eyes of Samson, as soon as he was in their captivity?

Samson's enemies would never allow him to see them again, but neither would they be seeing him either, because they all died together when God allowed Samson to avenge himself of his enemies.

I'd like to think that Samson was cited as a looker and a seer to the point that the Philistines feared his ability to see whatever he truly focused upon!

Samson's enemies were not going to allow him to return to his own camp to regain any since of strength that he might have lost, or to strengthen his ability to see once again.

He saw his way into their camp, but he would never be able to find his way out of their camp.

What Are You Looking At!

People do not always establish a legitimate reason for looking in the direction of another individual. They don't always tell you what it is that has got their attention fixed on you.

Their reason may be something that you really might not want to even be made aware of, considering the nature of their negative thought process!

Has anyone ever told you something and as soon as they had finished speaking with you, you wished that they did even know that you even existed on the face of the earth?

Some things that people say, will leave you in a tail spend, spiraling downward without the strength to pull up from the decline, being that the very nature of their information was so degrading.

Lots of people will say that you had better care about what other people think about you! But that advise is to be taken in the proper context with a grain of salt in every individual situation.

Hidden In the Light*

The very people who are not even qualified to make an opinionated assumption, are the very ones always forming an opinion and passing it on to be received as a legitimate newsreel from **HEAVEN! BULLETIN!! BULLETIN!!!**

When I say that I see me, I totally understand what I am saying to you. In spite of what people may think they see in me, no one sees me, like me! Some will fabricate or even exaggerate a story to arouse the interest of other people, but, I See Me!

I was never even concerned about those individuals, and could have cared less of whatever they might have been thinking about me.

I am not speaking in terms of psychosomatically deranged people or mentally challenged people who are slow to comprehend, I am speaking in reference to people who have not given themselves to the personal evaluation of self and the word of God.

Some people really become unrattled, and they get dangerously upset, whenever they notice that others are looking at them, even to the point

OF STARING IN THEIR DIRECTION. THERE ARE SOME PEOPLE THAT WILL DO YOU BODILY HARM, AND EVEN TAKE YOUR LIFE BECAUSE OF YOUR FOCAL AFFIXATION UPON THEM, FOR TOO LONG.

OFTEN TIMES, AS PEOPLE ARE LOOKING AT YOU, THEY BECOME SO AFFIXED IN OBSERVANCE OF YOUR EVERY MOVE THAT THEY FAIL TO NOTICE THAT YOU ARE ALSO LOOKING RIGHT BACK AT THEM. THEY DIDN'T EVEN NOTICE THAT YOU HAD NOTICED THEM LOOKING AT YOU.

YOU CAN NEVER KNOW WHAT IS ON THE INSIDE, LOOKING FROM THE OUTSIDE, FEELING THAT YOU HAVE MADE SOME TYPE OF AN ACTUAL DISCOVERY. SEEING WHAT A PERSON DOES, WON'T NECESSARILY ALLOW YOU TO KNOW WHO THAT PERSON IS!

Nothing Wrong With My Vision!

BUT I SEE ME! I KNOW WHO I AM BOTH IN THE NATURAL AND IN THE SPIRITUAL REALM. I AM NOT ASHAMED OF ME.

OTHER PEOPLE WILL TRY TO PSYCH YOU TO BELIEVE THEY HAD A BETTER ADVANTAGE OF SEEING YOU IN A WAY THAT YOU WOULD NEVER BE CAPABLE OF SEEING YOURSELF.

Hidden In the Light*

I would never want to believe that you are that shallow of understanding, as to be convinced that you have seen everything that there is to see of me, because there is more to me than what you see!

Many people look and search in the directions where they prefer to find you. They feel that they know where you belong and that you should never ever be found out of place as far as they are concerned.

I thank God that I see what the Lord has made of me, right now in the name of Jesus, and for the rest of my life, I agree with God.

I trust God with me! The blessing of Abraham that has come upon the Gentiles, is on my life right now, I have been with me all of my life, and I have seen myself in all of my struggles, and in the midst of all of my failures, my sins, and all of my mistakes.

God has already blessed me, I am now a Blessing, since being enlightened that it's already been done! If you can't wrap your mind around what I've said, or walk with me in this particular vein of understanding, you don't know God's word.

The freedom that I am now walking in at this time of my life, has been wonderfully orchestrated by the hand of the Lord, and my joy is full in the Holy Ghost!

I see me blessed, highly lifted up and favored of the Lord!

While others celebrate my hurt, I reverence my help! While they focus on my pain, I lay hold on my gain! While the secret weapons of the enemy are launched to destroy, Jesus is the center of my joy!

Conclusion

Ask and it shall be given, seek and ye shall find, knock and it shall be opened unto you: For every one that asketh recieveth; and he that seeketh findeth; and to him that knocketh it shall be opened.   St. Matthew 7:7-8

Hidden In the Light*

Looking In All The Wrong Places

Thank God for the everlasting light of Christ that can never go out! Light that can never be darkened nor extinguished by any means at all. The awesome power of the light has been in authority ever since from before the start of what is now recognized as the beginning. It was actually the light that showed us the initial start of the beginning process of the existence of humanity.

Writing from the perspective of the light has been an experience like no other, as there is nothing else in the cosmos like the light, even the Sunlight. I was riding the other day on my way to worship, when I realized that the morning sun was an unusually bright Amber color, very high luminosity. All I could do was just to thank God for the brightness of the morning sun; it was so beautiful and giving.

However, I could not help but to remember a plane trip that I had taken several years back whereas it was on a very rainy day. Dark clouds filled the sky, completely overcast, whereas the sun could not be visualized at all. But, as the plane ascended into the sky, we

Conclusion

EVENTUALLY SOARED ABOVE THE CLOUDS, AND TO OUR SURPRISE THE SUN WAS SHINING JUST AS BRIGHTLY AS IT WOULD HAVE ON THE SUNNIEST DAYS HAVING CLEAR SKIES WITH NO CLOUDS.

I SOON REALIZED THAT THE CLOUDS HAD NO BEARING ON THE ABILITY OF THE SUN TO SHINE BRIGHTLY OR NOT AT ALL, AND EVEN THAT THERE IS ABSOLUTELY NOTHING IN THE COSMOS THAT CAN ELIMINATE THE SUN'S ABILITY TO SHINE. THE SUN ALWAYS SHINES BRIGHTLY AND IS ALWAYS IN WORKING ORDER SINCE THE BEGINNING OF TIME. THERE ARE NO HUMAN HANDS OR HUMAN INTERVENTIONS THAT ARE ABLE TO EFFECTIVELY LESSEN THE POWER OF THE SUN'S TEMPERATURE, SUN RAYS, AND EVEN THE SUN'S LUMINOSITY.

WE HAVE TO TAKE ALL SORTS OF METHODS TO BLOCK OUT THE LIGHT OF THE SUN WHERE WE MAY HAVE DEEMED IT UNNECESSARY OR UNWANTED. THE CLOUDS WERE JUST THAT, THEY WERE JUST CLOUDS THAT ADORNED THE DOMINANCE OF THE SKY. THE CLOUDS COULD ONLY BLOCK OUT THE VISIBILITY OF THE SUNLIGHT SO THAT WE COULD NOT SEE THE SUN FROM THE VANTAGE POINT OF THE EARTH WHERE WE WERE STANDING. THERE WAS JUST NO WAY THAT WE COULD SEE THE SUN, BUT WE COULD SEE THE CLOUDS VERY CLEARLY.

SO IT IS WITH THE MANY HINDRANCES

Hidden In the Light*

which block out the visibility of Christ's light, to keep the average persons from seeing the light of the Lord, yet it doesn't have the power to stop the light of the Lord from shining brightly, just waiting on those that will see, have the light of the Lord illuminate their hearts and their minds. Alike the clouds in the sky we focus on our problems and the words of the unbelievers and the skeptics and the scoffers in our society, when the focus ought to be that of the light of Christ that can't be stopped.

We don't usually have problems seeing the hindrances that erect themselves by many diverse means to block out the light of the Lord we just seem to be concerned that God allowed the hindrances to be there. The only element on the face of the planet that truly has the power to stop you from seeing the light of the Lord is self! Jesus is ever shining in the souls of man everyday all day long. We have to remember to let the light of the Lord shine through for all men to see that Jesus is alive and well, living in us.

The true message in this book is relative to the invisible but extremely valuable things that are indeed hidden in the light that require more than an

Conclusion

ability to visualize or to discern with the natural eyesight. There would have to be a satiable appetite for the more in depth things of God that are not clearly seen as a result of a light switch that had been flipped on. We can no longer afford ourselves to aspire to the theory that it doesn't take all of that; and go beyond just the face value of the word of God which is often devalued as a real necessary mapped out plan for living.

If for a fact we are going to realize the things that are truly hidden in the light, the truth is that we will most definitely have to acknowledge the light. We as people often think that we do ourselves a favorable service by acknowledging that we are all prone to sin and to disobey the written word of God on a daily basis. We are most apt to quickly identify with our humanness as a legal right to continue on as living foul to the righteousness of God.

There are reasons that most people don't have the desire to acquire the hidden things of God, nor to explore the secluded realms of the spirit of God in holiness and righteousness, where the truer things of God are reserved for them that love Him and are truly

Hidden In the Light*

DEDICATED AND FAITHFUL TO THE CAUSE OF CHRIST IN THE EARTH.

THE TRUTH IS THAT WE DO PAY A PRICE FOR GOING DEEPER INTO THE SPIRIT REALM TO ACQUIRE THE POWERFUL THINGS OF THE SPIRIT THAT WILL PUT US IN AUTHORITY AND IN THE POWER OF THE SPIRIT OF GOD, MAKING US A MORE FORMIDABLE WEAPON AGAINST THE ENEMY. PEOPLE ARE ENCOURAGED AND EVEN TAUGHT BY THE EXAMPLES OF OTHERS WHO HAVE FLED THE SCENE OF THE ATTACKS OF SATAN IN THE CHURCH, THE MOMENT THEY CHOSE TO COME IN CLOSER TO THE SPIRIT OF THE LORD, REFUSING TO ABIDE ONLY ON THE SHORES OF SPIRITUAL LIVING, BUT LAUNCHING OUT INTO THE DEEPER REALM OF THE REALITY OF THE SPIRIT AND THE POWER OF GOD.

I HAVE SAID THAT MOST PEOPLE DON'T REALLY HAVE THE DESIRE TO BE POWERFUL IN THE SPIRIT OF GOD; HOWEVER THEY DO DESIRE TO SEE THE POWER OF GOD ON OPEN DISPLAY, WORKING THROUGH THE LIVES OF SOMEONE ELSE THAT HAD BEEN WILLING TO SUFFER THROUGH THE ATTACKS OF ALL THE ENEMY, EVEN TO THE POINT OF BEING LESS POPULAR WITH THE COMMON PEOPLE OF THE SOCIETY AND HAVING LESS FINANCIAL MEANS AND WEALTH MANY TIMES, OF COURSE THEY ARE PEOPLE THAT HAVE BEEN ABLE TO WITHSTAND THE WHILES OF THE DAILY CIRCUMSTANCES FOR

Conclusion

which under the weight many would crumble and faint.

It is extremely rare to find those things that are indeed hidden in the spirit of the Lord when you were never really looking for them even as it is always impossible to recognize them for what they are truly without having the proper spiritual discernment. Things don't just happen in the spirit realm for no reason at all. God has to ordain and set the things into motion for a specific purpose, which is also the reason that there has got to be a desire to discover the hidden things of God that are strategically hidden right in plain sight in the light.

My friend when I speak of things that are hidden in the light I am simply implying to you that God has Himself placed the greater things of the spirit in the light whereas those believers who desire to obtain the greater things of the spirit of the Lord will have to look intentionally in the light for those things. Too many of the people of the churches are looking in all of the wrong places for the things that are only going to be found in the light of the Lord.

People are accustomed to digging

Hidden In the Light*

INTO THE EARTH WITH A SHOVEL, WHICH ALLOWS THEM TO GO DOWNWARD DEEPER INTO THE GROUND; BUT THEY HAVE A PROBLEM WITH LOOKING UPWARDS TOWARDS THE SKY IN THE VERY SAME DIRECTION THAT JESUS WENT UP WHEN HE CAUGHT AWAY ON A CLOUD. AT LEAST WE KNOW WHICH WAY JESUS WENT WHEN HE LEFT THE EARTH TO BE BY THE SIDE OF THE FATHER ON THE THRONE.

TO BE TOTALLY HONEST WITH YOU I DO HAVE A REVELATION AS PERTAINING TO WHY IT IS THAT WE ARE SO PRONE TO LOOK DOWNWARD INTO THE EARTH FOR THE MYSTERIOUS FINDS EVEN IN THE SPIRIT. THE DAY THAT ADAM AND EVE SINNED IN THE GARDEN, WHEN GOD STEPPED FORWARD TO REBUKE THEM FOR THEIR INSUBORDINATE BEHAVIOR AND ACTIONS AGAINST THE INSTRUCTIONS GIVEN TO THEM BY GOD, GOD CURSED THE GROUND FOR MAN'S SAKE.

> *And unto Adam he said, because thou hast hearkened unto the voice of thy wife, and hast eaten of the tree, of which I commanded thee saying, thou shalt not eat of it: cursed is the ground for thy sake; in sorrow shalt thou eat of it all the days of thy life. Thorns and thistles shall it bring forth to thee; and thou shalt eat the herb of the field; in the sweat of thy face shalt thou eat bread, till thou return to the ground; for out of it wast thou taken: for dust thou art, and unto dust shalt thou return.*
> *Genesis 3:17-19*

Conclusion

When reading the scripture very carefully it is easily understood that neither the serpent nor Satan were sent away into a far away corner to prevent them from hearing the stern rebuke of the Lord as he cursed the ground for man's sake; and I would like for it to be known of you for the rest of your own natural life, that God never cursed male nor female, neither the man or the woman, anything believed otherwise is in error to the written word of God.

No woman has ever been cursed as a result of the sin in the garden. But, God did curse the serpent above all cattle and every other beast of the fields. Satan was already cursed, cast down from heaven, and sentenced to eternal death and destruction, whereas God would have no need to bother.

God did say to the woman that in child bearing she would also bear pain and sorrow, and of course it is so! Sorrow my friend is the direct result of sin for which the ultimate penalty for sin is death! The greatest sorrow for every mother is ultimately the death of her own child, and family. The woman is blessed with the ability as a mother to love like no one else in the whole family unit, even to the point that she can

Hidden In the Light*

SOON FORGET THE EXTREME PAIN SHE SUFFERED GIVING BIRTH, IMMEDIATELY LOVING HER BABY GIVING IT A NAME TO BE REMEMBERED FOR THE REST OF ITS NATURAL LIFE.

PERHAPS BEING JUST LIKE GOD IN THE DAY THAT HE FORMED US OUT OF THE GROUND; MOST LIKELY WHENEVER MANKIND WOULD DESIRE CHILDREN, WE COULD HAVE RETURNED TO THE GROUND BY THE LEADING OF THE LORD TO FORM AND TO FASHION OUR OWN SONS AND DAUGHTERS FROM THE DUST OF THE EARTH WITHOUT ANY AGONY AND PAIN TO THE WOMAN? PERHAPS GOD NEVER INTENDED FOR THE WOMAN TO BEAR CHILDREN IN HER WOMB? BUT, BECAUSE OF SIN GOD WOULD HAVE TO CLOSE UP THE GROUND, AND OPEN UP THE WOMB OF THE WOMAN AS TO INSURE THAT THE REPLENISHED MULTIPLIED SEED OF HUMANITY WOULD BE STILL LIKE GOD IN HUMAN FORM.

IT WAS A SLAP IN THE FACE OF SATAN THAT GOD WOULD NEITHER CURSE THE MAN OR THE WOMAN IN THE EARTH, FOR A TRUTH THE DEVIL MADE THEM DO IT! THEY WEREN'T PRONE TO MAKE SINFUL DECISIONS PRIOR TO THEIR CONFRONTATION WITH THE SERPENT AND SATAN IN THE GARDEN. GOD NEVER CURSED THE LIFE OF MANKIND OR HUMANITY, BUT HE DID PUT A CURSE ON LIVING, AS LIVING ON THE EARTH WOULD NEVER BE

Conclusion

heavenly for man on the earth, as that privilege would be forever denied to mankind as a result of the disobedience.

Satan heard everything that God had said to man; also he had been there in the beginning when God formed man out of the dust of the earth. It was for our sake or even rather for our benefit that God had even cursed the ground. God knew that Satan would forever make an attempt to duplicate and even to emulate the things that God had done, but God would never consent to allow Satan the ability to successfully reproduce the things in which God had Himself created in the earth.

Satan's desire to be like God was so intense that he would have copied God in creating his own trees, and grass. He would have produced his own demonic species of fish in the ocean, and he would have even created his own deceptive beast to roam the fields with a beautifully formed exterior, however destructively horrible on the inside. But, most of all; God cursed the ground to prevent any other humanlike beings the opportunity to be formed out of the ground and from ever coming forth ever again, for which the desires of Satan were forever rendered inoperable to

Hidden In the Light*

create a man of his own!

God determined that no other man woman boy or girl would ever be formed from the ground ever again even of himself. God may have allowed Satan to see the forming process of mankind, but He would never let him do it on his own. Man is God's creation for His own glory, even though man sinned all on Satan's plot and schematic idea to destroy the fellowship of God and man; the bottom line is that we still belong to God.

Satan's mind was forever blown over the mysterious manner of which God formed man out of the dust of the ground, and ever more assuredly God sent him into a fit of rage over the ability to put a form over that which had already been spoken into existence just like he had been spoken into existence, but God never took the time to place a form over Satan! God intentionally left him in the realm of the spirit, whereas Satan would have to use another human being to touch a human being.

The ground is forever a mystery to Satan; whereas God shut him out of it all together. I could only imagine the number of times in which Satan has made

Conclusion

an attempt to try to bring up the form of human flesh out of the ground since back in the garden, even though God said that it would never be so. God did say that mankind would return to the dust of the ground in death. Even as man had finished with the body of which he had sinned against God, Satan would not even be allowed to have the dead body as an undertaker.

It was indeed Satan's idea that Cain would kill his brother Abel over the jealousy of him pleasing God with his sacrifice to God. Neither of these boys knew what it was to be jealous of one another, but Satan filled the heart of one against the other. Satan had already reached Cain causing him to be lethargic and lazy and disinterested in giving God his very best, which he knew that it would have pleased God.

Satan did it for another reason that did not reach the forefront of the understanding of the men. Not only did Satan see the Lord Form man out of the ground and breathe the breath of life into him; he saw God's secret formula for which all mankind even beasts, birds and fish lived; he saw the infusion of the blood in the veins of mankind. Perhaps if he could spill the

Hidden In the Light*

blood of one of the men into the ground, just maybe another could stand up and live out of the same ground? But to the surprise of Satan; God knew exactly what Cain had done to his brother in that the voice of the blood was crying out from the ground. The life of the blood had been spilled where it could never ever be placed again, because God had shut up the ground, and cursed it for man's sake!

I understand now why it was that Satan disputed about the body of Moses when he had died, when God sent the Arch Angel Michael to retrieve the body of Moses. Michael did not do a lot of talking with Satan to convince him that he had no right to the body of Moses, he said to him; "Satan; the Lord rebuke thee!" In other words he said to him, you know what the Lord has said to you in the garden, and it is still so forever! Satan had to be reminded that God had never changed his mind concerning Satan and human flesh, dead or alive!

Therefore, I concede that it is never really man's idea to look downward into the ground seeking to find the hidden things of God there underneath the earth. Don't be so easily

Conclusion

DECEIVED; SATAN KNOWS WHERE HE FELL FROM EVEN THOUGH HE DOES NOT KNOW A WAY TO GET BACK TO HEAVEN. SATAN KNOWS THAT YOU DON'T FALL UPWARDS, BECAUSE HE FELL DOWN AND BESIDES HE KNOWS EXACTLY WHERE GOD IS MY FRIENDS!

WE NEGLECT TO REALIZE THAT SATAN WAS THERE TO SEE THE ANGELIC HOST OF GOD OPEN UP THE INVISIBLE ENTRANCE TO HEAVEN AS ENOCH WALK AWAY FROM THE MORTAL REIGN, STEPPING INTO THE IMMORTAL EXISTENCE OF GOD, BEING ABLE TO TESTIFY THAT HE HAD PLEASED GOD. SATAN WAS THERE WHEN ELIJAH CAUGHT AWAY ON A FIERY CHARIOT LEAVING FOR GLORY IN THE PRESENCE OF GOD. HE SAW THE PATHWAY, BUT NEITHER HE, NOR ANY OF THE FALLEN HOST OF HEAVEN, NOW TURNED DEMONS WOULD BE ALLOWED TO FOLLOW THAT SAME PATHWAY.

UNDERSTAND THAT SATAN HAS BEEN THERE TO SEE ALL OF THE OBEDIENT SAINTS OF GOD WHO HAVE LEFT THIS WORLD ASCEND UNTO THE THRONE OF GOD IN HEAVEN; HE SAW THEM ALL GO UPWARDS! EVEN AS HE HAS SEEN BODIES GO BACK INTO THE GROUND AND EVEN DOWN INTO THE SEA, HE HAS NOT BEEN ABLE TO PREVENT THOSE THAT LOVE THE LORD FROM GOING UPWARDS TO MEET THE ANGELIC HOST OF HEAVEN IN THE PRESENCE OF GOD.

HE HAS SEEN THEM ALL GO INTO THE

Hidden In the Light*

LIGHT TO BE RECEIVED ETERNALLY. WE WERE MADE FOR THE GLORY OF GOD, WHICH IS THE LIGHT OF THE LORD, TO GIVE REVERENCE AND TO SHOW THE WORLD THAT GOD IS ON THE THRONE AND THAT HE IS ALIVE AND WELL. IT ONLY MAKE SINCE THAT WE WOULD COME INTO THE LIGHT NOW WHILE WE ARE ABLE TO CHOOSE, AND ARE ABLE TO INFLUENCE THOSE WHO HAVE CHOSEN THE DARKNESS TO COME OUT OF THE DARKNESS AND COME INTO THE LIGHT.

WE BELONG TO THE LIGHT, THEREFORE WE BELONG IN THE LIGHT, ABIDING THERE AS OUR OWN DWELLING PLACE OF RESIDENCE IN THE REALM OF THE SPIRIT. NOT ONLY ARE THE THINGS OF THE SPIRIT HIDDEN IN THE LIGHT, BUT AS WE TAKE IT UPON OURSELVES TO LOOK INTO THE LIGHT FOR THE THINGS OF THE SPIRIT OF THE LORD TO ENHANCE OUR LIVES AS WE WALK THIS CHRISTIAN WALK IN THE SPIRIT, WE OURSELVES AS THE CHILDREN OF THE LIGHT AS LIKEWISE HIDDEN IN THE LIGHT!

WE ARE LIVING IN MUCH DARKENED TIMES OF OUR HUMANITY; SATAN HAS MANAGED TO DARKEN THE PERSPECTIVE REASONING OF THE UNDERSTANDING OF MERE HUMANITY, AND HAVE BLINDED THE MINDS OF THOSE WHO HAVE SET THEMSELVES IN AGREEMENT WITH THE SECULAR HUMANIST OF THE DEMON INFILTRATED SOCIETY. AS A

Conclusion

RESULT, THOSE WHO HAVE COME INTO THE CHURCH FROM THE WORLD THEY CAN'T SEE EVEN THAT THE SPIRITUAL REALM REALLY EVEN EXIST, THEREFORE THEY DON'T KNOW THAT THEY OUGHT TO LOOK INTO THE LIGHT TO ACQUIRE THE THINGS OF THE SPIRIT OF THE LORD.

SATAN CAN SEE THE LIGHT BUT HE CAN'T ENTER INTO THE LIGHT AS HE HAS BEEN FOREVER OUSTED FROM THE GLORY OF THE LIGHT, WHICH IS THE REASON THAT EVERYTHING THAT HE DOES IS DONE FROM THE DARK. IF EVER YOU WOULD DESIRE TO BE IN A PLACE THAT YOU WERE SURE THAT SATAN COULD NOT HAVE FREE COURSE TO YOU I WOULD SUGGEST THAT YOU FIND YOUR PLACE IN THE LIGHT!

www.ingramcontent.com/pod-product-compliance
Lightning Source LLC
Chambersburg PA
CBHW021826090426
42811CB00032B/2040/J